EAST END
PAST

First published 2004
by Historical Publications Ltd
32 Ellington Street, London N7 8PL
(Tel: 020 7607 1628   Fax: 020 7609 6451)

ISBN 0 948667 94 X
British Library Cataloguing-in Publication Data
A catalogue record for this book is available from the British Library.

Typeset in Book Antiqua by Historical Publications Ltd
Reproduction by Square Group, London SE1
Printed in Zaragoza, Spain by Edelvives

The Illustrations

We would like to thank the following for permission to reproduce illustrations:

Guildhall Library, London: *16, 21, 26, 34, 42, 63, 64, 65, 66, 70, 76, 101, 154*
Estate of Felix H Man/National Portrait Gallery *148*
National Museum of Labour History: *126*
The Salvation Army: *144, 145*
Richard Tames: *1, 2, 3, 4, 5, 6, 7, 12, 14, 19, 22, 23, 27, 29, 32, 37, 45, 49, 62, 71, 74, 75, 79, 85, 93, 95, 96, 97, 99, 100, 102, 103, 107, 108, 109, 118, 120, 127, 132, 133, 134, 141, 142, 143, 147, 149, 151, 152, 153, 155, 157-181*
All other illustrations were supplied by the publisher.

EAST END PAST

Richard Tames

HISTORICAL PUBLICATIONS

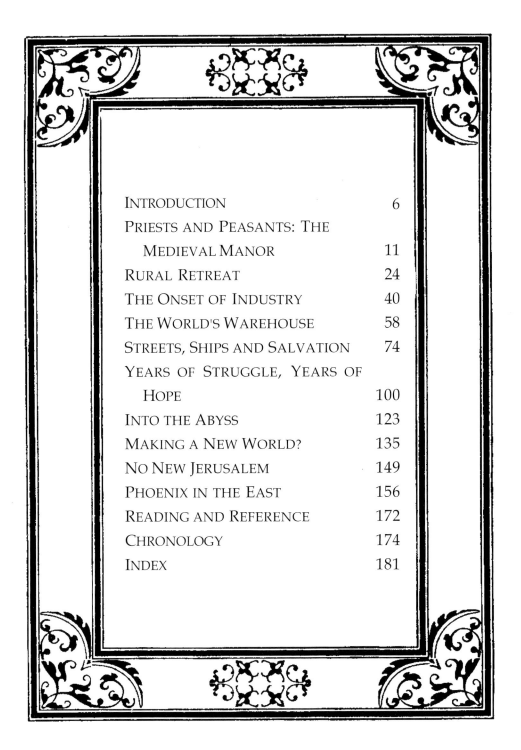

INTRODUCTION 6

PRIESTS AND PEASANTS: THE
    MEDIEVAL MANOR 11

RURAL RETREAT 24

THE ONSET OF INDUSTRY 40

THE WORLD'S WAREHOUSE 58

STREETS, SHIPS AND SALVATION 74

YEARS OF STRUGGLE, YEARS OF
    HOPE 100

INTO THE ABYSS 123

MAKING A NEW WORLD? 135

NO NEW JERUSALEM 149

PHOENIX IN THE EAST 156

READING AND REFERENCE 172

CHRONOLOGY 174

INDEX 181

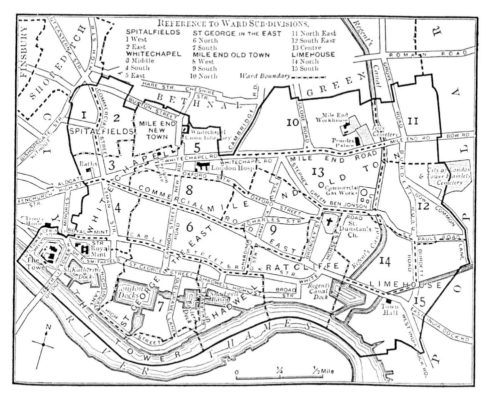

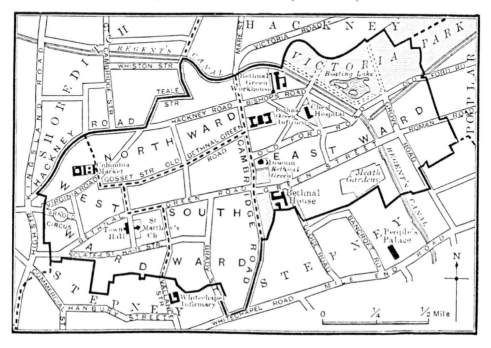

Map of Stepney (above) and of Bethnal Green (below) early 20th century.

Introduction

There is no need to say in the East End of what."
Arthur Morrison, *Tales of Mean Streets* (1901)

In this book the East End means the area of the modern borough of Tower Hamlets. It does not, therefore, include Hoxton, much less Hackney, nor Shoreditch, let alone Stratford. While many might dispute where the boundaries of the East End lie, none could challenge that Tower Hamlets is where its heart is. Whichever bells a Cockney must by legend be born within hearing of – St Mary-le-Bow or St Mary, Bow – birth between Aldgate and the River Lea is a certain qualification in fact.

'Cockney' in its origins was a disparaging term for Londoners in general and is recorded as early as 1600, as in "I scorne to let a Bow-bell Cockney put me down". Subsequently it would acquire narrower geographic connota-tions and be used as a qualifying adjective by learned contributors to the *Dictionary of National Biography* who wished to indicate such quin-tessential and life-affirming East End qualities as vulgarity, brashness, alertness, good humour and wit. The term 'East End', denoting the setting for lifestyles of deprivation, drudgery and drunkenness, stained by vice and punctu-ated by violence, only gained general currency in the 1880s. For most of its known history, for some fifteen centuries in other words, the East End consisted of fields and farms. Writing of Stepney at the dawn of the sixteenth century, the great Dutch scholar Erasmus declared that "wherever you look the earth yieldeth a pleas-ant prospect ... and the very bounds of heaven do delight you." Although industry and its attendant nuisances had already begun to befoul the riverside it was still possible a cen-

1. The Real Thing? Pearlies greet a tourist group outside the Bow Bells in Bow Road. Inside halves of 'warm' bitter await a cautious sampling.

tury and a half later for Samuel Pepys to bowl out to Bow in his carriage for an evening treat of skittles and cherries in the fresh air. London's eastern suburbs became famed for silk-weaving and shipbuilding but they were also a favoured location for almshouses, asylums and academies before they became synonymous with slums and squalor.

Standing at the gateway to what would become the world's greatest city and the capital of the world's greatest empire, the East End would serve both as the springboard from which that empire would initially be explored and the point of arrival for millions bearing strange cargoes, bringing new skills, fleeing persecution or seeking a better life in neighbourhoods which became known as Knockfergus, Little Warsaw or Chinatown. Tower Hamlets Town Hall is situated in Mulberry Place – not a reference to the tree but to the artificial Mulberry harbours cast there for D-day when the site was still occupied by the East India Import Dock. The local history of the East End is therefore inevitably global. And yet it is also

2. The Bow Bells pub, rated 'top boozer' by Fancyapint.

3. Multi-layered history in Hanbury Street – more or less correct despite the spelling mistakes.

Christ Church Hall

Built in 1719 as a French Hugeonot church it stood back from the road behind a paved, tree-planted, courtyard in which there was a pump. In 1740 La Patente church moved into the building. Their plaque of the royal arms, signifying the patent granted by James II, is still mounted in the hall. The Three Crown Court church in Wheler Street then joined La Patente and by the 1760's the congregation was noted for being large and prosperous. During this time John Wesley preached here. In 1787 it became a German Lutheran church, the Baptists then moved into the building and renamed it Jireh Chapel and during the period that it was occupied by the United Free Methodists Charles Dickens used the building for public readings of his works. In 1864, the building was extended to cover the courtyard and the original stone facade was destroyed. Christ Church bought the building in 1887 and it was converted for use as their church hall. The building was used by the matchstick girls to hold their strike meetings in 1888 organised by Annie Besant and Eleanor Marx-Aveling (Karl Marx's daughter). These led to the establishment of the British Trade Unions. As Christ Church Hall it has, in many ways, served the needs of the church and community in Spitalfields over the past century.

a world unto itself. In 1923 George Lansbury's *Daily Herald,* reporting the diamond wedding anniversary of Mr and Mrs Hickey of Bow, noted that neither had ever spent a night away from the East End and Mrs Hickey at 81 had yet to see either Westminster Abbey or the Tower of London.

The vigour and variety of the East End's population makes it a fertile compost for making mythic figures, from the Cockney costermonger personified by the impeccably bourgeois Albert Chevalier from Bayswater to Jack Warner's upright Dixon of Dock Green or Warren Mitchell's explosive Wapping xenophobe Alf Garnett. As a literary canvas the East End yet retains its appeal, whether as the setting for Peter Ackroyd's fantastical, time-shifting whodunnit *Hawksmoor,* Iain Sinclair's bizarre encounters and rambling reflections in *Lights Out For The Territory* or Gilda O'Neill's reminiscence-based evocations of the 'day before yesterday'. Caricature and cliché have characterised much writing about the East End. *The Oxford Book of London* contains two lengthy extracts from the novels of local journalist Arthur Morrison, three pages about Jack the Ripper, a passage from Charles Booth about the *chevras*

5. *No. 19 Princelet Street, successively a Huguenot silk-weaver's house, a synagogue and home to the reclusive David Rodinsky – and potentially a Museum of Immigration.*

4. *A dragon monument recalls the Limehouse Chinatown – only restaurants remain.*

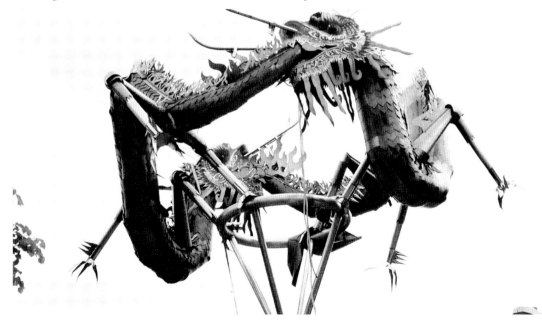

6. *Gasometers on the site of Congreve's rocket factory, Bow Back Rivers – part of the area designated for London's projected bid for the 2012 Olympics.*

which served as congregations and mutual aid societies among the poorer Jews and two pages about the Blitz.

By implication therefore today's East End is no longer authentic because it has lost what were once its defining characteristics – the docks have closed, the overcrowding and the Jews have gone and the Blitz is history. In the twentieth century alone the area has been transformed not once but repeatedly. In 1900 Tower Hamlets had a population of 600,000, making it more populous than Birmingham or Leeds. The numbers then fell precipitously for decades, even before the Blitz gutted it. By mid-century it was down to 230,790; thirty years later to 139,996. By 2001, however, it had expanded over the course of twenty years to reach 196,106, a dramatic reversal of a lifetime's trend.

A century ago Jack London wrote of (or wrote off?) East Enders as the *People of the Abyss*. But East Enders of that era were to become the creators of commercial television and Tesco's. The East End is where all the glass for the Crystal Palace was made and Brunel's *Great Eastern* was built. Its products have ranged from tarpaulins and tropical helmets to Dreadnoughts and dog biscuits, from the war-winning Baker rifle to Duckham's Oil and Pan Yan

Pickles. Whitechapel and Wapping were the homes from which Captain Cook and Captain Bligh departed to face murder and mutiny. Bromley-by-Bow was where Jewish economist David Ricardo lived when he was making his fortune in the City and Bethnal Green was where Jewish pugilist Daniel Mendoza settled in honoured retirement from the bare-knuckle ring.

The East End is the birthplace of the Salvation Army, the colour purple, 'Big Brother', boxing, the PDSA and IPA. Jeremy Bentham was born in Spitalfields as well as Bud Flanagan. Others born in Tower Hamlets include arch-swindler Horatio Bottomley, Abe Saperstein, creator of the Harlem Globetrotters, actress Angela Lansbury, hair-stylist Vidal Sassoon, children's illustrator Lucy Attwell and sixties cult photographer Terence Donovan. Graduates of the Jews' Free School include both the flamboyant diamond millionaire Barney Barnato and Sam Gompers, pioneer of American trade unionism.

The history of the East End is therefore much more than a colourful chronicle of cheery Cockney cabbies and charwomen, with the Ripper and the Krays thrown in for blood-chilling counterpoint. Five minutes walk from

7. The House Mill in the Three Mills Conservation Area at Bromley-by-Bow is Britain's largest surviving tide-mill and one of London's few Grade I listed industrial buildings. Built in 1776 by Daniel Bisson as a timber-frame structure with brick facing on three sides and weatherboarding on the fourth, it was used to grind grain for flour or distilling into gin, until blitzed in 1941. Threatened with demolition in 1971, since 1989 it has been re-roofed and restored. Water-powered mills are recorded in this area in the Domesday Book.

where these words are being written Gandhi established his *ashram* throughout the long weeks in which he antagonised imperial proconsuls across the conference table. Thirty years later the confrontational psychotherapist R D Laing would run a controversial 'anti-clinic' in the very same building. Five minutes further on, passing over the site where Chaucer's fashion-victim Prioress once held sway, one can stand next to an eighteenth century tide-mill and gaze across to where rockets were manufactured for use against Napoleon's cavalry at the Battle of the Nations. A quarter of an hour in the opposite direction would take the walker across ground on which Richard II met the rebel peasant army of Essex in 1381, past where Dr Barnardo began the crusade which would pluck fifty thousand destitute children from the streets of London and lead to where a church has stood for more than a thousand years, a church in which the only English samurai in history was married. You don't get that in the suburbs ....

Priests and Peasants: The Medieval Manor

HINTERLAND

During the roughly four centuries of the existence of Roman *Londinium* the area to its east remained largely unsettled. Down near the river's shoreline a short stretch of road ran straight east from where the Tower now stands to roughly the Ratcliff area, where there was a small settlement and possibly a landing-place for ships. Halfway along that road, at Shadwell, was a signal station, presumably to give the city forewarning of raiders or important shipping movements. Burials have been found there and on either side of the section of road between the signal station and Ratcliff. A much larger cluster of burials took place in the Spitalfields area and a further cluster to the north of that around Shoreditch.

One of the Spitalfields burials, unearthed in 1999 complete with a stone sarcophagus and shell-patterned lead coffin, was that of a high status pagan woman in her early twenties who had been brought up in southern Europe. She was probably the victim of a summer infection and was buried in Chinese silk decorated with gold thread woven in Syria. Her remains and costly grave goods are now in the Museum of London. Another significant burial, in the Aldgate area, was that of Classicianus, the Gaulish financial administrator appointed by Nero in AD 62 to revive *Londinium* after its devastation at the hands of Boudicca's rebel army. Classicianus died *c*. AD 65 and, in the absence of any other known candidate, might be considered the true founder of London's commercial greatness. Facsimiles of his tomb can be seen at Tower Hill and in the Museum of London. The original – or most of it – is on display in the British Museum.

Passing between the Spitalfields and Shoreditch burial clusters was the main road to Colchester, Roman Britain's initial, if short-lived, capital. This route crossed the River Lea at Old Ford, where there was another settlement, still small but larger than the one at Ratcliff and with a number of associated burials around it. A subsidiary feeder road, running from the Old Street area, may have joined the main artery at Old Ford.

Local names indicate Anglo-Saxon settlement attributed to tribal patriarchs. Stepney first appears as Stybbanhythe, later Stebunhithe, Stebba's landing place. Bethnal Green in its earliest form was Blithehale – Blitha's corner or nook. Wapping, traditionally thought to denote the settlement of Waeppa's people, may, however, derive from *wapol*, a marsh, which, until the sixteenth century, much of it was. These early settlers exploited the area's contrasting landscapes to advantage. The riverside marshland was valued for fishing and grazing, the adjacent cultivable area for raising crops and the forested area to the north, now partly occupied by Victoria Park, for wood for construction and fuel and pannage for swine, as well as for nuts and berries to vary the diet. During the Saxon period the bishops of London acquired possession of the sprawling manor of Stepney, which extended over all of what is now the borough of Tower Hamlets and northwards into Hackney and Islington with parts as far out as Hornsey. This they were to retain until the Reformation, although most of it would eventually be granted or sublet to other ecclesiastical bodies and secular tenants. In 1228 the Canons of St Paul's, for example, were granted an estate in Shadwell. Other religious institutions associated with the area were the Knights Templar, the nuns of St Mary, Clerkenwell and the priory of St Osyth in Essex, all of which held land in the parish of Stepney. The fact that the entire area was largely owned and administered by religious authorities may well have retarded its exploitation for residential or industrial purposes compared to other locations on the fringe of the capital, not because clerical control was inherently hostile to economic enterprise but because the land was more highly valued as an immediately convenient source of fresh produce and a healthy amenity and occasional refuge easily accessible from a city which was prone to epidemics, fires and casual violence.

In 870 London was taken by the Danes and its eastern hinterland must therefore have come under their temporary control. Following their defeat at Alfred's hands the city was reoccupied in 886 and the boundary with Danish-settled territories set at the River Lea.

8. *St Dunstan's church, Stepney. From a drawing by J P Neale, published in 1815. Most of the present building dates from the fifteenth century but inside there is a pre-Conquest stone carving of the Crucifixion.*

ST DUNSTAN

Stepney's parish church is dedicated to St Dunstan (924-88), the most commanding English churchman of his century, chiefly responsible for reviving monasticism after the ravages of the Vikings and also remembered as the deviser of the coronation service still used by English monarchs. Dunstan also had a personal connection with Stepney, serving, albeit briefly, as bishop of London before his elevation to Canterbury in 959. Popular veneration made him a saint long before the church canonised him officially in 1029. Firm evidence for the existence of St Dunstan's as a church, however, dates only from 1154.

DOMESDAY

The Domesday Book of 1086 lists the bishop of London as Lord of the Manor of Stepney (Stibenhede}. Like every other bishop in the country, with the sole exception of the saintly Wulfstan of Worcester, Maurice, London's bishop, was a Norman. Translated to his diocese in the year of the great Domesday survey,

he had also succeeded to the office of Chancellor and was therefore the king's chief minister. He retained high office for the next twenty years. In his own right Maurice held estates in distant Somerset and, by virtue of his office, other estates in Essex, Hertfordshire and Dorset. Only a portion of the Stepney lands was farmed directly on the bishop's behalf. Much was leased on to other landholders. Some of these were themselves great landowners – Ranulf Flambard was a former Chief Justice; the Bishop of Lisieux was the king's doctor; the king's chamberlain, William, who organised the monarch's domestic household, was another tenant; Engelbert is identified as a canon, presumably of St Paul's cathedral and therefore a personal colleague of Maurice; William de Vere and Hugh de Bernieres were presumably Norman knights and the female referred to only as "the wife of Brian" was presumably a knight's widow, who sub-let some of her land to Roger the Sheriff. The holdings of these sub-tenants were, however, modest, ranging in annual value from thirty shillings to six pounds, whereas the bishop's was valued at £48. There were still three Anglo-Saxon sub-tenants but they were small fry. Aelfric Chacepul had "land for one plough but the plough is wanting". Edmund, son of Algot, held a recently-built mill and Aethelwin, Beorthmaer's son, another one. The mills were recorded as being without land and must therefore have enabled their owners to make a living grinding local grain crops into flour. As the windmill was unknown in England until the twelfth century, these would have been watermills. Stepney's riverside location meant that its inhabitants were unusually well provided for in this respect because Hugh de Bernieres also had one and the bishop controlled four more.

The Anglo-Saxon peasants who tilled the soil were divided into villeins, who leased substantial holdings of up to thirty acres and worked their lord's land in lieu of rent, and bordars and cottars, who held only marginal amounts of land and were forced to rely on working for others for their subsistence. Although slaves existed in England none were recorded in Stepney; perhaps, with the great city of London so near escape was easier than in more remote parts of the kingdom. Women and children went unrecorded as, usually, did members of the clergy. Allowing for unrecorded dependents the population of Stepney in the aftermath of the Conquest has been estimated at between seven and nine hundred, scattered in eleven small settlements. The bishop's own direct holding was by far the most densely populated with sixty villeins and forty-six cottars. All the other holdings added together had only a dozen or so villeins, forty-odd bordars and half a dozen cottars.

The manor's lands were classified into arable, measured by how many eight-ox plough-teams it would need to cultivate it, meadow, pasture and woodland, the latter usually measured by the number of pigs which could be fed on its acorns and beech-mast. Measured in these terms the bishop's own direct holdings were far larger than any other, consisting of land for twenty-five ploughs, an equal extent of meadow, pasture unspecified and woodland for five hundred pigs. No one else had land for more than five ploughs or woodland for more than 150 pigs. Ranulph Flambard had no pasture but did have "a wood for making fences".

Finally the compilers compared how much each holding was worth and compared it with its value at the Conquest, twenty years previously. With the exception of the three marginal Anglo-Saxon tenants, whose holdings had neither fallen nor risen in value, all the others had fallen. In the case of the bishop the difference was minimal, from £50 to £48; but the others varied from 15% to 40%. In respect of three holdings it was also noted that there was land lying uncultivated.

Domesday Book also records one Stepney estate which did not belong to the bishop but was held directly from the king by one Robert Fafiton, who also sub-let part of it to Roger the Sheriff. It had once belonged to a Saxon canon of St Paul's, Sigeraed, and, not surprisingly "the Bishop of London claims that he ought to have it" – plus the 53 acres adjacent "which Hugh de Bernieres usurped to the loss of the canons of St Paul's and placed in this manor, according to the testimony of the hundred."

FOOD AND FAMINE

Over the course of four and a half centuries the dozen or so holdings recorded in Domesday were repeatedly sub-divided by sale or inheritance and their constituent parts recombined and sub-divided again. What are conventionally referred to as 'manors' were sometimes compact and coherent holdings in the possession of the same institution or family over long periods. The estate in Stepney held by the bishop of London's steward, William of Pontefract, in 1166 was still known as Pontfreit or Pomfret when it was bought for £300 by royal servant Sir John Abel in 1302 and, as the name of the estate, lasted into the fifteenth century. The Trentemans family held lands from the twelfth to the fourteenth century, their core holding being known as the manor of Bernes. Land held by Roger Huscarl in the reign of Richard I was still held by his descendants until at least 1356, when its nominal rent was a single red rose. But estates named for William of Pontefract's contemporaries, Ralph the Clerk, Bernard of Stepney and Salomon of Stepney, outlasted their patronymic proprietors by only a few decades. The enduring names of other manors, such as Hulls and Ashwyes, at least perpetuated the memory of their erstwhile possessors. More usually the manor, better conceived as a unit of economic management than as an archetypal mansion and associated farm, consisted of a main holding plus other, not necessarily contiguous, assets, such as marsh or forest some distance off. In the late twelfth century, for example, Brice of Shadwell acquired an estate consisting of marsh, meadow, a mill and annual rents from sub-leased lands, held by ten different tenants, ranging from two shillings to a pound of cumin. In 1400 a house known as Mewes Place (from the previously occupant family of Meau) was granted to the king's servant Louis Recoches together with some ninety acres of land in Stepney and with grazing for sixty pigs in the royal forest out at Havering.

As elsewhere throughout England, the main business of the bulk of the population was producing and processing food. Part was for consumption by its producers, part for the ecclesiastical proprietors of the land and some, no doubt an increasing proportion as the economy became monetized (Shadwell had 51 tenants paying a money rent by 1285), to meet the insatiable needs of the ever-expanding capital. The latter was less likely to be grain, which could fairly easily be brought up the Thames by ship, than products which were more liable to damage or deterioration if transported for more than a few miles, such as fruit, milk or eggs. Surviving accounts make it clear that much that was sold on to market passed through the hands of ecclesiastical proprietors first and was disposed of when found to be surplus to their own requirements.

The staple food of the medieval peasantry was grain. Only the better off ate white bread made from wheat. From as early as the thirteenth century Londoners drew much of theirs from commercial bakeries at Stratford so the people of Tower Hamlets would have seen batches passing through each day on their way to market. Much of the flour would have been ground in watermills ranged along the River Lea. The area also had the bonus of rich marshlands on which cattle and sheep might be grazed. Both types of livestock were valued for their milk as well as their meat and hide or wool. Cheese is recorded as a local product. Cattle which had been driven long distances to meet the demands of the London market were certainly fattened up for final sale by being grazed on the Isle of Dogs.

Another bonus was the Thames, which yielded not only substantial fish, such as salmon but also oysters and ducks. Eels were the poor man's most frequent treat. Perhaps

surprisingly in view of its proximity to the nation's largest city there were also hunting grounds in the parish of Stepney. When the bishop of London proposed to turn two areas into fenced-off parks for his own exclusive use in 1292 the citizens of the capital successfully obstructed him in defence of their traditional rights to hunt there. The bishop's manor house cum hunting lodge, in existence by 1207, stood on the site of the future London Chest Hospital.

The fact that the Tower Hamlets area was blessed with a diverse range of output did not, of course, mean that it was enjoyed by the cultivators – we may be fairly certain, however, that it was enjoyed by the residents of the wealthy religious houses which fringed the eastern rim of the City.

Although famine was obviously a much more frequent visitation in marginal upland areas, it remained a menace even in the fertile southeast well into the Middle Ages. Famine is documented in Stepney parish in 1270. All Europe was afflicted by successive rains that ruined harvests in 1315 and 1316, creating an unprecedented crisis in 1317, when even Londoners within the walls perished for lack of food. At Shadwell a tax exemption was granted in 1316 and by 1318 its local windmill was in ruins and there was no miller. By 1334 the manor house itself was so derelict that even its stairs and windows had been removed and the outbuildings stood in ruins. The Black Death plague epidemic of 1348-9, the almost equally severe outbreak of 1361 and a third eruption in 1369 not only carried off at least a third of the populace but also on each occasion severely disrupted agricultural work and therefore the food supply. Another famine afflicting the area is recorded in 1391, despite the drastic fall in demand caused by the decline in population occasioned by successive outbreaks of plague. Plague remained endemic and further major local outbreaks were recorded in 1407 and 1499. A new affliction known as sweating sickness reached epidemic proportions in 1485 and recurred in 1518.

Thanks to the recurrent disasters of the fourteenth century the balance between land and people shifted in favour of the cultivator, causing radical changes in farming practice. Following the second major visitation of plague in 1361 there was a widespread commutation of weekly labour services into cash payments in 1362-3, presumably because enforcement of servitude had become too problematic. Pomfret manor house was recorded as in ruins by 1362. Rents continued low throughout the fifteenth century and much land was made over from cultivation to grazing.

Although the general danger of famine receded in the fifteenth century purely localised disasters could still damage the food supply. Because virtually the entire area of Tower Hamlets stands fifty feet or less above sea-level, and much of it thirty feet or less, flooding was a constant threat. One indication of its frequency was the appointment by the Crown of commissions to inspect and repair stretches of the river bank. The earliest recorded was in 1297; there was another in 1324, nine between 1354 and 1381, five more between 1395 and 1407 and a further five between 1447 and 1480. When the Thames froze solid in 1410 and again in 1434 it would not only have disrupted the river's role as a source of nutrition but also presumably have been accompanied by temperatures severe enough to threaten livestock. Similar disruption must have accompanied the huge inundation of the Isle of Dogs when its protective embankment was breached in 1448-9. The flooded area was estimated at a thousand acres and sixteen years later four hundred acres were still useless for farming. In 1455 William Marowe, Mayor of London, bought flooded land at Poplar as a speculation but the damage was not fully recovered until 1488 and seems to have extinguished the farming community established at the southern end of the Isle of Dogs for three centuries.

Farming work was, of course, seasonal in its demand for labour. Outside peak periods associated with planting and harvesting, peasants might be set to building work, digging sand and gravel, transporting foodstuffs or maintenance tasks such as repairing river defences. There were also by-employments, such as gathering reeds from the marshes, to be used for thatching or woven into baskets, fish-traps and matting. From the fourteenth century onwards legal transactions relating to properties in Tower Hamlets contain references to workshops. The lime-burning which gave Limehouse its name was certainly being practised by 1335. Clay was being dug to make tiles by 1366. Brickmaking occurs in the fifteenth century, concentrated around Whitechapel, with Brick Lane named as such by 1485. By then it had become a large-scale business. When

John Bramston died in 1504 he bequeathed 10,000 bricks to London's Charterhouse, the same to the Priory of St Bartholomew in Smithfield and the same to his son and heir Hugh. The watermills of Domesday were matched by windmills from the thirteenth century. Some watermills were also adapted for fulling cloth. Out at Bow a dyeing industry was established on the banks of the Lea. In 1404 the will of William Dyer of Stratford-le-Bow bequeathed his dyeing equipment to his cousin, also William. Commercial brewing was established in Stepney by 1419. The industry appears to have attracted the involvement of Flemish immigrants, who brought with them expertise in making hopped beer, a far superior product to traditional ale because it not only tasted better but lasted much longer. In the reign of Henry VII Geoffrey Gate was twice authorised to take control of brewhouses around St Katherine's, either because their product was deemed too weak for local consumption or because they were sending too much abroad.

The river itself generated employment for ferrymen connecting the north and south shores of the Thames. One, known as Potter's ferry (perhaps taking its name from another local occupation) ran from Blackwall, another from where Island Gardens now stand and a third a short distance to the west of that one. Whether shipbuilding was established as a regular industry – rather than on an individual project basis – is uncertain. It is known, for example, that in 1356 Guy de Seintcler and John Straunge conscripted ships' carpenters from East Anglia to build ships and barges for the king in Ratcliff. In 1421 a ship was built at Limehouse for the Duke of Bedford. In 1485 the aspirational Cely family's trading vessel, the *Margaret Cely*, was repaired at Blackwall but there were no permanent docks or slips there. Fishing was a regular employment. A community of fishermen existed at Blackwall by the fourteenth century. In 1488 London's Mayor issued a proclamation forbidding "the casting of refuse into the Thames and commanding that no manner of person ... draw any net between Ratcliff Mill or Wapping Mill westwards towards London Bridge." Victualling ships had by then become a significant business for the brewers, bakers and butchers of Ratcliff and Limehouse, giving rise to the name of Butcher Row, which seems to have been hard-surfaced by the fifteenth

century, presumably on account of the volume
of traffic it had to bear. Specialist artisans by
then plying their trade in Tower Hamlets included several tailors, a potter, a brasier, an
arrowsmith, a white tawer (worker in tin and
soft metals) and a barber. Even more indicative
of the increasing economic sophistication of
the locality is the evidence of diversified businesses built up by a single individual. Richard
Etgoos, described as a yeoman by status at his
death in 1503, was primarily a lime-burner,
with operations at Limehouse and at Greenhithe
in Kent. His Limehouse premises included a
new house, land recently enclosed from former
marsh, a wharf, a boat, the *Katherine,* for bringing in the chalk which was his raw material,
a kiln and, adjoining his dwelling, four tenements for his employees or for renting out, a
tanhouse, a beerhouse and twenty-eight acres
of marsh. In addition to this he had another
four tenements, another wharf, a garden on
which he had built half a dozen more tenements, a patch of arable land and a further
thirty-two acres of marsh leased out to butchers
for fattening their stock prior to slaughter.

BOW BRIDGE

Credit for the building of the first bridge at Bow
is attributed to the consort of king Henry I
(reigned 1100-1135), who is variously known
as Matilda, Maud, Mahalde and Mold (1080-
1118). Most women of her era, even royal ones,
are known only as names or ciphers, petrified
in the conventional phrases of a monkish scribe.
But Matilda survives as a distinctive personality, a true Lady Bountiful, rightly remembered for good works, genuinely pious and also
literate.

Before it was built the River Lea was crossed
at, or possibly below, Old Ford and one tradition holds that the queen, after a goodly drench-
ing while fording the river, ordered two stone
bridges with a paved causeway between them
to be erected downstream across two branches
of the Lea. As queen Matilda certainly had both
the wealth and the authority to bring off such
a project. Her motives, moreover, may have
been as much spiritual as practical because the
building of bridges, being of benefit to pilgrims
and honest travellers, was regarded as a pious
act. The queen certainly took a strong personal
interest in Barking Abbey and getting to it by
land necessitated crossing the Lea at some point.
The nuns of Barking were charged with the

9. *Bow Bridge, by W. Bartlett, published in 1839. The bridge marked the boundary between Middlesex and Essex. Note
the presence of gas street-lighting.*

10. On Bow Bridge in c.1905. Note the corn merchants. The locality's association with landing and processing grain pre-dated Domesday.

responsibility of maintaining the bridges at Bow, with a grant of land from Matilda to provide funds for the purpose.

Apart from building Bow Bridge, Matilda's second connection with the Tower Hamlets area is that in 1108, on the advice of Richard of Belmeis, newly appointed as bishop of London, she founded England's first Augustinian priory, Holy Trinity at Aldgate, which was to hold the manor of Bromley St Leonard, including valuable mills along the Lea. The building of the Tower rendered the strip of land beyond the city walls redundant as a defensive feature and in 1125 it was granted to Holy Trinity. It later became known as the ward of Portsoken. Holy Trinity was destined to become the richest religious house in the capital, with property in 87 London parishes. A summary of the holdings and rights enshrined in over a thousand charters, wills, writs, leases etc. was compiled as a sumptuous cartulary in 1425-7 by Brother Thomas de Axbridge and survives as one of the special treasures of the library of the University of Glasgow.

The Victorian author of Matilda's entry in the *Dictionary of National Biography* asserted that "she was a warm patroness of verse and song; she gave lavishly to musical clerks, to scholars, poets and strangers of all sorts, who were drawn to her court by the fame of her bounty and who spread her praises far and wide" but concluded sourly that "the tenants on her estates were too

often fleeced by her bailiffs ... to provide funds for this ill-regulated generosity." Robert of Gloucester, however, chronicling her husband's reign a century and a half after her death, lauds her as a restraint on her often evil-tempered spouse and declared that "the goodness that she did here to England cannot all be here written nor by any man understood."

ST LEONARD BROMLEY

The origins of the priory of St Leonard at Bromley by Bow are obscure and disputed. It has been suggested that a religious house of some sort was established in that area around 960, with the encouragement of St Dunstan, to supply spiritual support for local inhabitants keeping watch along the Lea against Danish incursions. If so, it would also have been exposed to danger and is therefore most unlikely to have been a Benedictine nunnery. Another possibility is that it was founded by the Conqueror's energetic appointee as bishop of London, William, who is known to have founded or rebuilt many churches, or by his successor Maurice, bishop of London from 1086 to 1107 or by his successor, Richard de Belmeis. It would seem equally plausible to associate its foundation with Henry I's queen, Matilda, known to have been a generous patroness of the church, as a logical accompaniment to her bridgebuilding project. Its existence by the reign of Stephen (1135-54) is certain thanks to the survival of a charter granted by that monarch.

St Leonard himself is also rather a mystery. *The Catholic Encyclopaedia* dismisses the earliest, eleventh century, 'Life' of the saint as having "no historical value whatever". Leonard appears to have been a Frankish nobleman who as a monk found favour with Clovis (465-511), the king who made Paris the capital of what would eventually become France. As a result of the success of his prayers that the Frankish queen might be safely delivered of a child Leonard was rewarded with land at Noblac, near Limoges, where he founded a monastery. There is no trace of his cult before the eleventh century but thereafter it spread rapidly, as far as Poland to the east and Spain to the west. If, therefore, the priory of St Leonard at Bromley by Bow was founded early in the reign of Henry I it would rank as one of the earlier such dedications in England.

St Leonard's never became a wealthy house. In 1294 it owned sixty acres of land locally. At the time of its dissolution in 1541 it was valued at only just over £100. But its situation on the banks of the Lea was undoubtedly a pleasant one, removed from the bustle of London but within easy reach of it. The house certainly attracted the interest of some of the highest in the land and was chosen as their burial place by John Bohun, Earl of Hereford and Essex and Constable of England (died 1336) and Elizabeth (died *c.* 1373), sister of Edward III's consort, Philippa of Hainault.

It seems likely that St Leonard's would be attractive to those daughters or widows of the London bourgeoisie who shunned the married state in favour of a quiet and comfortable life. It is certain that Chaucer had St Leonard's in mind in creating the vivacious but vapid figure of his Prioress, Madame Eglantyne. Chaucer (1340-1400) certainly wrote with first-hand knowledge. A Londoner by birth, in the course of a varied career as courtier, diplomat and bureaucrat, he served for a time as a customs officer, in return for which he was granted a suite of rooms in the gatehouse at Aldgate, from which he would have looked straight down the road eastward out of the City, leading towards St Leonard's.

Chaucer describes in detail Madame Eglantyne's glamorous looks, fashionable clothes and accessories, polished manners and flirtatious charm – scarcely a portrait of spir-

11. *The prioress, from the Ellesmere Mss of Canterbury Tales, which dates from within five years of Chaucer's death.*

ituality but true to his method of satirising by presenting his characters as they seemed eager to present themselves to the world. Chaucer had travelled on the Continent and was fluent in Latin, Italian and French and was therefore surely mocking the Prioress in writing:

> "And frenssh she spoke ful faire and fetisly
> (exquisitely),
>   After the stole of Stratford atte Bowe,
>   For frenssh of Parys was to hir unknowe."

In other words, for all her pretensions, the Prioress's true origins were immediately betrayed by her unwitting deployment of Cocknified French. The tale Chaucer assigns to her – of the alleged murder of the boy saint Hugh of Lincoln – is notable for its vicious anti-semitism, implying that the simpering snob was also vindictive, vacuous and bigoted even by the standards of her day. Quite what are we to make of this? A London prioress – real or imagined – would never have met a Jew, as they had been expelled from England a century previously, in 1290, whereas the well-travelled Chaucer ...

Eileen Power presented a portrait of Madam Eglantyne in a pioneering work of social history, *Medieval People*, first published in 1924. Her painstaking researches into the records of bishops' visitations, the spasmodic tours of inspection which were made to check up on the management of individual religious houses, revealed that a prioress of St Leonard's had been denounced by the other nuns for a lengthy catalogue of managerial shortcomings – that she got the convent into debt; that she tried to get out of debt by selling off woods belonging to the convent, leasing out farms at low rates for long periods and promising annual pensions in the future in return for lump sums down; that she had failed to compile annual accounts; that she took frequent jaunts which were really social but which she pretended were on convent business; and that she had failed to repair a hole in the church roof or to give the other nuns new clothes so that they were forced to wear threadbare ones. This situation had arisen because the prioress had no head for figures but persistently made financial decisions without consulting anyone else. To avoid any recurrence of mismanagement the bishop ordered that the convent's seal should be kept in a box with three separate locks so that the prioress couldn't use it without consulting at least two other key-holders. She was also required to present annual accounts. (She did.) And just to make sure things didn't slide the bishop also arranged that a neighbouring rector should oversee the convent's business affairs.

Despite such reproofs the irrepressible prioress seems to have managed to continue to live merrily enough because her accounts reveal payments for visiting harpers and players at Christmas, for bonfire nights with bread and ale, for 'wassail' at New Year, Twelfth Night and games to mark the arrival of May – despite the bishop's injunction forbidding "all manner of minstrelsy, interludes, dancing or revelling within your holy place." And, of course, the church, far from encouraging nuns to go on pilgrimages actually forbade them to do so because it took them away from cloistered contemplation and exposed them to worldly temptation. So, in theory at least, Chaucer should never have included her among his band of pilgrims.

The remains of St Leonard's Priory were demolished in 1635, though the church itself continued in use.

THE CLERICAL FRINGE

The population of medieval London clustered most densely along the riverside to be near

12. The Gothic memorial arch at St Leonard's, honouring a Victorian vicar, leads only to a derelict churchyard since the destruction of the largely medieval church in World War II.

work. Many of the parishes crowded together there extended over a mere five acres, some even less. The city's religious houses tended to establish themselves along the line of the city walls or just outside them, where the environment was palpably healthier, far less noisy or noisome and there was abundant space for cloisters, gardens and even orchards. Apart from the institutions already mentioned, along the eastern side of the City were ranged several others. Closest in were the Minoresses of the Abbey of St Clare, founded in 1293 by the Earl of Lancaster and now remembered in the name of the Minories. Near their establishment was the foundation of St Katherine by the Tower, brought into being as a hospice for the poor by Queen Matilda (another one) in 1148 and destined to enjoy the special protection of subsequent Queens of England for almost seven centuries. That Matilda, consort of King Stephen, appears to have been prompted to make this gesture as a way of assuaging her grief over the loss of her two children, who were buried nearby in Holy Trinity, Aldgate. To the north stood the Priory of St Mary, Spital, first established in 1197 by Walter de Brune (hence Brune

Street in Spitalfields) and refounded in 1235 as an Augustinian house. It served as a hospice for the dying and also, uniquely, offered shelter to the mentally afflicted. The Cistercian abbey of St Mary Graces was founded by Edward III in 1350 in the immediate aftermath of the Black Death, possibly as a gesture of contrition with the lifting of what many took to be a scourge from God, although tradition holds that the king did it in fulfilment of a vow made while fearful of drowning at sea. Its site is now occupied by the old Royal Mint. At Mile End there was a leper hospital which Tudor historian John Stow dated to the reign of Edward II (1307-27). On the far side of the Lea there were Cistercians at Stratford Langthorne. The increase in population which fuelled the economic expansion of the twelfth and thirteenth centuries created a need for more places of worship for the laity. St Botolph without Aldgate was in existence by 1125. Between 1163 and 1180 William of Pontefract, a steward of the bishop of London, built a chapel on the

Isle of Dogs, dedicated to St Mary. The white chapel which gave its name to the surrounding district by 1340 was originally known as St Mary Matfelon (a name possibly of French origin) and certainly existed by 1280. It achieved parish status by 1320 and was rebuilt in 1362. St Mary, Bow can be traced back to 1311.

The lay subsidy of 1334 raised more from Stepney than from anywhere else in Middlesex, which implies a substantial and/or prosperous population. The poll tax returns of 1377 recorded 1,005 over the age of sixteen. Wealthy London citizens and even titled persons acquired residences in Tower Hamlets from the fourteenth century. Draper Sir John Pulteney, who served as Mayor of London in 1331-2, 1334 and 1337, acquired Poplar manor house; after his death in 1349 his widow married Sir Nicholas Lovayne (died 1375). The Black Prince is known to have stayed there in the summer between 1354 and 1358. Sir John Philpot (died 1384), Mayor of London, had the estate and manor house at Mile End known as Hulls.

13. *St Mary Matfelon, Whitechapel, in the 18th century. Originating as a chapel-of-ease to St Dunstan's, it was rebuilt several times but finally destroyed by bombing in December 1940.*

14. St Mary Bow, 2004. The post-war reconstruction in brick of the blitzed fifteenth-century stone tower is clearly visible.

HIGH DRAMA

The peasantry of Stepney parish led lives of monotonous hard labour, patterned by the passage of the seasons and the rituals of the church calendar. Doubtless the most dramatic events of their lives were also the most unwelcome – failed harvests, extremes of weather, outbreaks of disease afflicting the community or its livestock, fatal accidents and casual acts of violence. Unlike most of England's overwhelmingly rural population, however, their perspective on life and its possibilities must have been broadened by their proximity to what was by far the nation's largest city. At the least they would have been aware of the constant flow of traffic and travellers along the main road out of the capital into and out of England's then most prosperous and densely populated region – East Anglia. A few are known to have left the manor and prospered in the capital. The son of Elfsus, Robert, became a clerk in the reign of Henry II. John de Stebbenheath (died 1281) prospered as a fishmonger and held civic office.

Once, perhaps, in a lifetime – a lifetime averaging forty years or less – the people of the Tower Hamlets may have witnessed an event of historic significance. In 1132, within a quarter century of its foundation, the wealthy Priory of the Holy Trinity at Aldgate was devastated by fire, which doubtless had a disruptive knock-on effect for the administration of its estates. In 1158 the mighty Thames ran dry; presumably the accompanying drought damaged the subsequent harvest.

In 1299 a fire at Westminster obliged Edward I to convene a parliament at Stepney where third time Mayor of London Henry le Waleis (died 1301) acted as his host. Le Waleis, originally an immigrant from Gascony, had prospered as a wine merchant and first served as Mayor of London (the format Lord Mayor did not become customary until the fifteenth century) in 1273, then again in 1281 and a third time in 1298. He had also represented London in Parliament in 1283. The Parliament held at Stepney issued a proclamation against the importation of forged pennies and banning the export of English coins.

A decade later, in 1309, a magnificent tournament was held at Stepney to mark the coronation of Edward I's son and successor, the hapless bi-sexual Edward II whose disastrous reign so catastrophically confounded the high hopes of its inauguration. In the same year a whale was beached at Stepney.

In 1381 local inhabitants would doubtless have been caught up in the great Peasants' Revolt, which initially broke out in Brentwood, some twenty miles to the east. What began as a protest against the imposition of a third extraordinary poll tax in less than five years, to pay for the unpopular wars in France, soon escalated into an apocalyptic crusade for the abolition of serfdom itself. The Essex insurgents, matched by another massive contingent in Kent and lesser companies from Hertfordshire and other counties, converged on the capital. Surging towards the City's eastern wall, the rebels were admitted by sympathetic Londoners and an equally sympathetic Tower garrison yielded up the hapless Archbishop of Canterbury, Simon of Sudbury, and Treasurer Sir Robert Hales, identified as the master-minds behind the hated impost. They were dragged to Tower Hill and crudely decapitated. Dozens of the capital's Flemish community, disliked for their industriousness, suffered a similar fate. The monarch, Richard II, a mere child of fourteen, was exempted from the popular fury, which was fortunate indeed for a government which had for the moment totally lost its nerve. Remarkably the boy king retained not only a sense of self-possession but also an instinct for political survival, parleying with assemblies of rebels on successive days to buy time. One of these inconclusive confrontations took place at Mile End. According to the chronicler Jean Froissart "the king sent to them that they should all draw near to a fair place called Mile End whereat the people of the City did sport them in the summer season." At Smithfield rebel leader Wat Tyler's uncouth behaviour before the king provoked his murder at the hands of the royal entourage. The king's coolness in dispersing the crowd marked the first decisive step in the disintegration of the uprising.

Another populist outbreak occurred under the leadership of the shadowy Jack Cade in 1450. The main rising occurred in Kent as a protest against the incompetence of the government of Henry VI, tarnished by the disastrous endgame of the Hundred Years War. Once again Mile End became briefly a focal point of revolt as Cade's Kentish supporters effected a rendezvous there with an Essex contingent. The combined force gained admission to London but soon lost the sympathy of the Londoners as Cade lost control over them and they turned to plunder. Once again the malcontents were induced to disperse with promise of amnesty, though Cade himself was subsequently fatally wounded resisting arrest.

The continuing weakness of the periodically deranged Henry VI left him at the mercy of bolder spirits and in May 1471, the year of his death, London was again consequently threatened from the east when the naval adventurer Thomas Fauconberg brought a fleet of forty-seven ships to Blackwall in a botched attempt to snatch the monarch from alleged protective custody in the Tower. Acting on behalf of his cousin, 'Warwick the Kingmaker', Fauconberg laid siege to London for three days but failed to get past Aldgate and was pursued back as far as Stratford, caught and executed.

THE FOUNDERS

Richard Foxe (1448?-1528}, appointed vicar of Stepney in 1485, is honoured in Oxford as the founder of Corpus Christi college, despite the fact that he is alleged to have said of England's universities that "long continuance in those places is either a sign of a lack of friends or of learning or of good and upright life". Foxe was a companion of 'Henry ap Tuddor' when he was in exile and when he became Henry VII the vicarage of Stepney – which had been denied Foxe by the defeated Richard III – was the first of many rewards which accompanied Foxe's rapid elevation to the king's privy council and the bench of bishops, with Foxe holding successively the sees of Exeter, Bath and Wells, Durham and finally Winchester, the richest diocese in England. Foxe's tenure at Stepney can only have been a matter of months because in the same year the office passed to John Colet (*see below*). The vicarage, a prized living conveniently near the capital, was evidently used as a stepping-stone to higher preferment. It was Foxe who baptised the future Henry VIII at Greenwich, served as ambassador in negotiations with Scotland, France and Austria and was still hailed a century after his death as "not only a grave counsellor for war or peace but also a good surveyor of works and a good master of ceremonies."

John Colet (1467-1519), chiefly remembered as the founder of St Paul's school, became vicar of Stepney when he was just eighteen and held the post until he became dean of St Paul's twenty years later. The actual duties of ministering to the people of Stepney were almost certainly delegated to a curate because Colet himself was both very wealthy and much preoccupied with scholarship. But he certainly knew Stepney well, having been born and brought up in the Great Place, his father's house, which stood just west of the parish church, on a site now occupied by Stepping Stones urban farm. He also returned there to visit his pious mother, Christine, when he was a middle-aged man.

Colet's father, Sir Henry Colet, was a mercer who twice served as Mayor of London and amassed an immense fortune. Like nine-tenths of all the men who held that high office in Tudor times he was a self-made man from the provinces. John was the eldest child of eleven sons and eleven daughters – all of whom had died by 1498. While Colet was still studying at university his mother's family conferred on him the living of a Suffolk parish, which he held until his death and in the same year, 1485, his father's influence gained him St Dunstan's, Stepney. To these he later added the income from five other church offices. Having the means to study in France and Italy was therefore no problem. Teaching at Oxford Colet became one of a small academic clique which revolutionized the study of the Bible by applying a critical historical approach to its text, rather than simply reproducing the established opinions of

15. *John Colet. A critic of church corruption, he left no money for Masses for his soul.*

16. *A surviving part of Great Place, drawn in 1804.*

centuries of medieval commentators. Only in 1498 was Colet finally ordained as a priest. In 1499 he met the great Dutch scholar Erasmus, who became a lifelong friend, as did Sir Thomas More. Both men visited him at Stepney, Erasmus writing with evident eagerness:

> "I come to drink your fresh air, my Colet, to drink deeper of your rural peace. Wherever you look, the earth yieldeth you a pleasant prospect, the temperature of the air fresheth you and the very bounds of heaven do delight you. Here you find nothing but bounteous gifts of Nature and saint-like tokens of innocency."

In 1505 Colet left Oxford upon being appointed Dean of St Paul's. Ironically, returning to London coincided with his giving up the vicarage of Stepney. Colet's father died at the Great Place that same year and was buried in Stepney church, leaving John sole heir to vast wealth, which he used to found St Paul's school, making over most of his inheritance to the Mercers' Company to administer for the benefit of his foundation. The school was to admit 153 boys – matching the number in the New Testament account of the miraculous draught of fish. Colet remained an outspoken critic of what he regarded as the intellectual decay and moral corruption of the contemporary church and even dared to denounce Henry VIII's gratuitous warmongering against France. Colet's personal integrity, however, proved sufficient to protect him from the malice of clergy who fell below his own high standards. Colet succumbed to a third bout of sweating sickness in 1519, aged just over fifty. Out at Stepney his devout mother, having survived the birth – and deaths – of all her twenty-two offspring, lived on until 1523. Ten years later The Great Place came into the possession of the hugely acquisitive Thomas Cromwell, who had been chiefly responsible for enforcing the suppression of the monasteries and served Henry VIII as chief minister in succession to the disgraced Cardinal Wolsey. Cromwell acquired a fifty-year lease and set in hand extensive and expensive building work perhaps with a view to his own retirement from the cares of high office – a decision taken out of his hands by his own disgrace and execution in 1540.

Rural Retreat

London's eastern hinterland was transformed in the course of the sixteenth century by the interaction of four factors – the quadrupling of the capital's population; the dissolution of its religious houses; the establishment of a permanent royal navy; and the development of a global commerce. London's first true historian, John Stow (1525?-1605) witnessed this transformation in the course of his own lifetime and chronicled much of it in his pioneering *Survey of London* (1598). A resident of Aldgate, at the easternmost edge of the City proper, Stow was all too aware of the environmental impact of the expansion of the metropolis which had transformed the arcadia of his childhood, offering berries from the hedges and milk fresh from the cow, into the embryonic East End. This transformation had been symbolised to him by a former garden of the nearby Priory of Holy Trinity which had been converted from an object of contemplation to a field for cultivation "that served the markets with herbs and roots". Stow sighed for the days when Petticoat Lane "had on both sides fair hedge rows of elm trees, with bridges and easy stiles to pass over into the pleasant fields, very commodious for citizens therein to walk, shoot or otherwise to recreate and refresh their dull spirits in the sweet and wholesome air."

THE NEWCOMERS

London's population growth from 1520 far outran that of England as a whole until the mid-eighteenth century – despite outbreaks of sweating sickness in 1518 and 1551 and of plague in 1562, 1581 and 1643, when Stepney alone saw 2,228 succumb. Between 1520 and 1600 England's population rose from 2,400,000

17. *Part of a 19th-century engraving of the 1543 panorama drawn by Anton van den Wyngaerde – showing the Tower (left), Bermondsey Abbey (foreground) and Greenwich Palace (right rear) in a still rural setting.*

to 4,110,000 – by just under three-quarters, London's from 55,000 to 200,400 – almost quadrupling. In 1520 London's population was slightly lower than the aggregate (62,000) of the ten historic inland provincial centres of Norwich, York, Salisbury, Chester, Worcester, Exeter, Cambridge, Coventry, Shrewsbury and Gloucester. By 1600 it was nearly three times as great, although they also had grown in aggregate by 18%.

London needed immigrants if it was to live, let alone to grow. Even in the later seventeenth century, when smallpox had replaced plague as the endemic killer, deaths in the capital exceeded births by some 6,000 a year. A study of the years 1551-3 shows that half the newcomers to the capital came from 90 or more miles away. Many of these were fleeing poverty in economically marginal areas, a pattern that continued during the period 1580-1640, when population growth outstripped the expansion of employment opportunities, and particularly in the famine-troubled 1590s and 1620s. Others came from overseas. Flemish immigration had been officially sponsored by the Crown back in the fourteenth century, when their cloth-making skills were at a premium. By the sixteenth century the 'Dotch', a catch-all category which embraced Flemings, Dutch and Germans, had become prominent in brewing and were taking the lead in crafts based on novel, cutting-edge technologies, like printing and precision machinery, such as the manufacture of clocks or spectacles. Where these related to maritime commerce, as in the making of maps or navigational instruments, it was natural that their practitioners should gravitate to the riverside. There were also overseas immigrants from the opposite end of the skills hierarchy, with sufficient Irish present in Wapping by the 1590s to constitute a distinct community.

Rivalling the Flemish as skilled craftsmen were the Huguenots, persecuted Protestant refugees (the word 'refugee' was first applied to them) from France, who were welcomed by the boy king Edward VI in 1550. Stow, too, welcomed the arrival of the Huguenots: "God's blessing is surely not only brought upon the parish receiving poor strangers but also a great advantage hath accrued to the whole nation by the rich manufacturers of weaving silks and stuffs and camlets, which art they brought with them." Huguenot immigrants distributed themselves outside the jurisdiction of the City of

18. Originally built c.1520, the Prospect of Whitby at Shadwell adopted its present name in 1777. Dickens, Whistler and Turner all drank there.

London in Soho, Spitalfields, Chelsea, Greenwich and Wandsworth, so that they could practise their trades without having to conform to its regulatory framework.

HOUSING, HOMES AND WORK

The unceasing growth in London's population necessarily increased the demand for accommodation. Some of this was met by cramming more people into the existing stock of housing, the rest by the building of new homes. It being a seller's market, many of these new dwellings were poorly constructed. The chronicler Ralph Holinshed observed in 1587 that the common at Mile End

"was sometimes, yea in the memory of men yet living, a large mile long (from Whitechapell to Stepenheth church) and therefore called Mile End Green; but now at this present, by greedie (and as seemeth me), unlawfully inclosures and building of houses, notwithstanding hir Maiestie's proclamation to the contrarie, it remaineth scarce half a mile in length."

Stow, writing a decade later, endorsed this view of the spoliation of Mile End: "this common field, being sometime the beauty of this city ... is so encroached upon by building of filthy cottages ... that in some places scarce remaineth a sufficient highway for the meeting of carriages and droves of cattle."

The need for residential development coincided with the royal decision to confiscate the wealth of the religious houses, including their landed estates. For the Tower Hamlets area, dominated for centuries by ecclesiastical landlords, the effects were particularly momentous. At St Leonard's in Bromley the successor to Madame Eglantyne (rather a termagant as it happened) was pensioned off and her sisters cast upon the world, as were the residents of the area's other convents and monasteries. A land boom began, encouraging ambitious schemes of development. The Parliament of 1535-6, which passed the legislation confirming the dissolution of the monasteries, also authorised a project to drain 130 acres of Wapping Marsh, from Hermitage to Foxes Lane (roughly present-day Glamis Road). The under-

19. The Whitechapel Bell Foundry, 2004. A rare modern survival of an ancient craft.

taking was entrusted to a Dutch hydraulic engineer, Cornelius Vanderdelft, who, by way of encouragement was to gain title of half the land thus recovered. Ironically, the Dutchman drowned and by a further Act of 1541 his portion was reassigned to a mercer, Richard Hill, presumably a leading investor. The project was completed a few years later. Major breaches in the embankment in 1565 and 1571 led to the apparently perverse decision to consolidate the threatened landscape by building houses on it. Stow described the resulting settlement as a "continual street or filthy straight passage with alleys and small tenements or cottages inhabited by sailors' victuallers." Catering to the various needs of sailors was to become a central element in the economy of the riverside. The famed *Prospect of Whitby* public house claims to have been founded as far back as 1520, though then it was known, doubtless with reason, as *The Devil's Tavern*. The enterprising Richard Etgoos already had a beerhouse at Limehouse when the century opened. There were several inns at Blackwall by the 1540s and by 1553 there were at least seven ale houses in Poplar and Blackwall alone.

Development continued east of Wapping in a manner that Stow did not *entirely* condemn:

> "There hath been of late, in place of elme trees, many small tenements raysed towards Radcliffe; and Radcliffe itself hath beene also encreased in building eastward (in place whereof I have known a large high way with fayre elme trees on both sides) that the same hath now taken hold of Lime Hurst, Lime Host, corruptly called Lime House, sometime distant a mile from Radcliffe ... but of late years shipwrights and ... other marine men ... built many large and strong houses for themselves and smaller for sailors, from thence almost to Poplar and so to Blakewal."

Another major project, of 1542, resulted in the paving of the entire roadway from Aldgate through Whitechapel and Mile End out as far as Bow Bridge. This not only improved the flow of traffic but established a spine along which further commercial and residential developments could be ranged. In the shadow of the Tower and eastwards along the riverside towards Limehouse and inland as far as Whitechapel, manufactures were established which were deemed too noisy, smelly or dangerous to be satisfactorily conducted within the walls of the City itself, notably tanning, brickmaking and metalwork. The nation's leading bell foundry relocated from its original site in Billiter Street to Whitechapel in 1583.

LORDS OF THE MANOR

In 1551 Nicholas Ridley, Bishop of London made over to Edward VI the manor of Stepney and within a few months Edward made over to his chamberlain, Thomas, first Baron Wentworth of Nettlestead in Suffolk (1501-51)

> "in consideration of his good and faithful service before done ... the lordships of Stebunheth and Hackney, with all the members and appurtenances thereto belonging, in Stebbunheth, Hackney Way, Shoreditch, Holiwell Street, Whitechapell, Stratford at Bow, Poplar, North Street, Limehouse, Ratcliffe, Cleve Street, Brock Street, Mile End, Bleten Hall Green (Bethnal Green), Oldford, Westheth, Kingsland, Shaklewell, Newinton Street alias Hackney Street, Clapton, Church Street, Wel Street, Humbarton, Grove Street, Gunston Street, alias More Street, in the county of Middlesex, together with the marsh of Stebunheth etc."

The manor of Hackney was valued at £69 9s. 4d and Stepney at £140 8s. 11d. The Wentworths were to remain lords of the manor until the eighteenth century. The first Baron Wentworth, a career loyalist royalist, had supported Henry VIII's divorce; condemned Anne Boleyn; helped crush the Norfolk rising of 1549 and soon repaid Edward VI by helping him overthrow his domineering self-styled 'Protector', Edward Seymour, Duke of Somerset, who was in fact Wentworth's own cousin. Somerset was to be ousted in October 1551 and executed for treason on the flimsiest evidence the following February. By then Wentworth a father of sixteen children (all by the same wife), had died (and apparently merited a magnificent funeral and burial in Westminster Abbey) and the manor had passed to his son, also Thomas (1525-84). The second baron Wentworth was distinguished, although that is perhaps scarcely the appropriate word in the circumstances, as the man who lost Calais, England's last holding in France, to the French. Wentworth did send repeated warnings to the government that the enclave was undermanned and inadequately fortified but his own incompetence added materially to the ineptitude of the resist-

ance offered when the French mounted a surprise attack in 1557. Being himself taken prisoner, Wentworth, ransomed and later committed to the Tower, was lucky to be acquitted of high treason and therefore not to lose his head or his manors. Although he was not a traitor a less forgiving monarch might have held him blameworthy for failing to respond promptly to reports of the imminent French attack but Elizabeth I was reluctant to inaugurate her reign with a bloodletting. Wentworth eventually recovered sufficient favour to be appointed Lord Lieutenant of Norfolk and Suffolk but was never entrusted with any higher office, although he was kept busy with supervising musters of the militia in Tower Hamlets. He died at Stepney, where his second wife Anne was already buried. Wentworth may have been married a third time because a Stepney neighbour, the explorer Sir William Burrough (*see p. 31*) married a widowed Lady Wentworth.

Despite the second baron's blighted career, his eldest son, William, nearly managed to redeem the family's standing by making a brilliant marriage to a daughter of Elizabeth's most powerful and trusted counsellor, Lord Burghley – but the bridegroom died of plague within the year. The title therefore passed to the second son, Henry (1558-93), who also proved short-lived. He married the daughter of Sir Owen Hopton, Lieutenant of the Tower, but died at thirty-five. The Wentworths are commemorated in the name of Wentworth Street, off Petticoat Lane.

RESIDENTS OF RANK

The Lords of the Manor of Stepney may have been more notable for their absence than their presence and the same might have been said for Richard Pace (1482?-1536), vicar of St Dunstan's from 1519 to 1527. A brilliant scholar, he had been picked out for the rare and expensive privilege of studying in Italy and was subsequently employed on diplomatic missions through which his dedication, energy and tact raised him rapidly in royal favour, gaining him no less than fourteen church livings or offices and the Readership in Greek at Cambridge. It was almost certainly at Pace's suggestion that Henry VIII subsequently founded the prestigious Regius Professorships in Greek at both Oxford and Cambridge. Absentee though he may often have been, Pace chose to be buried at St Dunstan's, although, having been appointed a dean of both St Paul's and Salisbury cathedral, he might have chosen either of those prestigious locations as his final resting-place.

Despite the burgeoning of ribbon development along the river and the line of the Whitechapel Road, there were still numerous persons of eminence who continued to choose Tower Hamlets as a place of residence and even retirement. One such was Ratcliff-born City grocer Nicholas Gibson, son of John Gibson, a mariner. By 1526 Nicholas Gibson had become Prime Warden of the Grocers' Company and had begun to accumulate what became a bucolic hideaway with an orchard at Ratcliff. He also had a substantial commercial property on Lower Thames Street. In 1536 Gibson and his wife Avice, accepting their childlessness, used their fortune to found an almshouse for fourteen aged persons and a school for sixty poor children. This was administered by the Coopers' Company from 1549 onwards and therefore took its name from them rather than its founder.

Sir Gilbert Dethick (1519?-84) was probably of Dutch origin but his father had anglicized his name. Whatever his background, he rose steadily through the ranks at the College of Arms to become Garter King-of-Arms in 1550. Henry VIII employed him in diplomatic missions to Denmark and Cleves and granted him a mansion at Poplar, set in an acre of ground and this became the family seat of the Dethicks for a further two centuries. The antiquarian Francis Thynne (1545?-1608), who eventually became Lancaster Herald, also lived in Poplar at some point.

Sir Gilbert Dethick's second son, Sir William Dethick (1543-1612) also became Garter King-of-Arms, despite an ungovernable temper which led him on varying occasions to punch his own father, stab his brother, beat colleagues at the College of Arms and attack two priests at two separate funerals – but, although he was suspended from office several times, he was apparently good at his job. Universally detested for his vile temper – for which no doubt these days a psychological or even physical disorder might be blamed – he resigned his offices in 1605 to sulk on an immense annuity of £3,200. He was buried in St Paul's Cathedral.

A great house that came to be known as Kirby Castle was built at Bethnal Green in 1570 by City merchant John Kirby. A generation later

20. Kirby Castle, Bethnal Green. Built c. 1570, it was to be for most of its existence a mental asylum.

it was the home of the eccentric experimentalist Sir Hugh Platt (1552-1608). The son of a wealthy brewer, Platt studied at Cambridge and Lincoln's Inn but, having no need to work, dabbled in literature before turning to applied science, especially in relation to horticulture and farming. Residing successively at Bishop's Hall, Bethnal Green and then at Kirby Castle, Platt maintained extensive experimental gardens where he grew such exotics as tobacco and grapes from which he made his own wine. He claimed that his wine was commended by the French ambassador – although we must remember that he was a diplomat. Platt's wide-ranging investigations enabled him to discover that by excluding air from freshly picked fruit, it could be kept far longer than usual. Platt thus pioneered the bottling of fruit as a means of preservation. He also discovered that meat could be preserved longer if it was partly boiled in brine. Sir Francis Drake was impressed with the meat experiments when he came to Bethnal Green to see for himself. He also took note of Platt's efforts to keep water drinkable by adding powdered brimstone to it and changing the hogshead containers it was stored in much more frequently. By 1592 Platt was celebrated enough to have a delegation of privy councillors troop out to his home to witness demonstrations of a number of his inventions and discoveries. These were published in 1594 as *The Jewel House of Art and Nature, conteining divers rare and profitable Inventions, together with sundry new Experiments in the Art* of *Husbandry, Distillation and Moulding.* This was a compilation of five different tracts, suggesting improvements in such varied matters as brewing, fishing and casting metal. A second treatise, dealing with manures, was issued separately and was extremely valuable in mooting the idea of crop rotation and in promoting the use of marl to improve soil quality. In 1602 Platt, who was married twice and had three daughters, published a manual of household hints entitled *Delights for Ladies to adorne their Persons, Tables, Closets and Distillatories, with Bewties, Banquets, Perfumes and Waters.* This contained recipes for cosmetics and medicines, directions for preserving flowers and instructions on how to construct a sweat bath; it remained popular throughout the seventeenth century. Platt also issued a pamphlet describing how coal could be mixed with clay and other materials to create an economical domestic fuel; he is also credited

with the discovery of coke. Knighted by James I in 1605, Platt published his major work on gardening, *Floraes Paradisae,* in the year of his death, incorporating, the author asserted, knowledge "wrung out of the earth by the painful hand of experience." It was still being reissued in 1685.

MILITARY MANOEUVRES

Tudor England lived in constant anticipation of invasion and civil insurrection. The state demanded that loyal subjects fit to bear arms in its defence should regularly practise their use. Tower Hamlets, as its name proclaims, was traditionally the recruiting-ground for the garrison of the Tower of London. The area would also have been regularly combed for vagrants, foreigners and masterless men who could be pressed into military service in Ireland or the Low Countries. The settled male population at large was also liable for service as part of a home defence force. The earliest map of London, published *c.* 1559, shows archers practising in Spitalfields. To the west of them, in the fenced-off Artillery Ground, a man is firing a gun at a target. Like Finsbury Fields and Moorfields to the north and St George's Fields south of the Thames, open areas like Mile End were used for military exercises. In 1585, for example, the Grocers' Company contingent trained there for four days in the last week of April. The men were paid eight pence per day, plus food and drink.

The largest gathering of the Tudor period took place on 8 May 1539, when 15,000 men assembled at Mile End for inspection. The size and brilliance of the assembly greatly impressed those who witnessed it, even if the following account seems to describe it in terms of catwalk appeal as much as lethal capacity:

> "all the fields from White Chapell to Myle End and from Bednall Greene to Ratclyffe and to Stepney, were all covered with harness, men and weapons; and in especial the battaile of pykes seemed to be a great forest ... The Lord Mayor himself was in a fayre armour (the crestes thereof were gylt) and over that a coat of black velvet with half sleeves; and so was Sir Roger Cholmely, Knight, Recorder of London and all the other Aldermen and Shirifes, all well mounted on stirryng horses richely trapped and covered, with battleaxes in their hands and maces and chaynes about theyr neckes."

21. *Another 16th-century pub – the Anchor & Hope at New Crane Stairs, Stepney. Watercolour c.1870, by J T Wilson.*

Accompanied by musicians and attendants in white and marching in contingents behind thirty banners, they passed through the City to Westminster where the procession took six hours to march past the king, then wheeled northwards to return via Holborn to its starting-point.

SPRINGBOARD OF EMPIRE

Sir Thomas Spert (died 1541), memorialized on the south wall of the chancel of St Dunstan's, was the founder and first Master of Trinity House, and thus instrumental in nurturing the maritime expertise on which England's expansion as a naval power depended. Sometime master of the celebrated *Mary Rose*, in 1514 Spert obtained from Henry VIII a charter of incorporation for the Deptford Mariners' Guild of the Holy Trinity, later known as Trinity House, which undertook a wide range of responsibilities ranging from the training of pilots and the regulation of buoys and beacons to the maintenance of lighthouses. Its original headquarters was at Deptford Strand but in 1618 it moved to Ratcliff Cross and around 1650 ac-

quired the rental of the 'Great House' opposite St Dunstan's.

Although Deptford was selected as the main shipbuilding base for Henry VIII's royal navy Blackwall was already sufficiently established as a comparable centre of expertise for it to be selected in 1512 to re-deck and caulk the royal vessel *Peter Pomegranate.* More impressive still Blackwall was also used for the fitting out of two of his most prized warships the *Mary Rose* and the *Henry Grace à Dieu*, more familiarly known as the *'Great Harry'.* The *Mary Rose,* distinguished as one of the first ships able to fire a broadside, enjoyed a dramatic career of thirty years before meeting a disastrous end by capsizing in 1545. The rapidity of its end preserved it as an unintended time-capsule. Raised from the sea-bed in 1982 it is now the only sixteenth-century ship on display in Europe. It is also known that Peter Pett, son of Peter Pett (died 1589), royal shipwright at Deptford, was a shipbuilder at Wapping.

Stow praised Stepney as "one of the greatest Nurseries of Navigation and Breeders of Seamen in England, the most Serviceable Men in the Nation; without which England could not be England: for they are its Strength and Wealth". The capacity to repair ships or prepare and victual them for long voyages made the Thames' northern riverside an obvious point of departure for journeys of exploration. An ancient half-timbered building – surviving into the Victorian era but demolished by 1881 – was long known as 'Raleigh's House'. Although there is no indisputable documentary proof that Sir Walter Raleigh ever was a permanent resident of Blackwall many of his letters are headed as having been written there while he was on naval or other official business.

In 1553 Sir Hugh Willoughby (died 1554) set out from Ratcliff with three ships in his ill-fated attempt to find a North-East Passage to the riches of Asia. Ironically in view of the recently-established Wentworth connection with the locality, Willoughby's project had been prompted by the damage to his promotion prospects at court following the fall from grace of Somerset, whose protégé he had been. Willoughby himself perished, having got no further in his quest than the coast of Norwegian Lapland. A diary he kept of the venture was found with his frozen corpse and subsequently published by Richard Hakluyt. This revealed that the course they took was proof of

22. Plaque erected in King Edward Memorial Park, Shadwell by the London County Council in 1922 to honour navigators who set off from Ratcliff to explore the inhospitable northern seas.

the utter ignorance of navigation of all the senior officers involved. The extinction of his crew can likewise be blamed on their complete failure to prepare or provision adequately for their attempt to survive an arctic winter. Willoughby's pilot-general, Richard Chancellor, did, however, manage to reach Archangel, from where he was taken by sledge to meet Tsar Ivan the Terrible in Moscow. On returning to London Chancellor established the joint stock Muscovy Company to trade with Russia, exchanging English woollens for Russian furs.

The inauguration of Anglo-Russian commerce was achieved at a heavy price in misadventure. Often enough misadventure had no positive outcome at all. On 14 June 1563 Elizabeth I consented to come to Limehouse to view a mock sea-fight organised by Thomas Stucley (1525-78), a Devonian adventurer. On the 25th of the same month he left with six ships, one supplied by the Queen, ostensibly to plant a colony in Florida. In reality he embarked on two years of indiscriminate piracy against

French, Spanish and Portuguese shipping until even the Queen was forced to disown him and order his arrest. Stucley, hounded by debt and still driven by ambition, defected to the service of Spain and was killed, fighting on behalf of the Spanish crown, in Morocco.

William Burrough (1536-99) was on Willoughby's expedition when he was only sixteen. By the time he was twenty-four he was already 'captain-general' of a fleet of thirteen ships charged with rooting out Danish freebooters from the Gulf of Finland. As a trusted agent of the Muscovy Company Burrough penetrated as far inland as Moscow, taking every opportunity to gather topographical information which he would later reproduce in a map of Russia presented to the Queen in 1578 – a significant achievement in an era in which geographical knowledge was jealously guarded as a matter of state security. Burrough's Russian map has now been lost although another, of Norway and Lapland, survives in the British Museum. By 1579 Burrough was living at

23. Execution Dock – used for pirates from the 14th century until 1830.

Burrough's swashbuckling career is matched, if not outstripped, by that of Master-Gunner Edwarde Webbe. Born in the shadow of the Tower around 1554, he first sailed for Russia in 1566, a mere boy. During his second visit to there in 1571 he happened to be in Moscow when the city was taken by the Tartars and was carried off to the Crimea as a slave, but was successfully ransomed. Undaunted, Webbe was at the assault on Tunis in 1572, only to be taken and enslaved again soon after. Exchanging a galley-slave's oar in the Ottoman navy for service in the Sultan's army as an artillery expert, Webbe campaigned against his master's enemies in Persia, Spain and Portugal. Around 1588 Webbe was one of twenty captives successfully ransomed by the English ambassador to the Ottoman court. Having returned safely to England once more, Webbe tempted fate yet again, accepting an appointment as chief master-gunner to Henri IV of France and taking part in the battle of Ivry in March 1590. Webbe perhaps felt the hand of history on his shoulder at that point and quit settling in lodgings at Blackwall to compose a memoir recounting *'The Rare and most wonderful things which Edward Webbe an Englishman born hath seen and passed in his troublesome travails ... "*.

At the prompting of Sir Humphrey Gilbert (1539?-83), then a resident of Limehouse, Sir Martin Frobisher (1535?-94) undertook three voyages to find a North-West Passage. He at least did have a seafaring background, having lived in Ratcliff and been sent to sea as a boy. On his first voyage in 1576 he managed to penetrate northern Canadian waters and returned triumphant with an eskimo and a lump of iron pyrites, which an Italian alchemist pronounced to contain gold. This inspired a second venture which brought back two hundred tons of the worthless dross. When it failed to yield the expected pay-off the eager believers in its authenticity simply argued that it was a poor sample and a third expedition was therefore despatched which brought home yet more.

Despite the discredit, not to say ridicule, which accompanied the conclusive proof of the worthlessness of his 'treasure', Frobisher rapidly managed to regain royal favour and so distinguished himself in the fighting against the Armada that he was knighted.

In 1582 Sir Humphrey Gilbert himself led an expedition which took possession of Newfoundland, thus establishing the first domin-

Limehouse, where he composed his *Discourse of the Variation of the Compass, or Magneticall Needle,* which was published in 1581. In this work he pointed out that failure to observe compass variations rendered nearly all contemporary charts useless for purposes of practical navigation. By 1583 Burrough was in royal service, suppressing piracy and bringing in ten major malefactors to be hanged at Wapping and have their corpses washed over by the tides at Execution Dock. In 1587 he served as Vice-Admiral in Drake's marauding expedition to Cadiz but having fallen out with the arrogant Admiral, a Devon man like himself, Burrough was demoted to command of a single small ship in the fight against the Armada the following year. Retiring from active seamanship, Burrough busied himself with fitting out a fleet for Frobisher (see below) and "getting a good wife" in the person of Lady Wentworth. The last record of Burrough, in 1590, when he was still living at Limehouse, is an anonymous warning that he was in danger of assassination, though for what reason is uncertain. He is commemorated in the name of the Sir William Burrough Primary School in Salmon Lane.

24. Sir Humphrey Gilbert. He was an ancestor of librettist W S Gilbert.

ion of the British empire. Yet another Devonian on the make, Gilbert at least had had the polishing effect of an education at Eton and Oxford. But there was more to him than courtly style. In 1570 he won his knighthood the hard way, by defeating a major Irish chieftain. Elected MP for Plymouth the following year, he elected to settle in Limehouse with his new wife. But he remained eager to prove himself in the field and in 1572 led an abortive expedition in support of Protestant Dutch rebels in revolt against Spanish rule in the Netherlands. Returning to Limehouse to take a five-year "loitering vacation from martial stratagems", he devoted himself to mapping out grandiose enterprises to win him fame and fortune.

One of his more cerebral schemes was for *'The Erection of (Queen Elizabethes) Academy in London for education of Her Maiesties Wardes and others the youths of nobility and gentlemen.'* By implication a critique of his own university experience, Gilbert anticipated by a generation Sir Thomas Bodley's achievement at Oxford of establishing an institution (in Bodley's case named after him) as a copyright library by

25. Sir Martin Frobisher. Oil by Cornelius Ketel.

suggesting that all printers should be obliged to present his proposed Academy with "one copy, well bound", of everything they printed, as well as requiring that the Librarian of the Academy should have first pick of all imported books.

After his detailed proposal for finding a north-west passage to China inaugurated Frobisher's exploring career, Gilbert, encouraged, compiled a secret memorandum setting out '*How Her Majesty might annoy the King of Spain by fitting out a fleet of warships under pretence of a voyage of discovery and so fall upon the enemy's shipping, destroy his trade in Newfoundland and the West Indies and possess both Regions*'. Gilbert's phony exploration deception was ignored by the Queen but did prompt the granting of a charter for discovery and colonisation. Divided leadership and a mauling at the hands of the Spanish scuppered that enterprise and Gilbert's finances with it. Repairing to Ireland to repair his reputation, Gilbert won the backing of speculators in Southampton for an attempt to colonise Newfoundland and in August 1583 he at last did just that, landing at St John's Bay to found the first English colony in North America. A month later he and his ship were simply "devoured and swallowed up of the sea."

Another former East End resident who can be said to have uniquely distinguished himself was William Adams (died 1620). Born in Gillingham, he served a twelve year appren-

ticeship under Master Nicholas Diggins of Limehouse, qualifying as a Trinity House Pilot. Adams married Mary Hyn in St Dunstan's, Stepney but can have seen little of her as he was constantly at sea, sailing as far as North Africa and the Arctic. During the Armada emergency he commanded a supply ship, running provisions out to the main fleet. Serving as chief pilot of a Dutch expedition which intended to combine commerce with piracy as opportunity offered, Adams was, after storms and starvation threatened death, eventually shipwrecked in Japan, becoming the first Englishman to reach that country. Adams' remarkable talents as a navigator, shipbuilder, map-maker and self-taught linguist rapidly gained him a unique position as a technical adviser, interpreter and trusted confidant to the first shogun of the Tokugawa dynasty, Ieyasu, who elevated Adams to the rank of samurai, a distinction never before or since conferred upon a foreigner.

John Vassall (died 1625) came to England as a child refugee from religious strife in Nor-

26. *St Matthias, Poplar. Built by the East India Company in 1654 and rebuilt in 1775/6, it is here shown in 1795. It is the only surviving London church originally built during the Interregnum. Watercolour, artist unknown.*

27. In 1867-70 S S Teulon 'restored' St Matthias by cladding its neo-Classical interior with Gothic stonework. Closed in 1977 and vandalised, it was restored in the 1990s as a community centre.

mandy. He fitted out and commanded a vessel against the Armada and put up £25 towards the settlement of Virginia. Vassall is known to have lived at Ratcliff from 1589 to 1602 and married both his first two wives in St Dunstan's, where he also chose to be buried. His fourth son, William (1592-1655), born in Stepney, became one of the richest settlers in Plymouth, Massachusetts and then in Barbados.

'JOHN COMPANY'

Chartered in 1600, the East India Company was to become Britain's first global corporation. Its connection with the East End was early and enduring. In 1612 the company established a shipyard at Blackwall and it was there that most of its fleet was to be built. Although they were primarily trading vessels East Indiamen were of necessity heavily armed to undertake long voyages carrying high value cargoes through hostile and dangerous waters. As India had little use for the woollen cloth which was Britain's usual main export product the company's ships often went out in ballast carrying bricks or beer, both produced in the East End. The bricks were used to build European-style houses in the company's major bases at Calcutta, Madras and Bombay. The beer was for the consumption of the garrisons there. Supplying John Company's many needs created much employment in the East End. The company in return acknowledged its ties with Poplar in particular by building a chapel there in 1654 and establishing almshouses nearby.

RETIREMENT – OR REFUGE?

The deeply learned Jesuit Henry Garnett (1555-1606), a convert to Catholicism, served as superior to the English province from 1587 onwards. Of necessity – under permanent threat of death simply for being a Jesuit – he lived a life in the shadows. One of his known refuges was a house in Spitalfields. Garnett was finally arrested as a consequence of a large-scale round-up which followed the Gunpowder Plot of 1605. He suffered the agonising death reserved for alleged traitors – hanged (until not quite dead), drawn and quartered.

William Davison (1541?-1608}, having served Elizabeth I as an expert on Scottish politics and a diplomatic agent in the Low Countries, became one of her secretaries and in that capacity was responsible for presenting her with the death-warrant of Mary, Queen of Scots for signature. When Elizabeth subsequently claimed that she had not intended the warrant to be enforced the blame fell on Davison, who was condemned to two years in the Tower and a fine of ten thousand marks. This broke him financially, forcing him to retire to a house at Stepney, where he ultimately died and was buried.

When a major epidemic of plague broke out after the death of Elizabeth I in 1603 the prolific playwright Thomas Dekker of Whitechapel satirised the flight of the rich to hide themselves in the slummy suburbs for fear of marauding thieves:

> "In unsought Allies and unholsome places,
>   Back-wayes and by-lanes, where appeare fewe faces,
>   In shamble-smelling rooms, loathsome prospects,
>   And penny-lattice windows, which rejects
>   All popularitie; there the rich Cubs lurke,
>   When in great houses ruffians are at worke,
>   Not dreaming that such glorious booties lye
>   Under those nasty roofes: such they pass by
>   Without a search, crying there's nought for us,
>   And wealthy men deceive poor villains thus."

Stepney can scarcely have been the safest of refuges. In the 1603 plague outbreak 2,228 were recorded as having died there; in the next major outbreak, in 1625, the figure was over 3,700. Disaster on such a scale posed a major challenge to local administration and the adoption of extraordinary measures to deal with it. Mary Oswell and Elizabeth Scott of Ratcliff and Joane Hassam and Rose Write of Limehouse were appointed to search out and view corpses "in case and fear of Contagion of sickness now suspected". Each body accounted for brought a fee of fourpence. By July of 1625 1,623 victims had been interred in Stepney churchyard and the sexton had been granted permission to bury where he would, providing only that the site was at least seven yards in from the churchyard wall, in consideration of those living adjacent on its outside. On 7 August the vestry attempted to cut out opportunistic extortioners by setting limits to the fees which could be demanded for conveying corpses to burial. Approved carriers were ordered to carry red wands as a badge of their office. Deaths peaked in that month at 1,282. A further eight hundred died in September. A new burial ground was now essential and by 1627 a pond had been drained and the surrounding area enclosed at the expense of the Mercers' Company who were major landowners in St Dunstan's environs. A further onslaught of 1636 carried off nine hundred, in 1640 another 1,100. In the last great visitation of 1665 Stepney lost more inhabitants than any other parish in the entire capital – 6,583. Defoe recorded that it had been necessary to dig eight huge burial pits in different parts of the parish to accommodate the corpses.

CIVIL WAR

London remained in Parliamentary hands throughout the civil wars of the 1640s. Given that the eastern counties were also solid for Parliament and that the king had established his capital at Oxford, it was reasonable to suppose that any royalist assault on the metropolis would come from the west. Nevertheless the entire city was surrounded by an eighteen-mile enceinte of earth and timber fortifications, the circuit of which was walked by Scottish merchant William Lithgow in 1643. The ramparts he saw were fronted by a ditch both deeper and wider than the height of a tall man, supported by embankments and punctuated at key points by star-shaped artillery forts. The stronghold at Whitechapel commanded the main eastern route in and out of the capital and was mounted with seven bronze cannon. The sections of ditch nearest to the Thames may well have been flooded as an extra deterrent to assault. Erected at huge expense and manned at further expense, these defences were never tested in action and almost completely

demolished in 1647, following the decisive parliamentary victory in the second civil war. This decision may, if only briefly, have looked a trifle over-confident when, in 1648, royalist insurgents briefly seized Bow Bridge in the hope of provoking a rising in the capital. They were, however, soon chased off and pursued all the way to Colchester where they took advantage of that parliamentary stronghold's defences to force their pursuers to conduct a lengthy and costly siege, at the end of which the royalist leaders were summarily shot.

SPITALFIELDS SAGE

Nicholas Culpeper (1616-54) set up as an astrologer, apothecary and physician in Red Lion Street, Spitalfields around 1640 and rapidly acquired a high reputation, not least for giving free treatment to the ever plentiful poor, although he himself was ever in straitened circumstances. Culpeper claimed to have been cheated of his patrimony but added to his burdens by fathering seven children – perhaps the pressure which made him a driven man. During the civil war Culpeper fought for Parliament and was seriously wounded in the chest. In 1649 he risked the rancour of the

28. Nicholas Culpeper and his house in Spitalfields.

Royal College of Physicians by publishing an unauthorised English translation of its *pharmacopeia*. By making arcane medical knowledge accessible to the literate layman Culpeper threatened to jeopardise a powerfully organised professional monopoly and thus provoked a venomous response from pamphleteers who maliciously accused him of atheism, lechery, drunkenness and what was doubtless intended as the killer thrust – making a bad translation. The book nevertheless – or perhaps to some extent even on that account – enjoyed huge sales, with a second edition appearing in 1650 and a third in 1651. In 1653 Culpeper scored a similar triumph with *The English Physician Enlarged, with 369 Medicines made of English Herbs that were not in any impression until this.* The book went through five editions by 1698 and was reissued as late as 1809. Culpeper's other writings include works on the ancient physician Galen, anatomy, astrology, midwifery and contemporary politics. Many of these were still in draft at the time of his death and published subsequent to it. Nicholas Culpeper died at the age of thirty-eight, probably from the lingering effects of his war wound, compounded by overwork.

BETHNAL GREEN BOUNDER

Courtier, diplomat, architect, miniaturist, pamphleteer and promoter, the multi-talented Sir Balthazar Gerbier (?1591-1667) carved out an opportunistic career which ended in failure and obscurity. Gerbier came to London in 1616 in the entourage of the Dutch ambassador but soon attached himself to the household of the royal favourite, Charles Villiers, Duke of Buckingham, as a surveyor, in which capacity he designed the impressive water gate which survives to this day in Embankment Gardens, the sole remaining vestige of a once-imposing riverside residence. Gerbier was then taken into the royal household and knighted by Charles I who used him to liaise with foreign artists, notably Rubens and Van Dyck.

The precariousness of Gerbier's position was exposed with the onset of the civil war. In 1642 a mob attacked his house at Bethnal Green on the suspicion that Papists were being concealed there. In 1649, during the owner's (doubtless prudent) self-imposed exile, the house was ransacked on the orders of Parliament in the hope of discovering incriminating evidence which might be used at the king's trial for treason. Gerbier nevertheless felt secure enough to return after the king's execution and open a gentlemen's academy in his home, offering both academic and military instruction and social polish. The faculty tactfully included Cromwell's crony, Henry Walker, a former ironmonger who professed to teach Hebrew but was notorious as a forger and fraudster. After the all too predictable failure of this venture, Gerbier promoted an even more disastrous South American gold mining project before dying while attempting to revive his original career as an architect.

VETERAN VEGETARIAN

Around the time that Gerbier was abandoning Bethnal Green it became the chosen home of Roger Crab (?1621-80), who may well have been the original 'mad hatter'. Born in Buckinghamshire, he became a vegetarian, teetotaller and celibate at the age of twenty and served seven years in the Parliamentary army, claiming to have been severely wounded in the head, before adopting the trade of hatter. Crab's increasingly odd lifestyle has been attributed both to his headwound and to the effects of mercury poisoning associated with felt-making. After obeying the Biblical injunction to sell all his possessions and give the proceeds to the poor, Crab eventually settled at Bethnal Green in 1657. Dressed in sackcloth and subsisting by then on a diet of dock-leaves and grass, he claimed to live on three farthings a week. Like Culpeper, Crab gave out free medical advice to the poor and dabbled in astrology and prediction. Having previously suffered imprisonment for his radical religious and political opinions, Crab lapsed into quietism and was protected from further persecution by a reputation for personal sanctity which eventually allowed him to be buried at St Dunstan's, Stepney, notwithstanding his past eccentricities.

READMISSION

London's Jewish community was expelled by Edward I in 1290, although individual Jews, often skilled physicians, were known in the capital in the sixteenth century. In 1656 a delegation of Sephardi Jews, originally from Spain and Portugal but settled in Amsterdam, led by Menasseh ben Israel, pleaded success-

29. A 17th-century shop front on the north side of Bow Road, in 2004.

fully with Cromwell for readmission. In 1657 they obtained a burial ground behind what is now 253 Mile End Road. It remained in use until 1742. With their first synagogue established in a house in Creechurch Lane they settled mainly in the Houndsditch to Aldgate area, rather to the west of the future epicentre of Jewish residence. In 1704 they were able to take possession of the handsome synagogue at Bevis Marks which still survives as an active place of worship.

FRINGE BENEFITS

Despite the evident thickening of settlements along the riverside the still largely rural suburbs to their north continued to play an important role in the food supply of the capital and as an arena for recreation. By the sixteenth century vegetables appear to have become an increasingly significant part of the metropolitan diet. The wealthy may have been responding to the culinary advice contained in new vernacular printed manuals for healthy living but the poor were doubtless responding to the

rising price of meat and bread. Substantial mansions like Kirby Castle were complemented by substantial gardens whose surplus produce was sent off to market. Sir Hugh Platt experimented with manures to raise outputs including the waste ash which was a by-product of soap boiling. Dutch and Huguenot refugees brought with them novel horticultural techniques, such as the use of hot-beds.

In 1605 the Worshipful Company of Gardeners was established to regulate all gardening activities within a six-mile radius of the City. By 1617 it claimed to be employing "thousands of poor people, old men, women and children in selling of their commodities, in weeding, in gathering of stones etc." Such employments would remain a mainstay of the East End's economy for a further two centuries.

Many plots were, however, non-commercial ventures, divided off by crude mud walls and leased to City workers or local weavers who relished not only what they contributed to their kitchens but also the opportunity they afforded for restorative exercise or leisurely pottering in the fresh air.

For those prepared to walk an hour or so out of town there were the alternative possibilities of riparian recreation with rod and line. *The Compleat Angler,* published by the retired Fleet Street ironmonger Izaak Walton (1593-1683) in 1653, was written as a practical handbook to the sport but was destined to appeal to a far wider audience, thanks to its literary skill and the inclusion of descriptions of natural scenery, fishermen's tales and conversation and incidents at riverside inns. That the banks of the River Lea provide the main setting for Walton's masterpiece attests to its still largely rural character in the mid-seventeenth century. This is confirmed by the 1664 Hearth Tax returns which revealed that while there were 8,292 households crammed into the riverside parishes and a further 2,482 in Whitechapel, there were still only 217 households in Bethnal Green and in Bow and Old Ford only 175.

Further confirmation can be found in the pages of the diary of Samuel Pepys (1633-1703). As an unusually conscientious naval administrator Pepys was thoroughly familiar with Ratcliff, Shadwell, Limehouse and Wapping. Wapping was where he went to consult the cartographer Joel Gascoyne (1650-1705) who was to be found at 'The Signe of the Platte neare Wapping old Stairs three doares below the

30. The Harbour Master's house and pub at Limehouse, 1907.

Chapell'. During the panic induced by the Great Fire of 1666 Pepys loaded his most precious possessions (account books, cash and a parmesan cheese!) onto a cart and drove them out to Bethnal Green for safe-keeping at Kirby Castle, then occupied by his boss, Sir William Rider. When Pepys' duties permitted an occasional afternoon or evening off it was one of his chief pleasures to head eastwards – "after dinner by coach with my wife, only to take the air, it being very warm and pleasant, to Bow and Old Ford and ... played shuffleboard, eat cream and good cherries." The drive was usually accompanied by treats of some kind – pullets, eel pie, neat's tongue, "a noble supper" at Lady Pooly's at Bow or dinner at the Queen's Head, nearby.

SPITALFIELDS SILK

Before the advent of the Huguenots English silk-manufacture was restricted to the production of small items such as ribbons, garlands, girdles and fringes. The newcomers brought with them the expertise to manufacture 'broad silks' such as brocades, satins and velvets and the light and glossy 'lustrings' and 'alamodes'. Such silks might be used, not only for ladies' clothing but for men's as well and additionally for slippers, bags, fire-screens, bed-hangings and the upholstery of chairs and stools.

Spitalfields was already an established textile-producing area even before the great Huguenot influx of the 1680. This is clearly attested by an Order in Council of 1669 which chronicled the nuisance caused by contractors producing building materials needed to reconstruct the City after the Great Fire of 1666.

> "the inhabitants of the pleasant locality of Spitalfields petitioned the Council to restrain certain persons from digging earth and burning bricks in those fields which not only render them very noisome but prejudice the clothes which are usually dried in two large grounds adjoining and the rich stuffs of divers colours which are made in the same place by altering and changing their colours."

A subsidiary trade of cabinet-making was practised by Huguenots in the adjacent neighbourhoods of Bethnal Green and Shoreditch. This trade might be combined with upholstery, often using locally-made silks, or with the manufacture of coffins and therefore with the provision of undertaking services.

Most of the Spitalfields Huguenots came from the Saintange area and around Bordeaux. Regional antecedents were perpetuated through mutual assistance societies based on ancestral ties. These groupings, the forerunners of modern Friendly Societies, helped incomers from their *pays* who were either too aged or too feeble to support themselves or too poor to bind their offspring to apprenticeships. Meeting weekly, they might also consider mutual grievances, such as threats to wage-rates, and thus function as *de facto* trade unions. In 1675, for example, an early attempt to introduce new Dutch machinery which wove several ribbons or tapes simultaneously provoked co-ordinated riots and machine-breaking on four successive days throughout Stepney and as far away as Southwark and Stratford.

The Onset of Industry

SPITALFIELDS SILK

Following decades of vindictive harassment against Huguenots by the French monarchy the Edict of Nantes, by which Henri IV of France had promised toleration of worship to his Protestant subjects, was finally revoked by Louis XIV in 1685. Tens of thousands, for the most part industrious and thrifty artisans and traders, fled abroad, to the great enrichment of the lands which afforded them refuge, particularly the Netherlands and Great Britain. Some forty thousand settled around the fringes of London, where previous Huguenot refugees had already been living for over a century.

Spitalfields represented the largest concen-

tration of these newcomers. Some came with capital and others with the tools of their trade, some with little more than their lives. But all brought with them a tradition of mutual assistance, forged through the years of their persecution. The harsh winter of 1689 led them to introduce an institution which came as a novelty to their English neighbours – 'La Soupe' – a soup-kitchen to distribute broth and bread to the needy. It became a permanent fixture.

By 1700 there were at least nine Huguenot congregations established in Spitalfields. These also undertook a variety of charitable functions. Ten new chapels were built between 1687 and 1743, culminating in the imposing building at the corner of Fournier Street and Brick Lane. The admonitory motto above its sundial – *Umbra Sumus* (We Are Shadows) – fittingly foretold its chequered future history as a place of worship subsequently for Methodists (1809), Jews (1897) and Muslims (1976).

Spitalfields' relative isolation from the fashionable West End caused it to lose its distinctively French character more slowly than Soho. But, during the eighteenth century, intermarriage with English families inevitably carried with it the seeds of assimilation. Constant wars against France hastened identification with the host community and the anglicisation of names. Like many immigrants the Huguenots of Spitalfields became fiercely loyal to their adopted country.

31. Keeping the Faith – Fournier Street's chapel subsequently became a synagogue, then a mosque.

32. The dining room of the former Huguenot silk-weaver's house at 18 Folgate Street, Spitalfields.

33. *Apprentices at a Spitalfields loom being closely watched. Drawing by Hogarth.*

When Bonnie Prince Charlie raised the standard of revolt in 1745 they volunteered themselves, their sons, their servants and their employees in defence of the throne. The various branches of the powerful Ogier clan alone pledged a hundred and seventy men.

The Huguenots were no less staunch in defence of their own interests. The importation of cheap printed calicoes by the East India Company in 1719 led to physical attacks on women brazen enough to wear them. This was followed in 1721 by the passage of legislation banning their importation, though the East India interest was powerful enough to secure its repeal in 1724.

The prosperity that Huguenots so ardently defended was expended in support of a culture that put their community a cut above the average London artisan, giving birth to a Spitalfields Mathematical Society in 1717 and a Spitalfields Madrigal Society in 1741. Both in their different

ways represented a Huguenot fascination with order, pattern and complexity as represented in nature and art. Another indication of the community's capacity for self-advancement through self-improvement can be found in the names of registered local doctors such as Peter Bluzee, John Bossu, Daniel Delessars, Daniel Delmestre and Peter Le Clerc.

John Dollond (1746-61} was to found a business which, as the opticians Dollond and Aitchison, survives to the present day. Born in Spitalfields, Dollond was in his youth compelled by poverty to work as a weaver while educating himself, chiefly in optics and astronomy, in his spare time. In 1750 Dollond's eldest son, Peter (1731-1820), set up an optical workshop in Vine Street off Piccadilly, and then in 1752 he moved to smart premises in the Strand, the capital's centre for the manufacture of scientific and navigational instruments. John Dollond joined his son in the business and after many trials he invented the achromatic telescope which produced pure images, devoid of colour, a phenomenon Newton himself had pronounced impossible. For this John Dollond received the Royal Society's Copley Medal in 1758. Peter Dollond, more entrepreneur than experimentalist, became optician to George III and three times Master of the Spectacle Makers' Company.

The Spitalfields silk industry linked together a complex chain of raw silk importers, throwsters, dyers, weavers and mercers, upon whom subsidiary specialists in design and pattern-making and the manufacture and maintenance of machinery in turn relied – not to mention the neighbourhood's shopkeepers, publicans, hawkers etc. who depended on the spending-power of these wage earners. The concentration of silk-making in Spitalfields thus created a parlous communal reliance on the fortunes of a single trade. Anything that threatened the market for silks or the wages of its makers threatened Spitalfields as a whole. During the Seven Years War (1756-63) English manufacturers enjoyed a temporary boom in consequence of capturing French export markets but their post-war loss led to lay-offs which the government tried to cure by banning all imported silks in 1765. Although the ban remained in force until 1826 its effect was undermined by widespread smuggling. And it failed to prevent recourse to wage-cuts, which led to riots so violent that two of the insurgents were hanged, not at Tyburn but in the locality, as a warning to others. What became known as the Spitalfields Act, passed in 1773, represented an attempt to stabilise the industry after a decade of uncertainties and disorders. To placate the masters it forbade their employees to form combinations – i.e. unions. To mollify the journeymen it forbade masters from taking on more than two apprentices. When necessary, wage-rates would be fixed by magistrates at Quarter Sessions. The Act brought a measure of peace but could not of itself deliver prosperity.

NEW PEOPLE

Although the Huguenot influx was the most visible addition to the population of the eastern suburbs, there were other migrants, apart from the usual inflow from the Home Counties and English provinces, which maintained demographic expansion despite the deleterious effects of the 'gin mania' which afflicted the capital, peaking in the 1720s and 1730s.

The Irish came to enlist, sometimes in Britain's armed forces, sometimes in those of her enemies, or as members of seasonal harvesting gangs. They were often unwilling, or unable, to return to the poverty they had fled in their native land, which suffered major harvest failures in 1728-9, 1740-1, 1744-5 and 1756-7. Irish migrants were resented by many as rate-busters and, in an age of Protestant bigotry, when Britain was frequently at war with Catholic France and Spain, despised for their Catholicism. In 1736 a mob went on the rampage in Shadwell, demolishing an Irish-owned cookshop and tavern and ransacking two more pubs favoured by the Irish. Local magistrates called out Grenadiers from the Tower and arrested twenty-three of the rioters. The Irish would show that they, too, could riot, playing a leading role in 1768 in the struggle over blackleg labour in the coal-heaving trade which brought shipping on the Thames to a standstill. That particular confrontation put six hundred soldiers on patrol in the streets of the riverside parishes.

Following the readmission of the Sephardim, Yiddish-speaking Ashkenazi Jews began to arrive from eastern Europe. Unlike the Jewish mercantile pathfinders from the Netherlands, these were mostly artisans and petty traders, an economic distinction that reinforced the separate identity they maintained in language and worship. In 1692 the Ashkenazim opened their own synagogue at Duke's Place and in 1697 acquired a burying-ground at Three Colts Yard, later Alderney Road.

The name of the Black Boy tavern near Stepney Green, in existence by 1724, denoted another new presence. Black denizens, usually male, came as a by-product of the 'triangular trade' which linked West African slaving with West Indian plantations. Newspaper advertisements offering rewards reveal that some of these newcomers were runaways, who had either jumped ship or hoped to escape by finding one. The *London Post* of 1701 offered two guineas to whoever would return 31-year-old Peter to Capt. Morgan, commander of the *New Content* of Jamaica, then lying at Limehouse. The *Post Man* of 1702 offered only ten shillings for a slender, unnamed runaway who had fled from Mrs Thwaits of Stepney "and is supposed to be gone on board some Ship in the Downes". Fifteen-year-old Lewis similarly absconded from the home of Dormer Sheppard Esq. of Mile End Green in 1707 and was believed to be trying to return to 'Guiney'. Discovered aboard *HMS Roebuck* within weeks under the assumed name of Scipio, he was returned but immediately ran off to sea again. But not all were discontented. John Scipio (died 1760), bought by a Captain Snellgrove on the Guinea coast, was freed and outlived his former master by seventeen years, continued in service with other employers and died worth over £300. Unsurprisingly many black males were servants of sea captains or plantation owners but Dr William Connop, a Mile End apothecary, also had a black servant.

Those blacks who could not find a safe berth, however, might, like so many of the similarly marginalised Irish, turn to crime. In 1739 a black man, originally mistaken for a chimney-sweep, but subsequently identified as a member of a "great Gang of Robbers", was indicted at Newgate for a robbery and murder committed by night near St George-in-the-East. Another black, John Edenburgh, was sentenced to death at the Old Bailey in 1763 for horse theft. A notice of 1765, in contrast, noted approvingly that a black man had made repeated dives to recover the body of a foreigner drowned in a pond at Mile End.

Clustered around Wellclose Square, then fittingly known as Marine Square, Scandinavian merchants and sailors constituted another distinct presence, reflecting the important Baltic trade in timber and naval stores. In 1696 a new Danish church was built in Wellclose Square, adorned with statues by Wren's Danish master sculptor Gaius Cibber. Later a Danish coffee-house opened in the same square.

In 1726 a Swedish church was built in Princes Square, Wapping. Swedish residents of the East End included the botanists Pehr Kalm and Daniel Solander and the famous mystic Emmanuel Swedenborg, who lived in Wellclose Square from 1768 until his death in 1772.

St George's Lutheran church in Alie Street, opened in 1762, was intended to serve the local German community, many of whom were employed in the sugar-baking business nearby. The founder, Dietrich Beckmann, was himself the owner of a refinery. In 1765 an adjacent bilingual English-German school began to take in pupils. The church would survive until 1996.

NEW CHURCHES

In consequence of the continued growth of population further new parishes were established – Wapping in 1694, Limehouse in 1715, Bow in 1719, St George-in-the-East and Spitalfields in 1729 and Bethnal Green in 1743. This did not, however, imply a groundswell of solid support for the Anglican establishment. The highly mobile population of the suburbs east of the City offered a fertile breeding-ground for sectarianism. The weakening of traditional ecclesiastical authority which had accompanied the civil wars and their aftermath unleashed an era of theological experimentation which took half a century to bring in check. Even before that Tower Hamlets had given birth to the country's very first Baptist congregation in 1633, when John Spilsbury had been appointed its minister in Wapping. By 1689 there were other Baptist congregations at Limehouse and Mile End Green. In 1655 Captain James Brock of Mile End had opened his house to Quakers, thus inaugurating the Ratcliff Meeting, which bought land for its own meeting-house a decade later. In 1700 it spawned a

34. St John at Wapping. Watercolour by William Pearson (fl. 1798-1813). Only the tower would survive the Blitz.

35. *A burial service at St Anne, Limehouse. Hablot Brown after R. Garland.*

37. *Christ Church Spitalfields, a masterpiece by Hawksmoor, in the 1920s.*

36. *St Matthew, Bethnal Green, built 1743-6 to the designs of the City Surveyor, George Dance the Elder.*

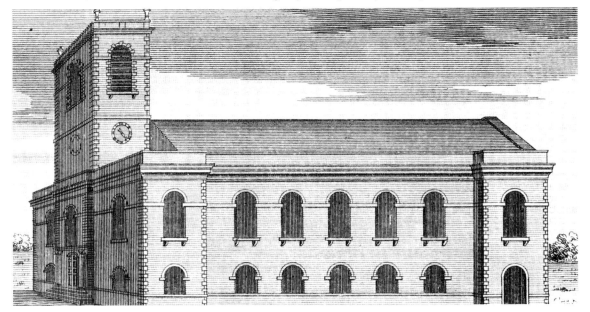

38. North-west view of the Danish church in Wellclose Square. Paid for by King Christian V of Denmark, the church was consecrated in 1696 and demolished in 1869 to make way for a school.

39. St George-in-the-East, Ratcliff Highway, built 1714-29 to designs by Hawksmoor.

sister meeting at Wapping. In 1684 Spitalfields was described by the Middlesex magistrates as "the most factious hamlet of all the Tower division, having had many conventicles in it" and that at least sixteen of these "as big as churches" were still meeting in private houses.

While welcomed as an economic asset and accepted as fellow Protestants, the Huguenots were, so long as they clung to a liturgy in French, unlikely to win back adherents to the established church. Alarmed by the spread of dissent, in 1711 a Tory administration promoted the Fifty New Churches Act, which allocated a fund of a million pounds towards the erection of places of Anglican worship. Three of these were to be built in Tower Hamlets to the designs of Nicholas Hawksmoor (1661-1736), Wren's dour assistant, who had only emerged as an architect in his own right in late middle age. St Anne's, Limehouse was begun in 1712 amid open fields, not completed until 1724 and not consecrated until 1730 when funds were at last raised to support a rector.

St George-in-the-East, begun in 1714, took until 1729 to complete. Christ Church,

40. South-west view of the Swedish church in Princes Square, Ratcliff Highway. Consecrated in 1728, the church closed in 1910 and was demolished in 1921. The remains of Swedish mystic Emanuel Swedenborg were repatriated in 1908 and the square was renamed Swedenborg Gardens in 1938 in his honour.

Spitalfields was built over the same time-span. Plagued by thefts and vandalism, it was originally budgeted to cost £9,129 16s. but finally came in over four times as high at £39,172 17s. 6d.

These spectacular new churches provided fine settings for fine music. John James became organist of St George-in-the-East in 1738. A "learned and sublime" performer, he composed voluntaries one of which was for many years attributed to Handel, and most of which were rapidly plagiarised by other organists. James, however, "even while attending to his duty at church ... indulged an inclination to spirituous liquors of the coarsest kind" and was also an enthusiastic fan of dog-fighting. Huguenot Peter Prelleur (1705-58), the first organist at Christ Church, led even more of a double life. At Christ Church he had command of the largest organ in the country, built by local master Richard Bridges, who also built the organs in the other two Hawksmoor churches. Handel himself made a trek out to Spitalfields to play this mighty instrument, which had over a thousand pipes. Prelleur, however, was far more than just an organist and in his *The Modern Musick Master or The Universal Musician* imparted instruction on singing and how to play the recorder, flute, hautboy, harpsichord and violin. Writing and teaching were certainly respectable enough as sidelines but Prelleur also composed music for the theatre in Goodman's Fields *(see p.57)* and played in the evenings at the Angel and Crown tavern in Whitechapel where he provided the music for an entertainment with the risqué title of *The Arabian Courtezan*.

NEW SCHOOLS
The provision of free schooling still depended on private or corporate munificence, which, in the case of Tower Hamlets, was pleasingly forthcoming. Draper Sir John Jolles had provided for a free school at Bow in his will of 1617. Prisca Coborn founded another school at Bow in 1701. A charity school opened in Mile

41. *Detail from John Rocque's map of London, c1746, showing the crowded area south of the Ratcliff Highway. Over on the south bank of the river elegant gardens still survive much closer to the shoreline.*

End Old Town in 1714. In 1719 Wapping brewer Henry Raine endowed a charity school in Farthing Fields, Charles Street, St George-in-the-East. Parmiter's School, Bethnal Green was established in 1722. Bancroft's School at Mile End opened in 1738. One of its first members of staff, the Revd John Entick (?1703-73) was dismissed for committing adultery with a colleague's wife (whom he did subsequently marry). Despite this disgrace he prospered as a prolific lexicographer and historian, acquiring over a dozen properties in Stepney.

There were also numerous private, fee-paying establishments. Although many offered little instruction of value some did have high standards and a focused purpose. The distinguished classicist Robert Ainsworth (1660-1743), who arrived in London *c.* 1698 from his native Lancashire, ran "a considerable boarding school" at Bethnal Green and espoused a most enlightened pedagogy which deprecated punishment and advocated the teaching of Latin as a living language. Ainsworth's Latin dictionary, published in 1736, was being reprinted as late as 1829. Allen Allenson ran a French boarding school at Mile End from 1754 to 1779 and at least a dozen other teachers are known in that area between 1741 and 1780, though half a dozen of them were women and many of their establishments appear to have been short-lived. At Bromley-by-Bow there were two specialised academies preparing youths for service with the East India Company. At Wellclose Square there was a well-known academy for Dissenting ministers.

OLD OCCUPATIONS

Joel Gascoyne's 1703 map of Mile End Old Town depicts significant clusterings of buildings along the line of the main west-east thoroughfare bisecting it but is still dominated by large, clearly-demarcated field boundaries. Agriculturally-related activities remained important in the northern and western parts of Tower Hamlets. In 1708 Ratcliff hay market was relocated to Whitechapel. The wide verges alongside the road at Mile End served as a major location for assembling herds of livestock, especially calves driven in from the specialist market at Romford. The numbers of beasts involved ran to tens of thousands per week. The cash generated and carried homewards by dealers constituted a standing temptation to

highway robbery. Fattening livestock (often using brewery waste) and raising ducks were other significant local specialisms. Corn chandlers, tallow chandlers and wholesale butchers were substantial members of the local bourgeoisie. Farriers and blacksmiths serviced the needs of passing riders, coachmen and carters.

Although the once open fields of what had been the sprawling medieval parish of Stepney housed a population of perhaps 100,000 by 1730, two-thirds of the area was still undeveloped at that date and two-thirds of that was under grass. Rocque's map of 1746 showed a more or less continuous straggle of roadside buildings as far as Stepney Green but beyond that to both north and south the land still consisted of gardens, orchards and open fields, punctuated only by a ducking pond, a bowling green and a brewhouse. The map itself stopped just east of St Dunstan's, Stepney because beyond that the publisher judged that there was little of interest to depict. The last thing shown before the border of the map is a cowhouse. The roadway immediately to its north is appropriately labelled 'World's End'. As late as 1795 *The Universal Magazine* could describe Poplar Marsh (the Isle of Dogs) as being "one of the richest spots of ground in England, for it not only raises the largest cattle but the grass it bears is esteemed a great restorative of all distempered cattle."

Market gardening remained important both as a source of supply for the markets of the metropolis and as a seasonal source of by-employment for East Enders. It also contributed to the management of the metropolitan refuse-disposal system by absorbing large quantities of human and animal waste. Some horticulturalists became more than mere routine suppliers of vegetables, fruit and flowers to the markets at Spitalfields and Covent Garden. One such was James Gordon (died 1780) whose plantsmanship earned him a European reputation. Gordon's success was based, paradoxically, on the fact that the soil of his nursery at Mile End Old Town was so poor and its site so exposed that if a plant could survive there it could grow anywhere. Trained under the talented Lord Petre of Thorndon Hall near Brentwood, Gordon went into business on his own account around 1740. By 1758 James Ellis, a Fellow of the Royal Society, was recommending him as a correspondent and supplier to the pre-eminent naturalist of the age, Linnaeus

(1707-78) of Sweden. Ellis thought Gordon much too modest about his expertise, which ran far beyond what was required for mere commercial success. In 1760 the Swedish botanist Daniel Solander (1736-82) took a room at Gordon's nursery to study there, considering it superior to the celebrated Chelsea Physick Garden. Solander would subsequently serve as a botanist under Captain Cook.

Gordon's prize exotics – camellias, magnolia and ginko – commanded premium prices which enabled him to invest in a range of glasshouses, to take over more land at Bow and to open a highly profitable seed-shop at 25 Fenchurch Street. In 1775 John Wesley recorded visiting "Mr. Gordon's curious garden at Mile End, the like of which I suppose is hardly to be found in England." Coming from a man positively notorious for his sobriety, his integrity and his inexhaustible appetite for travel this was no hyperbole but an informed compliment of the highest order.

AXIS OF DEVELOPMENT

Residential and commercial development eastwards was stimulated from 1722 onwards by the turnpiking of the thoroughfare from Whitechapel out to Shenfield along the Great Essex Road. Most coach services for more distant destinations, such as Harwich, started in the City itself but a few short haul services ran from Whitechapel, including daily coaches out to Barking, a twice weekly wagon to Chelmsford and a weekly one to Ongar. Such regular traffic was of great benefit to local inns. The *Three Cranes* is first mentioned in 1719, The *Grave Maurice* in 1723. By 1750 there were over 120 licensed premises in Whitechapel and some forty in Mile End Old Town, meaning that every tenth building there was a tavern or alehouse. There were fifteen on the north side of the Mile End Road just between the Trinity Almshouses and the present site of Queen Mary College.

Given the need to supply such outlets, as

42. *The Anchor Brewery, Mile End Road. Aquatint by D. Wolstenholme, 1820. Opened in 1757, the brewery came under the control of the Charrington family.*

well as the ever-growing commercial fleets reprovisioning on the river the stimulus to local brewing is self-evident.

In 1730 the Barley Mow brewery was established at Stepney by Salmon and Hare. William Burr's White Swan brewhouse at Stepney existed by 1736. The Anchor brewery established in 1739 by Waistfield and Moss in Bethnal Green moved to the Mile End Road in 1757. Successful brewers were amongst London's greatest capitalists. Burr was estimated to be worth £100,000 at his death in 1743. Benjamin Kenton (1719-1800) made a fortune by inventing long-lasting India Pale Ale (IPA) for the East India Company and left £63,550 in bequests. Benjamin Truman, proprietor of the Black Eagle brewery in Brick Lane was knighted.

Other industrial facilities also moved into the East End. The Whitechapel bell foundry moved to its present site in 1738, taking over and extending the premises of the former Artichoke inn. In 1748 the West Ham Water Company built a reservoir near the site of Bancroft's almshouses. Along the River Lea there were dye works and calico printers. Down by the Thames rope-making was a large-scale business, with four major works between Aldgate and Blackwall.

The most novel industrial enterprise was the manufacture of porcelain. The secret of making a 'soft paste' near-porcelain had been uncovered in Italy in 1575. Instead of using ingredients unique to China, European formulae substituted glass and later soapstone or bone ash. Experimental production in the London area began at Fulham in 1671 but serious commercial efforts only began in the 1740s with half a dozen enterprises starting up within a decade.

The Limehouse pottery was set up by Joseph Wilson in 1745 at 20 Fore Street near Dick (Duke) Shore, a site corresponding to 108-116 Narrow Street. Limehouse specialized in a glassy type of porcelain, mostly tea-pots and sauceboats, mainly decorated in under-glaze blue. These polychrome wares may have been decorated in Holland or by Dutch decorators brought over for the purpose. This may indicate that local standards of workmanship were low. The Limehouse output failed to sell well enough and a creditors' meeting convened in 1748, heralded the end of this short-lived works. Its very existence was forgotten until the rediscovery in 1927 of advertisements for its wares in the pages of the *Daily Advertiser*. A 1990 excavation by Dr Bernard Watney finally confirmed its location and amateurish standards of production. One of the partners in the Limehouse enterprise relocated to Bristol, where a porcelain works using Cornish soaprock opened in 1749 only to close in 1752.

The Bow porcelain factory, by contrast, became the largest of the eighteenth-century London works, although strictly speaking it was just outside the capital's boundary. Initially it was located on the north side of Stratford Causeway on the Essex side of Bow bridge; from 1749 it stood further east along the north side of the High Street by Marshgate Lane. The River Lea was nearby to provide smooth carriage for its delicate products and its associated marshland served as a convenient dumping-ground for the inevitable failures in the tricky processes of firing and glazing. It was in 1744 that Bristol clothier Edward Heylyn and Irish artist Thomas Frye (1710-62) took out their patent for "a new method of manufacturing a certain mineral whereby a ware might be made of the same nature or kind, and equal, if not exceeding in goodness and beauty, china or porcelain ware imported from abroad. The material is an earth, the produce of the Cherokee nation in America, called by the natives unaker." It seems inherently improbable that any such raw material could have been imported from America in sufficient quantities, at competitive rates, to make commercial sense, which may explain why production probably did not start at their New Canton works until 1747, when the patent-holders enlarged their partnership to bring in two wholesale china merchants, John Weatherby and John Crowther, as well as George Arnold, a City Alderman. Heylyn and Frye did incorporate calcined bone ash into their recipe, ox bones being readily available from local slaughterers serving London's butchers. This innovation was copied by virtually every other porcelain manufacturer in the country by the end of the century. In 1749 Frye took out a second patent in his sole name and on his death it was Frye who was to be acclaimed by his obituarist in the *Gentleman's Magazine* as "the Inventor and first Manufacturer of Porcelain in England." Years spent around searing hot furnaces seem to have taken their toll on the corpulent and gout-ridden Frye, who retired from factory management in his last years to return to art, producing miniatures and sketches of celebrities, including a portrait of the youthful Jeremy Bentham (1748-1832) who had been born in Spitalfields.

Bow forms and methods of decoration were as widely imitated as its recipe and Bow workers were readily taken on at Chelsea and Worcester. One of Frye's daughters, who had been employed as a china painter at Bow, married a Worcester china painter and went with him to work for Wedgwood. Robert Browne, a former Bow employee, was one of five partners who started up the Lowestoft factory in 1757, using the same phosphatic (bony) soft paste as Bow to produce the same blue and polychrome wares for the mid-market until declining into the souvenir trade.

Resisting a direct challenge to Nicholas Sprimont's up-market Chelsea works, Bow concentrated on meeting middle-range demand for blue and white wares and polychrome decorated pieces. Apart from plates, bowls and jugs, candlesticks proved another popular line, as were tablewares copied in imitation of silver. Other items included sucriers and inkwells. Despite its middle-market focus the works also managed to attract prestigious customers such as the Duke of Argyll, who had run up an outstanding account of two hundred pounds by 1756. Much also went for export, with items certainly reaching America by 1754. The factory lived up to its assumed title of 'New Canton', at least in marketing terms, often completing its Chinoiserie style items with pseudo-oriental factory marks. After gaining access to original works from the prestigious royal factory at Meissen in Saxony around 1752, a large range of figurines was produced. Initially these were copies of generic types, such as gods and heroes of classical antiquity, shepherds and shepherdesses etc., but the factory later diversified into a highly successful series featuring stars of the London stage, notably Kitty Clive, Peg Woffington and David Garrick. By 1765, however, three of the firm's founders had died and the management were not responding to changes in popular taste. The most significant loss seems to have been John Weatherby, whose demise was followed by a reduction in production standards. Sales had already peaked in the 1750s and a decade of decline ended with the sale of the factory, stock and equipment to William Duesbury of Derby between 1774 and 1776. Duesbury had himself been employed at Bow as a sub-contracting decorator and at Chelsea, which he also took over.

WORLDS APART? I

Although industrial development was evident in Spitalfields and Stepney, in Bethnal Green and at Bow, as well as along the riverside, it is evident that the eighteenth-century East End was far from the homogeneous proletarian mass that observers were to perceive in Victoria's reign.

Professor Peter Linebaugh's controversial study of *The London Hanged* throws much incidental light on the turbulent lives of the inhabitants of Wapping, Shadwell, Ratcliff and Limehouse, dozens of whom ended on the gallows at Tyburn. This is not, of course, to claim that this area was uniquely criminalized. The celebrated petty thief and escapologist Jack Sheppard (1702-24), one of the few ne'er-do-wells to make it into the staid pages of the *Dictionary of National Biography*, was born in White's Row, Spitalfields. The even more notorious, and similarly complimented Dick Turpin (1706-39) was a Whitechapel butcher's apprentice. Nor were all the inhabitants of the riverside impoverished. Rope-maker John Shakespeare (died 1772) occupied a three-storey house on the east side of Stepney Causeway

43. Jack Sheppard's spectacular escapes from Newgate made him a popular, if short-lived, hero. Sir James Thornhill painted Sheppard's portrait shortly before his execution.

with fifteen panelled rooms and seven marble chimneypieces and four more of Portland stone. He also owned thirty tenements and six acres of land locally and left £31,000 to his ten children, plus £1000 a year to his widow.

Although the riverside parishes had long been notorious for their taverns and bawdy-houses, settings routinely conducive to drunkenness and violence, even a cursory examination of the recorded trial proceedings of the Old Bailey reveals the near impossibility of drawing a sharp distinction between a class of respectable, industrious poor and an underclass of the idle, vicious and parasitic. The culture of working life itself continually blurred the line between honest and criminal behaviour wherever foremen, clerks and officials invoked the 'customs of the trade' or 'London courtesies' to supplement their incomes with kickbacks or bribes euphemised as 'fees' or 'tips'. Expected levels of 'wastage' became institutionalized as routine deductions from otherwise unspoiled or undamaged bulk cargoes. Collusion and embezzlement were built into the handling of valuable and easily divisible cargoes, such as tobacco. The circumstances of daily life, the vagaries of climate, fashion, harvest failure or war too often thrust even the diligent and law-abiding into criminality through sheer desperation or momentary impulse. Natural catastrophes inflicted not only material damage but innumerable reverberations of personal misfortune on individuals already over-burdened with debt, children or illness or dependent on intermittent employment, as in 1703, when a hurricane drove ships at anchor all the way from London Bridge to Limehouse, or in 1714 and 1749, when there were major outbreaks of cattle disease which must have blighted the lives of hundreds of drovers, graziers, slaughterers, butchers, tanners and leatherworkers.

Less than half the population of the riverside parishes was London born so even fewer had local family roots to sustain or restrain them. Apart from in-migrants from the countryside and Ireland, their numbers were constantly added to by sailors discharged after the annual arrivals of the West India and East India fleets, by soldiers discharged at the end of campaigns and youths discharged from workhouses. Although most of those who appeared before the courts were labelled as having an occupation, typically they had found work in whatever

way they could as a labourer, porter, waterman, hawker, harvester, coal-heaver or in 'the needle trades' before turning to larceny, counterfeiting, pickpocketing, prostitution, receiving or robbery. Rag Fair, near Rosemary Lane, off Wellclose Square, offered a convenient location for the disposal of clothes, wigs and buckles forced from their possessors at the point of a weapon. This highly-organised institution was also where similar items stolen in provincial cities as far distant as Coventry and Norwich were regularly turned into cash.

Living on the margins of economic survival and often at the edge of legality the inhabitants of the riverside parishes were prepared to defend their interests with collective violence. In 1763 merchant seamen marched in protest against threats of wage-cuts. In the same year Charles Dingley's Limehouse sawmill was demolished by a mob of hand-sawyers who saw his introduction of new machinery as a menace to their livelihoods. In April 1768 discontent among Spitalfields weavers spilled over into a movement among the predominantly Catholic coal-heavers of Shadwell and Wapping to secure a rise in wages. When this shut down the Port of London, John Green of the Round About tavern in Shadwell tried to recruit blackleg labour. He was besieged on two successive days until the strikers were driven off by gunfire which left at least two dead. After Green's sister was brutally murdered in retaliation, the justices hanged seven alleged ringleaders on a gallows specially erected at Stepney Green. The use of sailors as blacklegs in May led to further stabbings and beatings and another fatality. The introduction of troops and further executions then led to the collapse of the strike. When, in 1773, coal-heavers combined with watermen and weavers to petition the King all marches were instantly banned for fear of escalation into similar major disorders.

LOCAL HERO

One positive product of the riverside culture of bawdy and brawling was Jack Broughton (1703/5-89) 'the father of English boxing', and (third) champion of all England from 1729 until 1750. An early exemplar of the role of sport as a ladder out of East End poverty, Broughton was born in Wapping and was a waterman by trade until a fight with a fellow waterman convinced him he was wasting a talent which

44. James Figg (on the left) versus Jack Broughton. An 18th-century mezzotint.

could be put to more lucrative use. His skills were soon to be honed by pugilistic pioneer James Figg (1695-1740), the first ever English champion. Broughton made his first appearance in the ring at a booth, run by the second champion, George Taylor, at Adam and Eve Court off Tottenham Court Road. In 1743 Broughton opened his own academy, known as Broughton's Amphitheatre, in Hanway Street, just north of Oxford Street.

In the same year he laid down the first rules of boxing to command general acceptance until they were superseded by the Pugilistic Society's London Prize Ring Rules in 1839. The most important rules were that a combatant was to be allowed thirty seconds to recover after a knock-down and that no man was to be hit while down or wrestled below the waist.

Because many of Broughton's pupils were young men about town who cared about their appearance and did not want to end each lesson cut and bloody, Broughton also introduced the use of gloves, known as mufflers, stuffed with wool or horse-hair. These were worn, however, only during practice sessions. Real contests continued to be bare knuckle affairs. After a long life Broughton was honoured with burial in the West Cloister of Westminster Abbey, his pallbearers being the most celebrated prizefighters of the day, most notably Daniel Mendoza.

WORLDS APART? II

To the north of the riverside parishes and especially eastwards, away from overcrowded Spitalfields, there was spaciousness rather than squalor, graciousness rather than grime. One clear indicator of social and environmental desirability was the favour these localities enjoyed as places of residence and retirement. Almshouses were erected by Dame Jane Mico at Stepney in 1691, by Trinity House on the Mile End Road in 1695, by the Skinners nearby in 1698, by the Drapers' Company at Bromley St Leonard in 1706, by a Captain Fisher in 1711

45.   Fournier Street in 2004. Note the roof-level weavers' lofts. Current residents include Gilbert and George, and Tracy Emin.

and under the terms of the late City official Francis Bancroft's will at Mile End in 1735. The London Hospital, founded in 1740, moved out from Prescot Street on the south side of Goodman's Fields to a supposedly more healthful locality at Whitechapel in 1757. Kirby Castle became a private mental asylum, where the poet Christopher Smart and Alexander Cruden, author of the famous *Concordance to the Bible*, were both to be immured. Derek Morris's painstaking study of Mile End Old Town in the mid-eighteenth century depicts a burgeoning

suburb of distinctly bourgeois character, which doubled in population between 1740 and 1780. Ten-roomed Fitzhugh House at Mile End, built in 1738, was one of over a hundred similar-sized residences, representing one in seven of that locality's housing stock. This has gone, but nearby Malplaquet House of 1741 remains, as does Ireland Terrace of 1717. Twenty-five households were wealthy enough to employ a male servant. The most imposing residences were ranged along Stepney Green where typical inhabitants drew their fortunes from the East India Company or the Hudson's Bay Company or from City insurance companies, distilling or slave-trading. Other inhabitants of the neighbourhood included retired admirals, scholars, a Member of Parliament, a former Lord Mayor, a Garter King of Arms and the illustrious explorer Captain James Cook. Dozens of households were headed by women, mostly annuitants or widows, indicating a residential area that was both pleasant and safe. Mile End appears to have been well policed by the standards of the day, the local constables and watchmen being supplemented by the gatekeepers of the turnpike who kept a vigilant eye on suspicious-looking travellers, especially at night. Compared with the affrays, brawls and burglaries which were a regular

46.   The Trinity Hospital, Mile End, drawn by Matthew Garbutt in 1896, for a monograph published that year.

47. *The Brewers' Company almshouses, Mile End, depicted in 1828 by Thomas H. Shepherd.*

48. *The London Hospital, founded in 1740, moved to a green field site in Whitechapel Road in the 1750s. The new building was finally finished in 1759. This view by William Bellers (1757) does exaggerate the rural nature of its surroundings.*

49. *37 Stepney Green dates from 1694 and was owned by the Gayer family whose wealth came from the East India Company. Note the fine shell door-hood. The building now houses a Careers Centre.*

51. *Captain James Cook. Oil painting by Nathaniel Dance. Cook mapped more of the world than any previous navigator.*

50. *Bancroft's almshouses in the Mile End Road. Lavish in scale, they were paid for by Bancroft's abuse of his office. They were abolished in 1884.*

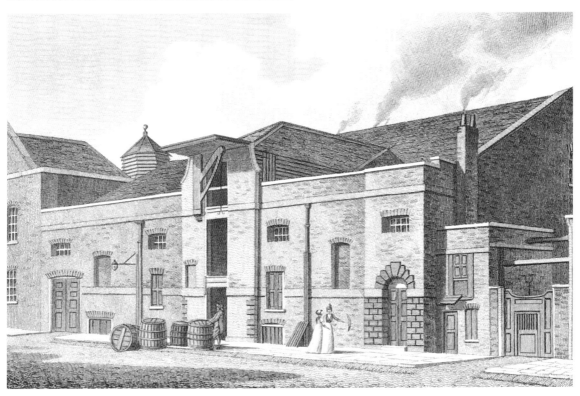

52. The second Goodman's Fields theatre in Ayliffe Street, c.1820.

feature of life down Wapping way the typical crimes of the Mile End area were relatively minor – bullying apprentices, disputes between neighbours, stealing ducks, dishonest servants and lodgers or being robbed while drunk.

This well-heeled, orderly neighbourhood supported not only the normal range of local tradesmen dealing in daily necessities but also four apothecaries, two clockmakers, a linen-draper, a jeweller, a cabinet-maker and individual makers of chairs, snuff, stays and guns. Leisure hours could be passed in a local coffee-house, an Assembly Rooms or from 1702 at the Spring Gardens pleasure ground, just west of St Dunstan's, Stepney.

From 1729 the quality could even visit a new theatre, which opened to the public in Goodman's Fields. The first proprietor, drama-tist Thomas Odell (1691-1749) put on four different plays successfully in a former silk throwster's workshop in Leman Street but was forced to close by the hostility of the City authorities. In 1733 Odell's leading man, Henry Giffard, had purpose-built premises erected to the designs of Edward Shepherd in Ayliffe Street. Giffard's libellous play *The Golden Rump* provoked the passage of the Licensing Act of 1737 which imposed censorship on the English theatre until the 1960s. Giffard attempted to evade its provisions by putting on short concerts before and after his plays and claiming that he was charging admission for these rather than the dramatic 'interval' between. This threadbare ploy at least permitted the sensational debut of the untutored David Garrick as Richard III in 1741. Garrick soon moved on to the West End and the legalised 'patent' theatres secured the closure of their suburban rival in 1742.

The World's Warehouse

Between the opening of the Limehouse Cut in 1770 and the advent of the railways in the 1840s the development of the East End was most profoundly shaped by the commerce which coursed along its riverside and transformed the livelihoods of those who lived within reach of it. Halfway through this transition the nation's first census, conducted in 1801, would reveal that Stepney, with a population of 113,000, was already more populous than Liverpool, Leeds, Manchester, Edinburgh, Bristol or Birmingham and had more than twice as many inhabitants as Norwich or Newcastle. Neighbouring Bethnal Green, with a population of 22,000 in 1801, already had more residents than Oxford and Cambridge added together.

The dynamic development of the Thames riverside took place against a background of global warfare with all its attendant uncertainties, aggravated by arbitrary natural disasters and the occasional dramatic human catastrophe.

In 1791 the Thames flooded Wapping and in July 1794 fire devastated Ratcliff, consuming 458 houses, 36 warehouses and twenty public buildings. In December 1811 the same area was traumatised by the mysterious Ratcliff Highway murders, a series of apparently motiveless killings of horrifying savagery. The first incident involved the deaths of a draper, his wife and child and a shop-boy, bloodily done to death with a chisel and a maul. The second left a publican, his wife and a maid with fractured skulls and deeply cut throats. A suspect – one of over forty detained in the ensuing panic – hanged himself before committal. In 1826 the Royalty theatre in Well Street, first opened in 1787, burned down. It was rebuilt as the New

53. A dramatic depiction of the supposed scene at 29 Ratcliff Highway in December 1811. In fact the bodies of the murdered Marr family were discovered by a neighbour who had forced an entry into the locked household.

54. *The Royalty Theatre in Well Street, depicted by Daniel Havell in 1826. It was originally built in 1786/7, and rebuilt in 1828. It collapsed three days after reopening, killing ten people.*

Brunswick but only three days after its reopening, it collapsed, killing ten people. In 1832 the East End would cower before a novel and hideous spectre – cholera.

Although the East End would later come to be seen as a *locus classicus* of victimhood, a cul-de-sac of limited horizons beset by poverty and ignorance, violence and vice, in the eighteenth century it was still a springboard of opportunity – to the west, central London represented the largest concentration of wealth and population in Europe, to the east the Thames led to all the oceans of the world. Two very different lives illustrate the possibilities open to talent and daring.

At the age of fifteen Thomas Stothard (1755-1834) returned from boarding school in Ilford to live with his widowed mother at Stepney Green. Whatever original ambitions his family might have had for him were curtailed by his father's death and Stothard was apprenticed to a pattern-designer in Spital Square. When he had served out his articles he returned once more to live with his mother, now in apartments at Bethnal Green, and began to paint

portraits of friends. Showing sufficient promise of artistic ability Stothard became a student at the recently established Royal Academy Schools in 1777, exhibiting for the first time in 1779, the year in which he commenced a fruitful career as a book illustrator. Stothard's work typically involved providing pictures for editions of Bunyan, Milton, Defoe and other classic works of English literature. Elected RA before the age of forty, in 1814 he won the competition for designing an armorial shield for the Duke of Wellington and in the same year was appointed Librarian of the Royal Academy, a post he held until his death. A lifelong friend of the eminent sculptor Flaxman, Stothard also designed silverware, David Garrick's monument in Westminster Abbey, decorations for the staircase of Burghley House and unrealised schemes for the state rooms of Buckingham Palace.

If Stothard's career was one of conventional bourgeois success, the much shorter life of Joseph Druce (1777-1819) was a roller-coaster of drudgery, crime, adventure and personal tragedy. The son of a Limehouse distillery

55. A caricature of city folk sampling sporting life in Bethnal Green. The man cleans his gun, while his wife yawns at the boredom of it all. A dog holds a second fowling-piece at an improbable angle.The artist is H. Bunbury (1760-1811) who specialised in people making fools of themselves.

worker, Druce was born and baptised in Shadwell. After working in a ropeworks and on a fishing smack, he was arrested for house-breaking and theft at the age of fourteen. Convicted at the Old Bailey and sentenced to death, his youth earned him the lesser punishment of transportation to New South Wales. Pardoned in 1801, Druce worked as a bushranger, a policeman and then a sailor. Sailing to New Zealand he befriended a Maori chief who became ill but recovered thanks to Druce's nursing. Druce then married one of the Maori's daughters and completed the reinvention of himself by adopting the name George Bruce. When his wife died, however, he abandoned his new life, left his baby daughter in an orphanage and returned to England aboard *HMS Porpoise*. By 1815 Druce, now Bruce, was in Shadwell workhouse but in 1817 he was admitted to Greenwich Seamen's Hospital, where he died after completing an account of his remarkable odyssey, opaquely entitled *The Life of a Greenwich Pensioner*.

SPORTING SUPERSTAR

The life of 'Mendoza the Jew' illustrates yet another extraordinary exodus from East End obscurity. Francis Place, 'the radical breeches-maker of Charing Cross', asserted that a single man transformed public attitudes to the Jews:

"I have seen many Jews hooted ... cuffed, pulled by the beard, spit upon and so barba-rously assaulted in the streets, without any protection from the passers-by ... Dogs could not be used in the streets in the manner many Jews were treated. One circumstance ... put an end to the ill-usage of the Jews ... About the year 1797 Daniel Mendoza, a Jew, became a celebrated boxer and set up a school to teach the art of boxing as a science, the art soon spread among the young Jews and they became generally expert at it. The consequence was in a very few years seen and felt too. It was no longer safe to insult a Jew unless he was old and alone..."

56. *Richard Humphreys versus Daniel Mendoza (right). The fight was at Odiham in Hampshire on 9 January, 1788. Mendoza sprained an ankle after 29 minutes. He won both the re-match and a third contest. Coloured engraving by T Grozer after R Einsle.*

Traditionally boxers had squared up toe to toe, slugging it out in a brutal confrontation in which punching power, weight and height usually proved the decisive factors. Short, stocky Mendoza (1764-1836), however, was just five feet seven inches tall and weighed eleven stones, making him a middleweight at best and therefore, in theory, physically disqualified from successful pugilism at its highest level. What Mendoza brought to the sport was a revolutionary emphasis on mobility, using fast footwork to dance out of the reach of an opponent and then to close in to inflict a flurry of rapid combination punches. As Mendoza himself put it – the first principle is to be perfectly a master of the equilibrium of the body. His pioneering treatise on *The Art of Boxing,* appeared in 1789.

Mendoza was recognized as the sixteenth British – and therefore in effect world – champion between 1791 and 1795. As such he attracted not only popularity in the sporting world but

the notice of royalty itself, becoming the first English Jew to meet and converse with his sovereign. A baronet was proud to act as his second at the ringside. Mendoza was also the first British sportsman to achieve superstar status, his likeness appearing on souvenirs and tributes ranging from cheap pottery to handsome medallions. His fighting fame reached far beyond the capital. When he visited Edinburgh he was presented with a gold medal and elected honorary president of its Gymnastic Society.

In retirement Mendoza became landlord of the Admiral Nelson at Whitechapel and lived at Paradise Row, Bethnal Green in a neat house that still survives. In 1816 he published his prodigiously titled *Memoirs of the Life of Daniel Mendosa, Containing a Faithful Narrative of the Various Vicissitudes of His Life and an Account of the Numerous Contests in Which He Has Been Engaged with Observations of Each; Comprising also Genuine Anecdotes of Many Distinguished Characters, to Which Are Added Observations on the Art of Pugilism; Rules to be Observed with Regard to training & c.* Mendoza's last competitive fight was in 1820, when he was in his mid-fifties. Defeated by a much younger opponent, he took a public benefit later that year and thereafter confined his exercise to the fives court. Mendoza died in Horseshoe Alley, Petticoat Lane, minutes from his Aldgate birthplace, leaving a widow and eleven children.

Daniel Mendoza inaugurated an association between boxing and the East End that has endured ever since. Many of his early successors were also Jewish. Isaac Bitton (1778-1838) – 'Old Ikey' – was renowned for his strength and coolness. He effectively confined his fighting career to the years 1801-4 and, ballooning to seventeen stones, became content to serve as a second to others and then opened a successful school for boxing and fencing.

'Dutch Sam' Elias (1775-1816), who was born in Petticoat Lane, was only five feet six and weighed a mere 134 pounds. A formidable puncher who is credited with inventing the uppercut, he trained on gin and fought over a hundred bouts, losing only twice but he still died in poverty. He was nevertheless followed into the ring by his son, 'Young Dutch Sam', who became the English welterweight champion In 1825. Barney Aarons (1800-50), an Aldgate fishmonger's son, was deemed Dutch Sam's successor as the hero of the Jewish community and hailed as 'the Star of the East'. Aaron's career lasted from 1819 until 1834 when he retired to take up his father's trade. His son, 'Young Barney' (1836-1907) won the lightweight championship of the USA in 1857 in an eighty-round contest lasting two hundred minutes, becoming the first Jew to win an American title.

DEVELOPING DOCKLANDS

Between 1700 and 1770 London's maritime commerce nearly doubled; between 1770 and 1795 it did double, with the metropolis handling roughly two-thirds of the nation's entire international trade. From the middle of the eighteenth century onwards therefore the Pool of London became increasingly congested, with three times as many ships crammed into the Upper Pool as it had been intended to accommodate. The limited length of quayside – a

57. *Social reformer and magistrate Patrick Colquhoun was a successful Glasgow merchant and promoter of poor relief schemes and soup-kitchens.*

third of what Bristol could offer – compelled many ships to lay waiting at anchor or bear the extra expense of unloading from mid-river by lighter. Overcrowding caused long delays in unloading, exposing imported goods to decay and weather damage and creating tempting opportunities for theft through which mercantile profits haemorrhaged away.

In 1797 the public-spirited magistrate Patrick Colquhoun (1745-1820) published his *Treatise on the Police of the Metropolis,* which led to the formation of London's oldest police force. Originally known as the Marine Police Force, it came into existence at Wapping in 1799, the annual cost of £5,000 being shared between the Exchequer (£980), which was losing revenue, and the West India merchants (£4020), who were major victims of theft. Dependent on the harvest for their products West India merchants landed all their goods in a concentrated period between June and October, when river congestion was at its worst. Colquhoun elaborated on the duties and organisation of the new force in a further pamphlet on *The Commerce and Police of the River Thames,* published in 1800.

58. *The headquarters of the River Police in Wapping High Street c.1900.*

The most effective answer to both the problems of congestion and theft, however, was the creation of immense enclosed docks which would both accelerate cargo-handling and provide security against pilferage. In 1799 Parliament authorised the construction of a dock on the Isle of Dogs "for rendering more commodious and better regulating the Port of London" and to ensure that "West India produce might be effectually secure from loss by theft or other causes and the public revenue greatly benefited". Promoter Robert Milligan (?1746-1809) assured for the West India Dock Company a twenty-one-year monopoly on the handling of West Indies produce – outward as well as inward. The design of the docks was entrusted to William Jessop (1745-1814), engineer of the Grand Union Canal.

With an import dock of thirty acres and an export dock of twenty-four the West India dock could accommodate over six hundred vessels. The wharves were flanked by five-storey warehouses. High walls and a wide ditch deterred incursions by river gangs. The defences were patrolled by a force of a hundred guards armed with muskets, pistols and swords and supported by another body of a hundred special constables. The importance attached to the project was underlined by the fact that the opening ceremony in 1802 was conducted by Henry Addington, the prime minister.

Meanwhile another project was going ahead upriver with the creation of the London Docks in Wapping, authorised in 1800 and opened in 1805. Entered directly from the Thames at Shadwell, this facility was also surrounded by a high wall. The designer was Daniel Alexander (1768-1946), Surveyor to Trinity House. Water occupied 35 acres of the ninety-acre site, which afforded two and a half miles of quay and jetty frontage, capable of accommodating three hundred vessels. Adjacent four-storey brick warehouses could store over 200,000 tons of goods. With the exception of goods coming from the East or West Indies, the London Docks secured a twenty-one year monopoly on handling the importation of tobacco, rice, wine and brandy.

The East India Docks, located between Blackwall Reach and Bugsby's Reach, handled Britain's Asian trade, most notably tea and spices. The supervising engineer was John Rennie (1761-1821). Capable of handling up to 250 ships a time, the complex consisted of parallel eighteen-acre import and nine-acre export docks entered via a three-acre basin and three locks. Protection was supplied by walls seven yards high. The goods passing through the East India Docks were of such high value in relation to their bulk that large storage warehouses were not required, most imports being shifted quickly along the newly-built

59. The West India Docks on the eve of their completion in 1802. By William Daniell.

60. *The opening of St Katherine Dock, 25 October 1828. The Ivory House (left with tower) was one of London's first iron-framed buildings. After a painting by W J Huggins.*

Commercial Road to the East India Company's warehouses in Cutler Street in the City.

The development of St Katherine's Dock beside the Tower of London was authorised in 1825 but before work could begin in 1827 over 11,000 people were displaced from the historic and crowded enclave which had grown up there over seven centuries. They received no compensation – unlike the ancient Foundation of St Katherine and the owners of the buildings.

Designed by Thomas Telford (1757-1834), St Katherine's Dock was constructed in less than two years and was opened in 1828. In a masterstroke of project management the contractor, Thomas Cubitt (1799-1855), instead of having to pay for the disposal of the extracted spoil, transported it upriver and used it to stabilize the marshy area west of Buckingham Palace, newly designated as a royal residence, which he would develop as the fashionable residential areas of Pimlico and Belgravia. Despite their relatively small size St Katherine's docks could handle up to 120 vessels and had warehouses six storeys high so close to the quayside that goods could be lifted straight out of ships in a fifth of the time it normally took to manhandle them by stages from ship to shore. This also cut opportunities for pilferage and meant that St Katherine's came to specialise in high-value goods such as ivory, carpets, marble, shells and perfumes as well as more expensive bulk products like rubber, sugar and indigo.

The proliferation of new dock facilities stimulated the construction of new communication links to distribute the increasing volume of goods being handled. The Commercial Road was opened in sections from 1803 onwards. East India Dock Road and West India Dock Road were opened in 1809 and West Ferry Road in 1812. In the same year Regent's Canal Dock was opened, so that when that canal was completed in 1820 it connected the riverside with the country's extensive system of inland waterways, which meant that bulky goods could be conveyed by water to destinations as distant as Leeds or Liverpool. Between 1824 and 1830 the scholarly but apparently not entrepreneurally gifted Sir George Duckett (1777-1856) had the short Hertford Union Canal cut through land south of what is now Victoria Park to link the Regent's Canal and the River Lea. The transit fees were, however, set too high and Duckett went bankrupt in 1832. The Regent's Canal Company finally bought 'Duckett's

Canal' in 1857.

In 1832 Brunswick Wharf was built to accommodate a new type of craft – the paddle steamer – which plied passenger traffic along the river and round the coasts of Kent and Essex. To cope with the demands of an increasing volume of traffic Bow Bridge was rebuilt in 1839.

The growth of riverside commerce and the continuing improvement in local communications encouraged further industrial development. Huddart's Patent Cable Manufactory was established at Copenhagen Place, Limehouse in 1800. After a distinguished career as a surveyor and commander in the navy of the East India Company Joseph Huddart (1741-1816) had turned his practical experience of seamanship to account by inventing a process for equalising the strains on the yarn in ropes. Huddart's would later manufacture the cables for the London-Blackwall railway which initially used stationary traction engines rather than locomotives. Huddart himself was honoured by appointment as an Elder Brother of Trinity House and election as a Fellow of the Royal Society. In 1808 the Albion Brewery in Whitechapel Road was built. In 1811 the Royal Mint left the Tower of London to occupy purpose-built neo-classical premises designed by

James Johnson and Robert Smirke. Brown Lenox, manufacturers of anchor cables, relocated from Ratcliff to Millwall in 1812. In 1817 the Ratcliff Gas Light and Coke Works was established, one of the earliest in the capital; Stepney's gasworks did not come on-stream until 1838-9. Along the line of the Limehouse Cut there were works for the manufacture of potash, lime, soap and rope – and the Mount Pleasant Eel Pie House. By 1819 the Isle of Dogs to the south of West India Docks had a rope-works, an iron foundry and an 'oil manufactory'. A decade later there were also a flour mill, a factory making iron cables and a second shipyard. By the same date there was a new brewery at Bromley-by-Bow, a gasworks in Poplar and a sail-cloth factory in Limehouse.

In 1821 the first Thames-built steamship, *City of Edinburgh*, was launched at Blackwall. Scottish engineer William Fairbairn's shipyard opened at Millwall in 1835 and in 1839 David Napier established another one nearby. The fortunes generated by expanding maritime commerce established local shipowners and shipbuilders as the locality's bourgeois elite. Irish-born Sir Robert Wigram (1743-1830) trained as a doctor in London and served as a surgeon on East Indiamen before eye trouble

61. The Limehouse Basin, where the Regent's Canal meets the Thames. A view by Thomas H. Shepherd, published in 1827.

62. A lock at the Limehouse Basin, 2004. This formerly key commercial node has become a smart marina, overlooked by up-market residences.

compelled him to become a wholesale druggist, a trade he plied so successfully that he was able to reinvest his capital and build up a fleet of over twenty ships. In 1810 Wigram became first chairman of the East India Dock Company. He also served as MP for his native Wexford, was created a baronet and sired 23 children. John Perry (1743-1810) represented the third generation in a family of Blackwall shipbuilders. In 1799-90 he built Brunswick Dock, the first on the north side of the Thames, which was capable of berthing twenty-eight East Indiamen and sixty of the sloops engaged in the Greenland whaling trade. From 1806 it became known as the East India Export Dock. Perry's apprentice George Green (1767-1849) became his son-in-law and took over the business, specialising in the construction of frigates. He and his son Richard Green (1803-1863) would become renowned for their local philanthropy. Joseph Somes (1787-1845) began in the coastal coal trade but prospered by buying redundant East India Company vessels

and chartering them to the government for the transportation of convicts and troops. He later acquired interests in whaling, sailmaking, chandlery and the colonization of New Zealand. By 1842 Somes' fleet of forty-odd vessels made him the largest private shipowner in the world. When he died at his mansion, New Grove, he was worth £434,000. St Clement's Hospital, Bow Road occupies the site of his home.

CHURCHES AND CHAPELS
The gigantic new docks and warehouses which edged the Thames might be regarded as so many temples to Mammon but the just claims of the Lord were not entirely overlooked, although to many lives He had already become an irrelevance. In 1816 the rector of Bethnal Green described his flock in terms which blended disgust with dismay:

"it consists of a population of about 40,000,

63. *Palestine Place, the centre of the missionary operations of the London Society for Promoting Christianity amongst the Jews. Built from 1813 onwards on the site of Bishop Hall Farm, it consisted of a chapel, schools and fourteen houses. Although Cambridge Heath Road was notably filthy when this picture was made, Palastine Place was noted as always clean. It was demolished in 1895 to make way forBethnal Green Infirmary. Lithograph c.1840, artist unknown.*

generally the lowest description of people ... Every Sunday morning, during the time of divine service, several hundred persons assemble in a field adjoining the churchyard, where they fight dogs, hunt ducks, gamble ... 'This on the Sunday?' At all times, chiefly on Sunday, Monday and sometimes Tuesday; Monday is the principal day; one or two thousand men and boys will on these occasions leave their looms..."

By the middle of Victoria's reign the East End would be regarded as a spiritual wasteland of unbelief but in the era of the evangelical revival its surviving religious life remained vigorous, at least if judged in terms of real estate. In 1809 Wesleyans purchased the former Huguenot chapel at the junction of Fournier Street and Brick Lane. All Saints, Poplar was established as a parish separate from Stepney in 1817 with a handsome neo-classical church in East India Dock Road built to designs by C Hollis. In 1817 also an Independent chapel was opened in West Ferry Road. A rebuilt St Paul's, Shadwell was consecrated in 1821, St Philip, Newark Street in 1823, St Stephen, Tredegar Road in 1827 and in 1828 St John's, Bethnal Green, designed by the doyen of British architects, Sir

John Soane. Nonconformists strove to keep pace with the Established Church. In 1832 the Brunswick Methodist chapel was built in Three Colt Street, Limehouse and in 1836 a Congregational chapel opened in Harley Street (now Grove) opened. But a further eight new Anglican churches were opened for worship between 1839 and 1841.

THE DEMISE OF SPITALFIELDS SILK

The outbreak of war against France in 1792 brought on a crisis in the Spitalfields silk industry more severe than any in memory. A local doctor declared of the weavers that

"it is not in the power of language to describe their long and continued miseries, not brought on by idleness, intemperance or a dissolute course of life but human wretchedness, absolutely produced by want of employment ... whole families without fire, without raiment, without food."

Another eyewitness of 1797 wrote that "the poverty and distress of these people at this time are inconceivable ... very generally a family in every room with very little bedding, furniture

64. *South-east view of St Leonard Bromley. The area in the foreground was consecrated as extra burying-ground in 1813. By then the manor house to the left had been demolished. In 1843 St Leonard's was substantially rebuilt in brick. Watercolour 1797, artist unknown.*

or clothes. The few rags on their backs comprise the principal part of their property." In 1795 the charitable and farsighted magistrate Patrick Colquhoun founded a soup kitchen in Spitalfields which became a permanent institution in 1797 when the Spitalfields Soup Society was founded.

A measure of prosperity returned by 1805-6, only to be blighted by Napoleon's continental blockade which reduced the area to mass unemployment again by 1808, further worsened by the Milan Decrees of 1812 which held back supplies of raw silk. The long-term implication of these afflictions was attested in 1814 by the opening of an Infirmary for Asthma, Consumption and other Diseases of the Lungs in Brushfield Street.

After a brief recovery at the end of the French wars acute depression returned in 1816-17 when the labour market was flooded with discharged ex-servicemen. Good times were back by 1823 but in 1824 the Spitalfields Act was repealed and import restrictions completely removed by 1826. Over the following six years one employer, Barrett Wadden, is known to have cut his workforce from three hundred to sixty. By

1832 it was reckoned that two thirds of the looms in Spitalfields and Bethnal Green were idle. In Bethnal Green alone six thousand were registered for parish aid. The parish being quite unable to bear this burden middle-class philanthropists set up a Bethnal Green Benevolent Society to distribute food and clothes among the needy. Many masters relocated to Essex or even as far as Somerset in search of cheaper labour in an attempt to stay competitive. It was reckoned that weavers who stayed worked not the customary ten but fourteen hours a day for a fifth less pay in order to survive.

The implosion of the Spitalfields silk industry brought in its wake the erosion of the cultural societies which had been such a characteristic feature of Huguenot life in prosperous times. Although a love of flowers lingered on, the once flourishing Horticultural Society foundered, as did others devoted to madrigals and mathematics.

Cultural impoverishment was accompanied by civic corruption. Not all Huguenots were models of rectitude. Born in Bethnal Green, Joseph Merceron (1764-1839) settled in Brick Lane and built up a miniature bureaucratic empire by becoming parish treasurer, a JP, Chairman of the Watch Board and a member of the commissions for sewers and local taxation. Local offices he was unable to fill in person he packed with relatives or trusted henchmen. Having a near-monopoly of local administration enabled him effectively to control over twenty licensed premises and to lower rate charges for friends and clients and raise them on those who dared to cross him. Threatened with an audit in 1804, he resigned but, as no replacement could be found, was re-elected and continued to hold office until 1818 when he was finally found guilty of misappropriation, fined £200 and imprisoned for eighteen months. Upon Merceron's release he repaid the funds he had been convicted of taking and regained control of his former offices, either in person or through his son or son-in-law – except that of magistrate. He died allegedly worth £340,000 – 'though he always appeared to be in poor circumstances.' Astoundingly his memory is commemorated in the name of Merceron Street El and Merceron House in Globe Road.

Fortunately for the people of Spitalfields there were still some of the comfortable classes who retained a sense of *noblesse oblige*. Quaker William Allen (1770-1843) of Steward Street prospered in the silk trade but was really passionate about chemistry. In 1797 he became a founding member of the Spitalfields Soup Society. He also sponsored a school for pauper children. Allen later became a Fellow of the Royal Society and founded the firm of Allen and Hanbury which became renowned for the manufacture of medical supplies. Fellow Quaker Peter Bedford (1780-1864), who inherited Allen's silk business, took a special interest in the social salvation of delinquents, memorialized by the establishment of reformatory Bedford Institutes, initially in Wheeler Street and later in Ratcliff, Bethnal Green and Hoxton. Sir Thomas Fowell Buxton (1786-1845) a director of the brewing firm of Truman, Hanbury and Buxton at the age of twenty-two, became a firm supporter of Allen's Spitalfield's charities. In 1816 Buxton made an impassioned speech at the Mansion House on behalf of impoverished Spitalfields weavers and raised £43,369 on the spot. Buxton also continued Bedford's work on the improvement of prison regimes and for the benefit of Spitalfields founded a savings-bank and a salt fish market.

Allen, Bedford and Buxton were all also prominent in the movement for the abolition of the slave trade.

ACADEMIA IN ARCADIA

Despite the increasing industrialisation of the immediate riverside areas localities inland to the north continued to attract institutions and residents in search of a healthful and semi-rural environment. In 1783 the Merchant Seamen's Orphanage Asylum was established in Merchant Street, Bow and in the same year an Evangelical Academy was founded in Mile End Old Town.

In 1795 the London Hospital opened a medical school. The founder, Sir William Blizard FRS (1743-1835), also took the lead in founding the Royal College of Surgeons and became its President in 1814.

In 1810 a Baptist Academy was established in Worcester House at Stepney Green before moving into purpose-built premises there in 1830. In 1815 the philanthropic Blackwall shipowner George Green built a school at Woolmore Street, Poplar. Green paid for four further Poplar schools as well as a sailor's home and a row of almshouses. In 1816 Father Barber founded Wade Street (later Holy Family) RC School – a long overdue act of provision for the East End's substantial and gravely disadvantaged Catholic community. In 1822 the Jews' Free School, opened in 1817, moved to its permanent home in Bell Street, Spitalfields, though that was more appropriate for its accessibility than its healthfulness.

In 1840, on the eve of his death, another philanthropist, the eccentric, but generous, insurance-broker, John Thomas Barber Beaumont (1774-1841) established the New Philosophical Institute in Beaumont Square, Mile End. Trained at the Royal Academy Beaumont had initially practised successfully as a miniaturist and was appointed official painter to the Dukes of York and Kent. During the invasion scare of 1802-3 he raised a company of volunteer riflemen who, most unusually, he trained to be the equals of professional soldiers in their standard of musketry. Beaumont also founded the County Fire Office and the Provident Life Institute and Bank of Savings, which were respectively the first properly constituted friendly society and workman's savings bank. Another financial wizard associated with the area was David Ricardo (1772-

1823), now remembered as second only to Adam Smith as a founder of the discipline of economics. Of Dutch Jewish descent, Ricardo was disinherited by his wealthy stockbroker father when he converted to Christianity at twenty-one to marry. Undismayed by familial rejection and undeterred by the slightness of his own formal education, Ricardo set himself to becoming seriously rich as a dealer in government securities. During this period he lived for some years at Bromley-by-Bow where four of his eight children were baptised between 1803 and 1810. It is reasonable to assume therefore that the area was still at that time a sufficiently attractive place of residence for a man on his way to making the modern equivalent of millions. When Ricardo did leave it was to assume the style of a country gentleman at Gatcombe Park, Gloucestershire, the present home of Princess Anne, the Princess Royal.

AN EMERGING EAST END

By the time of Ricardo's exodus to the countryside the quickening pace of urbanisation was increasingly apparent. The East London Waterworks Company had established a plant at Old Ford, Bow to supply the needs of new households. Whitechapel Mount, a relic of the civil wars much augmented by decades of waste-disposal, was demolished in 1807. Contrary to much speculation it yielded little of interest to archaeologists but permitted the building of residential streets along the new Commercial Road, a process vigorously pursued by the Mercers' Company from 1817 onwards. Much residential building, however, was ventured by small-scale speculators and consisted of short streets or even single terraces. Some were named after popular heroes – Rodney Terrace, Wellington Place and Nelson Street. Others had the often all too temporary or deceptive allure of the exotic or the picturesque – Canton Place or Prospect Place. Even more were named after

65. Bow Workhouse painted c. 1796. Clearly built as a substantial mansion, this would seem to have been taken over to house the poor as opinion hardened against out-relief payments.

66. Old shops at 84-98 Cable Street, Stepney. The name of the street recalls local rope-making and it was originally just a cable's length – six hundred feet – from end to end. Watercolour by Frederick Calvert (fl. 1811-44) c.1830.

themselves or their children. Directly east of St Dunstan's there were streets named for Catherine, Richard, John, James, Samuel, George and Edward. Immediately to the north-west were those named for Alfred, Ernest and Henry – and also for John, James, Edward and George.

Further signs of changing times included the demolition of Poplar manor house in 1810 and the opening of Poplar workhouse in 1817, the suppression of the annual Bow Fair in 1823 and the laying out of Tredegar Square from 1828. In 1830 the last pirates were hanged at Execution Dock and by the terms of the great Reform Act of 1832 a Parliamentary Borough of Tower Hamlets came into existence, somewhat belatedly recognising both the commercial and demographic significance of the sprawling suburbs emerging to the east of the City.

De-ruralisation encompassed the final extinction of market gardening. Most operators had typically occupied patches of land varying from three to six acres in extent. But in 1775

cowkeeper Joseph Wilkinson of Bishop's Hall also had fifteen acres of garden, plus a further six south of Old Ford Road for growing fruit. As late as 1795 horticulturalists occupied some 140 acres or 28% of Bethnal Green's surviving agricultural land, as opposed to 160 still put to grass and 190 to arable. Over the course of the following half century almost a hundred acres of this garden ground was lost, mostly to building, though some was simply taken over by squatters or used for dumping refuse. By 1851 only 47 acres were still under cultivation.

The same story was repeated further east at Bromley St Leonard. In 1816 some sixty acres were still occupied by market gardeners and nurserymen. But the Allport family, who had been in business as market gardeners since at least 1751 and had branched out into the nursery and seed trades, began to sell off part of their holding from 1807 and had disposed of it all by 1832. The Mandeno family, who cultivated multiple patches of land here and there, hung on until the 1840s. By then, however, the advent of the railway had effectively deprived Tower Hamlets' horticulturalists of any advantages of cost or freshness they once derived from proximity to London markets and made it far more profitable to convert land to residential use to accommodate the non-stop flow of inmigration.

A DREAD VISITATION

The outbreak of cholera, first recorded in India in 1817, reached Russia by 1823 and Hamburg by 1831. From there it entered Britain via Sunderland, making its way inexorably southwards. The first case in the East End was recorded on 12 February 1832. Sarah Ferguson, a tough youngster who "gained a living by picking up coals and timber along the riverside ... even in the most inclement weather" – i.e. she was what was commonly known as a 'mudlark' – died within eight hours of feeling unwell, her extremities having turned quite blue in that brief interval. Cholera was new to the medical profession, unknown in its causes, horrifying in its effects and terrifying in the speed with which it could spread.

Because the nature of the contagion was not understood the treatment given was the opposite of what was required. The bacterium causing the illness produced a profuse diarrhoea requiring copious intakes of water and salts to replace what had been lost. Instead doctors prescribed emetics, enemas and purgatives and in some cases even resorted to bleeding.

The London Hospital, in common with other voluntary hospitals, refused admission to infectious cases as a matter of policy, though it did set up an isolation ward for existing patients who became infected. Poplar alone had already taken the precaution of establishing its own isolation hospital in advance of the outbreak. Another was set up in two houses in Vinegar Lane in St George-in-the-East. Many of the poor, however, refused to allow their sick to be taken to these facilities, fearing, not without reason, that in the case of death the corpse would be used for dissection. At one point a mob assembled in Vinegar Lane, threatening to pull down the house and to lynch the surgeon "exclaiming that they were 'Burking' the poor wretches who were admitted" – a reference to the notorious Edinburgh body-snatchers, Burke and Hare. A bold spirit rushed out, however, dragged one of the ringleaders inside and, after the patients had testified to their humane treatment, thrust him out to reassure the crowd which shamefacedly dispersed.

In Limehouse, Shadwell, Wapping, White-chapel and Bethnal Green cholera wards were created in workhouses which were already overcrowded. The Admiralty made the frigate *HMS Dover* available as a floating hospital, mooring it at first off Limehouse, then off Hermitage Pier at Wapping. After the crew refused point blank to attend the sick three female nurses were procured to assist Surgeon Inlay. Most of his patients, however, were taken, not from the East End, but off collier ships arriving from the northeast, the original point of outbreak.

Emergency regulations required that cholera victims be buried within twelve hours of death. This conflicted with the deep-rooted Irish custom of holding a wake during which the deceased was put on public display for friends and neighbours to pay their respects. On occasion, therefore, the recently established Metropolitan Police were obliged to break into houses and remove corpses by force.

By the time the cholera epidemic had passed it had killed more than eight hundred in the East End, out of some three thousand in the capital as a whole – about a third as many as would die in Paris in just the first month of its onslaught there. To put the outbreak in perspective the number of deaths it caused was considerably lower than the annual number of tuberculosis mortalities – and over twice as many victims caught cholera and recovered as caught it and died.

Streets, Ships and Salvation

The urbanisation of the East End continued relentlessly throughout Victoria's reign but without the benefit of any overall planning to balance the need for housing against complementary needs for employment, sanitation, recreation or education. The volume of building needed to accommodate the area's ever-expanding population can be gauged from the fate of the dead. Between its opening in 1845 and its closure in 1876 the less than ten acres which comprised Victoria Park cemetery was crammed with some 300,000 burials – in just over thirty years.

Apart from the need to employ and accommodate in-migrants to the metropolis much development was stimulated by major improvements in communications. Prominent among these were broad boulevards intended to improve the flow of through traffic. Old Ford Road was straightened in 1844, Commercial Street laid out in 1849 and Burdett Road opened in

1862. Bethnal Green Road was constructed between 1872 and 1879 and Wapping High Street widened, both by the Metropolitan Board of Works. By 1856 there were eighteen buses daily running westwards towards Chelsea. In 1870-1 a horse-drawn tram service was inaugurated from Aldgate via the Mile End Road into Essex. In 1872 a complementary route linked Poplar with Bloomsbury.

So much for the roads. In 1840-1 a railway service was opened to link Blackwall with Fenchurch Street. 1nitially the carriages were hauled by cables, with departures every fifteen minutes. Passengers boarding at intermediate stations were obliged to continue to the terminus. Locomotives finally took over in 1849.

In 1843 the Wapping-Rotherhithe tunnel finally opened. Built by Sir Marc Brunel (1769-1849) and Isambard Kingdom Brunel (1806-59), it represented an engineering triumph, the first in the world to be driven under a flowing river. Initially projected in 1798, the task had overwhelmed two previous constructors and had taken the Brunels two decades to complete. But its completion had little immediate impact as funds had run out before access roads could be completed. Unusable for traffic, the tunnel remained a curiosity and ultimately an embar-

67. West India Dock station, on the newly-opened London-Blackwall Railway, in 1840.

68. The Blackwall railway terminus, depicted in The Builder 14 October 1843. Note the paddle-steamers plying a passenger trade from the landing stage.

69. An unlikely assembly of people in the Thames Tunnel, though it did attract tourists. The stall is selling German books.

70. *A funeral arrives at the gates of the 'City of London and Tower Hamlets Cemetery'. Lithograph c.1860, by George B. Moore (1806-75).*

rassment until it was bought by a railway company in 1865 and converted for its use. It still carries the Underground from Wapping to Rotherhithe.

Little value was attached to the preservation of the relics of antiquity. In 1842 much of the medieval chapel of St Leonard, Bow was demolished and in 1845 the Bishop of London's manor house was similarly knocked down. The church was largely rebuilt in brick but incorporated some of the oldest medieval arches. The rapid transformation of the former marshland to the south of the great docks may, however, have provoked the publication in 1853 of Benjamin H Cowper's *Descriptive, Historical and Statistical Account of Millwall, Commonly called the Isle of Dogs*. The opening of Tower Hamlets cemetery in 1841 and of Victoria Park in 1845 at least preserved two substantial open spaces from disappearing beneath the apparently unstoppable avalanche of bricks and mortar.

The population of Poplar more than doubled between 1831, when it stood at 17,000, and

1861, when the parish alone passed 44,000. With its environs Poplar by then encompassed 79,000 souls, a figure which would expand to 157,000 by 1881. Cubitt Town in the south-east corner of the Isle of Dogs, was one of the few ventures which recognised the desirability of providing scope for jobs as well as houses. It was developed from 1842 onwards by the building contractor William Cubitt (1791-1863) who established a materials yard and workshops for his own business in Wharf (now Saunders Ness Road and sub-let the rest of the land he had leased from the Countess of Glendale for use as timber wharves, a saw-mill, cement factory and shipyard and for speculative building. Street lines followed those of former drainage ditches. The houses built were intended to attract artisans who would work in the new industrial facilities proliferating along the shore-line. In 1847 the first purpose-built school on the Isle of Dogs was opened. Cubitt retired from business in 1854 to devote himself full time to public life, serving as MP for Andover (1847-61) and Lord Mayor of

71. Three children of one family who died in June 1877, are recorded on this gravestone in Tower Hamlets Cemetery. They are grim evidence of a life at the mercy of epidemics.

London for two terms (1860-62). He also helped finance the building of Christ Church, which enabled the Isle of Dogs to become a parish in its own right in 1857.

By 1841, the population of Bethnal Green exceeded 80,000, making it more populous than Norwich or Newcastle. The prolific journalist and novelist George Reynolds (1814-79) took advantage of the newly-opened Eastern Counties Railway to present readers with a doleful bird's-eye view of the locality:

> "The traveller upon this line may catch ... a hasty but alas! too comprehensive glance of the wretchedness and squalor of that portion of London. He may actually obtain a view of the interior and domestic misery peculiar to the neighbourhood; he may penetrate with his eyes into the secrets of those abodes of sorrow, vice and destitution. In summertime the poor always have their windows open and thus the hideous poverty of their rooms can be readily descried from the summit of the arches on which the railroad is constructed. And in those rooms may be seen women half-naked, some employed in washing the few rags they possess, others ironing the linen of a more wealthy neighbour, a few preparing the sorry meal, and numbers scolding, swearing and quarrelling. At many of the windows men out of work, with matted hair, black beards and dressed only in filthy shirts and ragged trousers, lounge all the day long smoking ... Around the doors children ... shoeless, dirty and uncared for, throng in numbers – a rising generation of thieves and vagabonds....".

Stygian observations were reflected from a street level perspective by Hector Gavin, the author of *Sanitary Ramblings: Being Sketches and Illustrations of Bethnal Green* (1849). Gavin noted

> "the enormous number of dwellings which have been constructed in defiance of every law and principle on which the health and lives of the occupants depend."

Piped water was available only three times a week for two hours at a time and even then at a very low pressure. Of Bethnal Green's four

72. *Most education of the poorer classes was undertaken by church schools. This illustration depicts the Trinity School Church in Peel Grove, Bethnal Green, in 1859.*

73. *Bethnal Green's new town hall. From The Builder, 17 July 1852. This Gothic version was replaced by a Baroque one in 1910.*

hundred roads only 14% were granite laid and only 40% had paved footpaths, Less than 10% of its houses were connected to sewers. By 1851, the year in which Bethnal Green acquired its own Town Hall, there were only 47 acres of market gardens left in the parish. Between 1871 and 1881 the population of the area rose by 6,857 to reach 126,961, crammed into 16,606 houses. This meant that Bethnal Green was more populous than such major provincial cities as Leicester or Nottingham. By 1874 there was only one brickfield left in the locality, although there were still over four hundred cows being stall-fed in byres to supply the residents with no doubt highly dubious milk.

LIQUID HISTORY

Although shipbuilding had been a significant East End activity for four centuries, during the middle decades of the nineteenth century, as shipbuilders made the double transition from sail to steam and from wood to iron, the Thames-side industry was to be responsible for some of the most innovative vessels of the day. Undoubtedly great fortunes were made but shipbuilding remained a hazardous venture, subject to rapid changes in technology, cash-flow problems, labour disputes, cancelled contracts, fires, explosions and the caprice of weather and wars. Even successful firms, therefore, often sought security in niche markets or by diversifying into civil engineering. Shipbuilding also helped to sustain a network of associated industries which provided further employment for local residents. These included

the Blackwall Iron Works in Yabsley Street, opened in 1847, as well as smaller-scale, specialised manufacturers of pumps and hoses. Rope manufacturers included Frost Brothers, West & Co., Soanes and Co. and Huddart & Co. Used rope was in turn recycled to make paper. Provisioning ships proved to be a lucrative market for East End brewers and manufacturers of biscuit, pickles, clothing and specialised maritime gear, as the investigative journalist Henry Mayhew observed in 1849:

> "every other shop is stocked with gear for the ship or for the sailor. The windows of one house are filled with quadrants and bright brass sextants, chronometers and compasses ... Every public house is a *'Jolly Tar'* or something equally taking ... All the grocers are provision agents and exhibit in their windows tin cases of meat and biscuits and every article is warranted to keep in any climate ... The corners of the streets, too, are mostly monopolised by slopsellers, their windows parti-coloured with bright red and blue flannel shirts, the doors nearly blocked up with hammocks and well-oiled 'nor-westers' ..."

The trail-blazer in early iron construction was the self-taught Scottish engineer Sir William Fairbairn (1789-1874) who opened a shipyard at Millwall in 1835 and, over the next fourteen years, built a hundred and twenty iron ships there. Fairbairn also patented a technique for using steam-power to hammer ships' rivets. When he decided to relocate his business back to Manchester, where he had made his first fortune, Fairbairn's yard was sold to John Scott Russell (*see below*).

Thomas J Ditchburn (1801-70) and Charles Mare (1815-98), having lost their recently-established Deptford yard in a fire, took over the premises of bankrupt shipbuilders William and Benjamin Wallis at Orchard Place, between Bow Creek and the East India Dock Basin, in 1838. Beginning with small paddle-wheelers, they progressed to cross-Channel boats and in 1845 built the Royal yacht *Fairy*. This prestigious commission marked a turning-point in the firm's fortunes. Whereas their average output between 1838 and 1844 had been barely 900 tons, it now soared to 6,000 tons thanks to orders from the Admiralty and the rapidly expanding P & O shipping line. As Mare and Ash the company switched increasingly to civil engineering projects, fabricating the iron roof of Fenchurch Street station, the tubular sections for Fairbairn and Stephenson's Britannia Bridge over the Menai Straits and the present Westminster Bridge.

Following Mare's bankruptcy in 1855, by which date the firm had expanded to employ 3,000 workers, it was re-founded as the Thames Ironworks and Shipbuilding and Engineering Company Ltd. As such it was easily the largest concern on the Thames with the capacity to construct 25,000 tons of warships and 10,000 tons of commercial vessels at the same time. From this mighty enterprise ironclads would be launched to equip the navies of Russia, Prussia, Portugal, Spain, Sweden, Denmark, Greece, the Ottoman Empire and Japan. In 1843 the marine engineers, Joseph and Jacob Samuda opened a Millwall shipyard which was to be distinguished for its state of the art technology. The Samuda yard pioneered the production of ironclads for the Royal Navy, including *HMS Thunderer* and *HMS Prince Albert*, as well as ships for the Brazilian, Prussian and Japanese navies, cross-Channel steamers, passenger liners for P & O and an experimental atmospheric railway for Brunel. Joseph D'Aguilar Samuda (1813-85}, descendant of a Sephardi Jewish line, also served as Liberal MP for Tower Hamlets (1868-80).

In 1850 John Scott Russell's yard constructed the yacht *Titania* for the railway engineer Robert Stephenson. Russell's also produced mail steamers for the Australian route. The construction of Brunel's mighty *Great Eastern*, at 20,000 tons by far the largest vessel ever attempted, was dogged by technical and financial problems. When completed the hull had become so embedded on its site that new hydraulic rams had to be specially commissioned to shift it. After months of frustration and delay it was finally launched in 1858 – sideways to avoid running ashore on the opposite bank.

This testing project was immediately followed by another for Scott Russell when *HMS Warrior* was hastily commissioned in response to a French initiative – *La Gloire*, the first warship with an armoured hull, launched in 1859. Regarded as a strategically provocative act, the launching of *La Gloire* sparked off a war-scare which caused thousands of Britons to enrol in volunteer rifle units. Joseph Samuda himself enrolled as an officer with the Tower Hamlets Volunteers. Scott-Russell, meanwhile busied himself with designing a ship which would out-gun and out-run any potential opponent. *Warrior* featured an armoured citadel of iron plates and teak three feet thick to house its guns. She also had armoured protection to both bow and stern and internal water-tight compartments. The actual work of construction was subcontracted to the Thames Ironworks. Intended to be ready in nine months, *Warrior* took twice that long to complete, thanks to the coldest winter for half a century. The project also nearly bankrupted the builders who had to be rescued from collapse by the Admiralty. When finally launched in 1860 *Warrior* instantly became the most feared ship afloat but, ironically, was destined never to see action. It survives, splendidly restored, at Portsmouth.

London Yard in Cubitt Town was opened in 1856-7 by Robert Baillie, Joseph Westwood and James Campbell. Although primarily concerned with building ships the yard's varied ventures also included a miniature steam yacht for an Egyptian pasha, bridges for Indian railways and an iron-framed palace for the Sultan of Turkey.

Thames shipbuilders suffered badly from the financial fall-out of the great City crash of Overend, Gurney & Co. in 1866. The sector was further battered by the severe winter of 1866-67 which damaged all the riverside trades – and was accompanied by London's last outbreak of cholera. One of the survivors was the yard

75. *Plaque to the chemist William Perkin, who discovered the first aniline dyestuff in 1856. (See p.81)*

74. *Monument to Joseph Bazalgette, who masterminded the reorganisation of London's sewerage system. The project resulted in the construction of the Abbey Mills Pumping Station. The monument is on the Embankment.*

which had only just been opened by the future Sir Alfred Fernandez Yarrow (1842-1932). Having learned his trade at the marine engine builders Ravenhill, Salkend & Co. of Ratcliff, Yarrow, still in his early twenties, set up for himself at what many sceptics would have thought an entirely appropriate location – Folly Wall on the Isle of Dogs. There he not only survived the crisis of 1866-7 but prospered. Between 1868 and 1875 Yarrow concentrated on river-launches, building over three hundred and fifty, then switched to torpedo-boats in 1876. In 1893 Yarrow's would launch *HMS Havock* and *HMS Hornet,* the first of an entirely new type required by the Royal Navy – the destroyer.

WORLDS OF WORK

Although there were some high value-added trades such as gun-smithing and bespoke tailoring, much East End industry was concerned with the manufacture of the everyday necessities of working-class life. The prevalence of businesses making starch, soap, candles, brushes and floor-cloths implies that 'the great unwashed' were increasingly less content to be so. Other significant industries included paper and printing, clothing, trimmings and footwear and furniture-making. Major new employers of the period included Bryant & May, whose match factory opened at Bow in 1861, Millwall Dock, opened in 1866, Abbey Mills sewage-pumping station, opened in 1877 and Beckton gas works, which came on-stream in 1878. The Albion brewery was rebuilt in 1855.

One of the more unusual businesses, located at 190 St George's Street East, Ratcliff Highway was that of Charles (actually Johann Christian Carl) Jamrach (1815-91), a German-born importer of exotic wildlife who built up a virtual monopoly of supplying menageries, zoos and circuses throughout Europe. His customers included American showman P T Barnum, the Ottoman Sultan and Dante Rossetti, who kept wombats as pets. Cage-birds and goldfish were imported in bulk for the domestic market. Jamrach's colourful establishment contrasted dramatically with the drabness around it and supplied endless copy for journalists as well as being featured in Bram Stoker's *Dracula* and stories by H G Wells and Mark Twain.

A short walk to the east from Jamrach's would have taken a curious visitor to the site now occupied by Gosling House, Cable Street. Here,

76. A 'Fire proof sugar refinery' in Leman Street. The sheer size of this nine-storey building is evidence of the increasing scale of industrial enterprises in the East End. Lithograph 1851, artist unknown.

77. A weaver at Spitalfields, end of 19th century. A few elderly workers kept up the craft into the 1930s.

while still a teenager, the future Sir William Perkin FRS (1838-1907} created the world's first aniline dye, mauve, and in doing so revolutionised the chemicals industry, with ramifications that would transform whole realms of human endeavour from fashion and furnishing to medicine.

POVERTY AND PHILANTHROPY

Despite the highly visible development of its economy the East End was characterised by equally visible concentrations of poverty. One specific and clearly identifiable factor behind this was the influx of Irish fleeing the catastrophic famine caused by potato blight in 1844-46. There had been a distinct Irish community in Wapping since the late sixteenth century and a section of Cable Street is marked on a map of *c.*1810 as Knockfergus. The newcomers represented a dramatic influx of desperate souls, seeking economic salvation where they could. Their willingness to work for the lowest rates stimulated greater efforts at unionisation among dockers eager to exclude them from competition. Workhouse returns show their most common occupations as labourer, hawker,

78. Old weavers' houses at Bethnal Green at the turn of the 20th century. Note the large upper windows to give maximum light in the weaving-loft. Note also the paucity of street-lighting and the absence of trees.

rag-sorter, washerwoman, charwoman or domestic servant. A minority found work demanding some level of skill in tailoring or bootmaking. Others were drawn into crime or prostitution. Investigative journalist Henry Mayhew, writing in the 1850s, referred to Commercial Road and Ratcliff Cross as 'Irish nests'. A decade later hundreds of the female offspring of the 1840s immigrants would find work at Bryant & May's match factory. The area around Furze Street would become known as 'the Fenian barracks'. The White Swan at Shadwell would be so much patronised by the Irish that it was known by all as 'Paddy's Goose'.

Contemporary observers were clear that the situation was growing worse, rather than better. In 1861 the Rector of Limehouse observed, with barely concealed distaste, that his "parishioners are for the most part poor, comprising a large number of persons employed at the Docks and engineering and ship-building yards ... There is an increase of low lodging-houses for sailors ... and the removal of the more respectable families to other localities." Increas-

ingly this would be the phenomenon remarked upon by social observers – not so much the visibility of the poverty as the invisibility of a middle class. The French historian and philosopher Hippolyte Taine, writing in 1872, thought Shadwell worse than anything he had ever previously encountered:

"by the vastness of its distress and by its extent ...(it) is in keeping with the hugeness and wealth of London. I have seen the bad quarters of Marseilles, of Antwerp, of Paris, they do not come near to it ... Beggars, thieves, harlots, the latter especially, crowd Shadwell Street. One hears a grating music in the spirit cellars; sometimes it is a negro who handles the violin; through the open window one perceives unmade beds, women dancing. Thrice in ten minutes I saw crowds collected at the doors; fights were going on, chiefly fights between women ... The bystanders laughed; the noise caused the adjacent lanes to be emptied of their occupants; ragged, poor children, harlots – it was like a human sewer suddenly discharging its contents ... "

In 1841 Bethnal Green was the second poorest parish in London; by 1871 it *was* the poorest. Writing of Bethnal Green in 1868 the *Illustrated London News* declared that "a large part of the population, at the best of times, is on the verge of pauperism." In the 1870s Bethnal Green workhouse usually accommodated around a thousand paupers. Relief was also paid out to about 1,500 vagrants annually. The 1881 census reveals that of the 395 inmates of the Whitechapel Union Workhouse at South Grove, Mile End Road less than half had actually been born in Tower Hamlets. Over seventy were of Irish birth, three were Scottish, three Welsh, five foreign-born and another fifty had been born more than fifty miles from London.

The East End had not only its own poor to contend with but was also a dumping-ground for paupers whom other communities preferred to remove from among themselves. St Clement's Hospital was built in 1849 as the City of London Union Workhouse. Grove Hall asylum at Bow housed hundreds of crazed and demented ex-servicemen. Even the dead were a burden on the living. In the first two years of its use 60% of the burials in Tower Hamlets cemetery were at public expense because the families of the deceased were too poor to pay for either a plot or a funeral. By 1851 the figure was 80%.

To some at least of the comfortable classes the immiseration of so many in the capital of a country which regarded itself as the world's leading nation constituted both a danger and a reproach. The flight of the better-off to the ever-expanding suburbs deprived the East End of the sort of local leadership which had traditionally administered local charities. Besides which casual doles to the deserving were scarcely an appropriate response to the scale of the challenge which had emerged. What was to be done? And who was to do it? The rich and the religious between them attempted a variety of remedies. Among the bourgeoisie who did remain in the locality the ship-owning Green family of Blackwall were notable for their benefactions. In 1847 George Green built Bow Lane School. His son Richard Green supported schools which taught and to a considerable extent also clothed, some two thousand children in the Poplar area. Richard Green also founded a Sailors' Home at Poplar and a Merchant Seamen's Orphan Asylum.

Allegedly the richest woman in the kingdom, Angela Burdett-Coutts (1814-1906), daughter of the radical MP Sir Francis Burdett and heir to the Coutts banking fortune, was to give away some £4,000,000 in the course of her lifetime and to make the East End a special target for

79. Handsome Poplar Vestry House – an expression of civic pride amidst poverty.

80. Angela Burdett-Coutts, open-handed heiress.

81.   *Columbia Market, built by Angela Burdett-Coutts, opened in 1869. It was to be a failure. It had the atmosphere of a church, with admonitory texts around the walls, and bells that rang hymn tunes. Worse, it was not allowed to trade on Sundays – this in a Jewish area.*

her bounty. Advised by Charles Dickens, whom she considered to be in touch with, as well as in sympathy with the poor, the heiress supported a range of projects and programmes ranging from soup kitchens, night-shelters and Ragged Schools to training courses for girls to go into domestic service and funds for boys to become self-supporting by joining the 'Shoe Black brigade'. She paid for stables for costermongers' donkeys and in 1862 opened Columbia Square Buildings as 'model lodgings'. Her most ambitious scheme, however, was Columbia Market, a flamboyant Flemish Gothic confection designed by H A Darbishire and opened in 1869 at a cost of £200,000. Believing that the poor were often cheated by stall-holders passing off underweight, inferior or adulterated goods, she hoped to mitigate such evils by providing a cathedral for honest commerce. Well-intentioned but fundamentally misconceived, the venture proved a costly failure almost from the outset, boycotted by wholesalers, stallholders and customers alike. The City Corporation took it over in an attempt to rescue all concerned from embarrassment but handed it back, defeated, in 1874. Briefly reo-

pened in 1884, Columbia Market was partly let as workshops and eventually used as a shelter during the Blitz. Pevsner, viewing its decayed grandeur a decade later deemed its preservation essential, but it was demolished in 1959. Considering what property developers have done with abandoned warehouses and redundant factories one can only fantasise about what they might have made of such a misplaced gem. Burdett-Coutts' generosity was recognised by the naming of Burdett Road. She further gave a magnificent drinking fountain in 1862 to adorn Victoria Park. She was ennobled as a baroness in her own right in 1871.

Unlike the Baroness, who opted for a scatter-gun approach, American banker George Peabody (1795-1869) chose to put his funding behind a single focused programme. Peabody had already made himself a millionaire out of dry goods before settling in England to become the leading financier of Anglo-American commercial relations. In 1862 he decided to mark a quarter century of success by putting some of his wealth back into the country which had made him even richer. Peabody's chosen concern was the provision of decent housing for

82. *Lodging houses in Columbia Square, also erected at the expense of Angela Burdett-Coutts.*

83. *The drinking fountain in Victoria Park - another gift from Angela Burdett-Coutts in 1862.*

84. *George Peabody. His generosity was rewarded by burial at Westminster Abbey – for one month only. His body was then repatriated to the USA.*

the steady, sober man of modest means. Reasoning that it was all too easy for even an otherwise industrious man to be dragged down into the underclass if he returned from work each day to a squalid slum inhabited by drunks and derelicts, Peabody determined to provide a firmly-managed environment in which picked tenants could be sheltered from harassment and temptation. In 1864 the first ever Peabody Buildings were opened at the junction of Folgate Street and Commercial Street. Fortress-like in their solidity, the block featured retail premises on its Commercial Street frontage; their rents helping to subsidise the rents charged to domestic tenants. A single entrance, easily supervised, guarded against unwelcome intruders. These 'model dwellings' really did serve as a model for other charitable providers. In 1867 a Peabody estate was completed in Shadwell. Peabody himself was honoured with a statue which still stands behind the Royal Exchange, its gaze directed towards Old Broad Street where the office of Peabody, Riggs and Co. once conducted its business.

Edward Denison (1840-70), the son of the bishop of Salisbury, an Etonian and Oxonian, took on the task of being almoner of the Society for the Relief of Distress in the District of Stepney and in 1867 settled in lodgings in Philpot Street, Mile End Road. Over the course of the following eight months he built and endowed a school, where he taught Bible-

85. Peabody Buildings in Commercial Street, 2004.

86. Peabody Buildings in Shadwell, opened in 1867.

classes and gave lectures to working men. Personal contact with the prevailing poverty around him convinced Denison that casual doles were no answer to its extinction and he determined to study systems of poor relief and entered the House of Commons in 1868. Cursed by poor health from youth, Denison set out for Australia in the hope that the voyage would strengthen his constitution and enable him to study emigrant conditions. Instead the voyage killed him. The letters he wrote to friends during his brief sojourn in the East End were published posthumously in 1872 and proved an inspiration to many.

'Dr' Barnardo (1845-1905) is commemorated by the children's charity which still bears his name. Dublin-born and initially anxious to become a medical missionary in China, Thomas John Barnardo first lodged at 30 Coborn Road while he studied at the London Hospital. His involvement as a volunteer in nursing victims of the 1866 cholera epidemic showed him there was benighted ignorance enough to be fought locally without going halfway round the world. His special concern was the homeless 'street Arab' children who survived by begging, scavenging and thieving and, where opportunity offered, even by such honest work as they could get. Barnardo established his East End Juvenile Mission in 1867 and in 1870 the first 'Barnardo home' was opened at 18 Stepney Causeway.

Within a decade the penniless Irish student became the flamboyant, autocratic and controversial head of the fastest-growing children's charity in the country. A tireless fund-raiser, Barnardo would garner in some £3,500,000 over the course of four decades. In 1876 he opened a Girls' Village Home out in the country, at Barkingside on the fringe of Epping Forest. Eventually he would create over ninety homes and agencies through which some 55,000 children would pass, acquiring a training in domestic, industrial or maritime skills as they did so. If only a minority adopted Barnardo's fervent faith, many more were saved from lives of degradation or crime. Barnardo's Ragged School of 1877 at 46 Copperfield Road is now a museum which perpetuates the memory of his achievement.

There were other programmes similarly focused to meet the needs of a particular disadvantaged group. In 1854 a Soup Kitchen for Poor Jews was opened in Leman Street and in 1859 a Board of Guardians of the Jewish Poor was established to administer on-going relief to the less successful members of that community. In 1856 a Strangers' Home for Asiatics was opened in West India Dock Road to accom-

87. 'Dr' Thomas Barnardo, whose motto was – no destitute child ever turned away.

88. Hope Place in Stepney. In 1868 Barnardo acquired two small cottages here to establish his first Home of the East End Juvenile Mission.

89. *Young boys in the printing office of Dr Barnardo on Stepney Causeway, c.1905. Barnardo's also developed training programmes for disabled children.*

90. *Dr Barnardo used photographs of waifs and strays to solicit money from the rich. This picture of a 'street arab' was very effective. Barnardo also kept a photographic archive of all the children taken into his care.*

modate lascar seamen who through accident, illness, drink, debt, disease or robbery found themselves abandoned to their fate in a land whose customs were alien and whose language they rarely comprehended beyond a few basic phrases.

Like Barnardo, William Booth (1829-1912) was driven by deep religious conviction. The son of a bankrupted builder, Booth knew from painful personal experience the ease with which one could fall from bourgeois comfort into proletarian squalor. Driven by hunger from his native Nottinghamshire, the friendless Booth found uncongenial work as a clerk in a London pawnbroker's, daily witnessing the humiliations of the poor – until he was sacked for refusing to work on the Sabbath. Repelled by the pietistic complacency of ultra-respectable Methodists, Booth became a freelance evangelist in 1865, preaching in a tent pitched in a disused Quaker burial ground. (A sundial in Vallance Road Gardens now marks the spot.) Although constantly harassed by the uncomprehending and the hostile, Booth and a growing band of dedicated disciples conducted services in a dancing academy until

91 & 92. *Soup kitchens in the East End in 1867, a period of great distress. The upper scene is at Spitalfields, the lower at Ratcliff Highway. Adults are shown eating-in while children carry theirs home.*

93. *Statue of 'General' Booth on Mile End Road.*

they acquired the former Eastern Star alehouse – "notorious for immorality" – at 220 Whitechapel Road. Further premises were acquired as the movement expanded its appeal – the Effingham Theatre, the Ebenezer Hall and the People's Market. By 1878 Booth's mission was sufficiently well-established for it to be reconstituted as the 'Salvation Army'.

Booth believed that emigration offered the shortest route out of poverty. Both Burdett-Coutts and Barnardo shared this view. Barnardo was responsible for despatching over 18,000 children overseas. A one-way ticket to the Cape, Canada or the Antipodes would both remove 'surplus' population from the metropolis and in doing so not only offered the individuals concerned the chance of a better life but fulfilled far larger purposes at the same time – supplying the 'empty' lands of the empire with much-needed labour and banishing from the homeland the dread spectre of revolution. Ragged schools made a point of selecting candidates who had proved themselves sufficiently "steady and industrious" to merit subsidy. The Bethnal Green Medical Mission, which ran a

Sunday School for hundreds of children continued to send emigrants to Canada until 1925. Although this was the destination most favoured by Booth and Barnardo as well, the discovery of gold in Australia made it a popular option from the 1850s. Many who chose that course were carried by the fleet of Blackwall ship-owner Richard Green, whose vessels had a reputation for greater comfort than most, an important consideration on a voyage measured in months, not days. In 1851 the Canterbury Association established a community in New Zealand specifically for emigrants from the East End. Unlike freewheeling Australia the organizers of the New Zealand settlement were concerned to target potential emigrants with practical craft skills.

Churches and local government co-operated with charities in the emigration process. On 7 May 1870 representatives of the East End Emigration Club witnessed the departure of 757 migrants to Canada, with the rector of Whitechapel, the Reverend J Cohen, accompanying them as their chaplain. Another group left the following day. The Poplar Board of Guardians had put £100 towards the scheme and the emigrants themselves paid £3 per head but the bulk of the £4,500 required was contributed by Kelsall's Emigration Charity, the Manufacturers' Relief Fund and the British and Colonial Emigration Fund, chaired by the Lord Mayor. In the same year the East End Emigration Fund supported the passage of another 1,035 people to Canada, all but forty-eight of whom came from the East End. The Family Emigration from the East End of London Committee sent another 974. In *East and West London*, published in 1875, the clerical author, Harry Jones, noted how the formerly smart hotel at Blackwall, once noted for its whitebait suppers, had become a rather dilapidated, but busy, depot for emigrants to New Zealand. Between May 1874 and August 1875 no less than 17,000 migrants had left for that destination. As a still overwhelmingly rural society, however, New Zealand appealed primarily to would-be settlers from Scotland and Germany rather than from the East End.

HEALTH

Emigrants to frontier societies faced hazards quite unknown to East Enders – extremes of weather, hostile peoples and animals and unfamiliar diseases. But the life they left be-

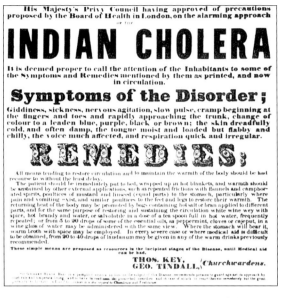

His Majesty's Privy Council having approved of precautions
proposed by the Board of Health in London, on the alarming approach
OF THE

INDIAN CHOLERA

It is deemed proper to call the attention of the Inhabitants to some of
the Symptoms and Remedies mentioned by them as printed, and now
in circulation.

Symptoms of the Disorder;

Giddiness, sickness, nervous agitation, slow pulse, cramp beginning at
the fingers and toes and rapidly approaching the trunk, change of
colour to a leaden blue, purple, black or brown; the skin dreadfully
cold, and often damp, the tongue moist and loaded but flabby and
chilly, the voice much affected, and respiration quick and irregular.

REMEDIES;

All means tending to restore circulation and to maintain the warmth of the body should be had
recourse to without the least delay.
    The patient should be immediately put to bed, wrapped up in hot blankets, and warmth should
be sustained by other external applications, such as repeated frictions with flannels and camphor-
ated spirits, poultices of mustard and linseed (equal parts) to the stomach, particularly where
pain and vomiting exist, and similar poultices to the feet and legs to restore their warmth.   The
returning heat of the body may be promoted by bags containing hot salt or bran applied to different
parts, and for the same purpose of restoring and sustaining the circulation white wine wey with
spice, hot brandy and water, or salvolatile in a dose of a tea spoon full in hot water, frequently
repeated; or from 5 to 20 drops of some of the essential oils, as peppermint, cloves or cajeput, in a
wine glass of water may be administered with the same view.   Where the stomach will bear it,
warm broth with spice may be employed.   In every severe case or where medical aid is difficult
to be obtained, from 20 to 40 drops of laudanum may be given in any of the warm drinks previously
recommended.

These simple means are proposed as resources in the incipient stages of the Disease, until Medical aid
can be had.

THOS. KEY,
GEO. TINDALL, *Churchwardens.*

94. *An official notice detailing the symptoms of cholera
and the best treatment for it.*

hind also had its dangers. Accidents were common in the docks and in factories where safety standards were minimal. Burns were a major risk for occupations such as iron-founders and sugar-boilers. Cholera returned in 1848-49, 1853-54 and, in a final and most savage outbreak, in 1866, when three-quarters of London fatalities occurred in St George's-in-the-East. However, unlike the isolated inhabitants of the prairie or the outback, at least the people of the East End benefited from a continually improving range of medical provision, belatedly upgraded systems of sewerage and drainage and new public facilities to aid in the unending battle against sweat, smoke, soot and grime. The London Chest Hospital, a pet project of the Prince Consort, who laid the foundation stone in 1851, specialised in the treatment of tuberculosis and thus met an especially pressing local need. In 1854 the London Hospital acquired a new medical college, "the most convenient, salubrious and handsome ... in the Metropolis." By 1876, when the Queen came to

95. *Washhouses in Oldcastle Street, Aldgate, now the headquarters of the Women's Library.*

open a new wing, the London, with 790 beds, was the largest hospital in the country.

Poplar hospital opened in 1855, its main purpose being to provide emergency treatment to men injured working along the riverside. The North Eastern Hospital for Children was opened in Bethnal Green in 1867. Poplar and Stepney Sick Asylum for the Poor (now St Andrew's Hospital) was opened in 1871. The East London Nursing Society, founded by a Mrs Wigram in 1868, was concerned to provide out-patient support for people ill in their own homes.

Charles Dickens himself supported the efforts of Dr Nathaniel Heckford (1842-71) to start a children's hospital in an old warehouse at Butcher Row, Ratcliff, dubbing it 'A Small Star in the East'. Heckford had won the gold medals for both medicine and surgery in his qualifying year at the London and in 1866 had taken charge of the Wapping District Cholera Emergency Hospital. Dickens' publicity brought in funds for the construction of purpose-built premises for what was initially known as the Shadwell Hospital for Women and Children in

Glamis Road, Shadwell. But by the time it opened in 1875 Heckford had died before he was even thirty.

In 1852 a Municipal Baths and Wash House was opened in East India Dock Road. In 1856 Poplar Baths opened. Turkish baths in Exmouth Street, Cannon Street Road and Whitechapel Road were valued for the treatment of muscular strains common among men handling heavy loads.

SPIRITUAL INFRASTRUCTURE

The 1851 religious census revealed an average East End church attendance of only 15%. The poor, of course, valued Sunday as a day of rest from their exhausting labours and were under no social pressure from peers, neighbours or employers to attend services. Often they also felt excluded by their own shabbiness and by the social gap between themselves and the clergy and the language they used. To some extent low attendance figures reflected a lack of provision as church-building failed to match the growth of population. St George-in-the-East could accommodate only a quarter of its total

96. *The former Presbyterian church on the Isle of Dogs was originally built for the many Scottish craftsmen employed at Scott Russell's shipyard. It is now an arts centre.*

population. Provision in Stepney and Poplar was scarcely better. Dozens of new churches were, however, to be built between the 1840s and the end of the century as the ancient parish of Stepney was further subdivided into more than sixty further parishes. Although many of the new churches were of indifferent architectural quality, others were distinctive creations by such leading figures as Vulliamy, Railton, Blore and Blomfield. Further separate provision was made for Catholics, Methodists and Presbyterians and through idiosyncratic initiatives like the Tower Hamlets Mission founded by Frederick Charrington in 1870.

But buildings were, perhaps, less important than what went on inside them. The challenge of presenting the gospel to an uncomprehending and often hostile lumpen proletariat attracted some of the most remarkable churchmen of the age.

Concisely characterised as a pioneer in bringing 'hope and incense' to the East End, Charles Fuge Lowder (1820-80) had come under Anglo-Catholic influence at Oxford. Joining an Anglican mission in Ratcliff in 1856, he became one of a small team of clergy who introduced a liturgy of elaborate solemnity and colour in the parish church of St George-in-the-East, thereby provoking disorders so riotous that the church had to be closed until services were resumed under police surveillance. Lowder, meanwhile, raised funds to build St Peter's, London Docks, of which he became the curate in charge when it opened in 1866. Lowder's unstinted devotion to the victims of the cholera epidemic of that year instantly transformed him into a folk hero and made his theological stance locally unassailable. He is supposedly the first Anglican priest to bear the title 'Father', a mark of deference conferred on him spontaneously by a community which wished to give him the respect that local Catholics gave to their pastors.

As an historian J R Green (1837-93) would both contribute to his academic profession by founding the *English Historical Review* and with his *Short History of the English People* would enjoy a popularity to rival that of Macaulay. Yet Green had graduated from Oxford after an academically undistinguished career. It was to be in the East End, first at Hoxton and then, from 1866 to 1869 as incumbent of St Philip's, Stepney that he was to develop through the painstaking composition of sermons which could touch a largely unlettered congregation

97. Statue of Richard Green, shipowner and philanthropist, in East India Dock Road.

the fluent accessible style which enabled him to write a history of the common people for the common people.

Despite an Eton and Cambridge education Stewart Duckworth Headlam (1847-1924) held heterodox opinions from the outset of his clerical career, outspokenly championing the poor against the rich, defending the theatre and dancing as wholesome pastimes and advocating the repeal of the blasphemy laws. Headlam became curate of St Matthew's, Bethnal Green in 1873 but was sacked in 1877 for a series of sermons which presented Christ as a revolutionary. Without a parish to tend Headlam established the Guild of St Matthew to promote Christian Socialism. It soon had four hundred members, a quarter of them Christian ministers. Headlam's tenure at St Michael's, Shoreditch lasted from 1881 to 1884 after which he turned to editing *The Church Reformer*. Passionate for every form of education, from swimming to Shakespeare, he sat for sixteen years on the London School Board and for seventeen on the London County Council. He believed that the rich should be taxed to provide free

98. A celebrated photograph of 'Hookey Alf' of White-chapel, by John Thompson, published in Street Life in London , 1877. Alf's arm was crushed in an accident in the London Docks. He was taken to the London Hospital where it was amputated. His hook was probably supplied by the Hospital's Samaritan Society.

99. The Old Globe, 2004. A typical Victorian corner-site public house with multiple entrances – both features intended to maximise passing trade.

schooling and free school meals and that, far from teaching obedience and gratitude, schools should aim to make children "discontented with the evil circumstances which surround them." This turbulent priest is appropriately commemorated in the school named for him in Tapp Street, E1.

TIME OFF

While Wapping and other riverside locations had been notorious for the number of their drinking establishments since Elizabethan times, the public house came to occupy a central role in East End life in Victoria's reign. While the comfortable classes celebrated the tranquillity and joy of family evenings at home, those forced to endure the most wretched housing conditions easily succumbed to the contrary attractions of public houses brilliantly lit with gas, sparkling with mirrors and enlivened with boisterous gaiety. Whereas the eighteenth century tavern had been frequented by men of affairs as well as their servants and employees

the mid-Victorian gin palace with its counter bar, noisy, flashy atmosphere and often deliberately limited seating was shunned by the respectable, although the more privileged 'aristocracy of labour' did often use the upstairs rooms of larger establishments to hold the branch meetings of trade unions and, even more, of the friendly societies which served as the artisan's self-financed welfare state. Many employers routinely paid weekly wages in pubs, especially to outdoor workers like building labourers. Not surprisingly much of the cash received went straight over the counter, a phenomenon which could easily be exploited by collusion between the employer and the publican. More positively public houses also functioned as labour exchanges for men seeking work and as savings banks where landlords administered subscription clubs through which 'regulars' could accumulate funds for Christmas or the purchase of new boots. The pub was also the working man's club, providing a base or venue for social groups devoted to pigeon fancying or various team sports. Alcohol consumption per head peaked in the 1870s. At that time Wapping High Street had twenty licensed premises, although admittedly it also had seven coffee rooms. Even the short section of Bow Road around St Mary's church

100. *The Rose and Crown, Bromley-by-Bow, 2004. A pub has stood here since c. 1720, then overlooking a village green with a pond and a pillory.*

102. *The former Royal Oak, 2004. Note the archway (right) for carriages.*

101. *The Vine Tavern, Mile End Road, 1901. Seventeenth-century in origin, it was demolished in 1903 as a traffic obstruction. Painting by Waldo Sargeant.*

103. The Star of the East, 2004. Polychrome tiles and 'Moorish' details echo the name of the pub.

104. The lake in Victoria Park, early 20th century.

had four pubs on the north side, three on the south and three more just round the corner in the High Street of Bromley-by-Bow.

During the middle decades of the nineteenth century the Saturday night 'free and easy', an amateur sing-song enlivened by repartee and individual 'turns', encouraged the enlargement of some public house premises to provide concert rooms with stages where not only customers but paid professional artists could appear. Out of such experimental ventures music hall was born. Unlike the theatre proper the music hall expected its patrons to smoke, drink, eat and chatter throughout performances. Audiences were expected to be enthusiastic rather than respectful. Heckling and repartee punctuated the patter routines and comic songs which became the characteristic staple of an evening programme normally running over three or even four hours.

Many halls took their name from a proprietor. Forrester's was originally The Artichoke, opened *c.* 1825. The Eagle in the Mile End Road, opened in 1848, became better known as Lusby's. Wilton's in Grace's Alley, off Cable

Street, was originally built in 1828 as a pub, the Prince of Denmark. Thirty years later it was extended and lavishly outfitted with mirrors, mahogany and a massive gas chandelier to create "the handsomest room in town". Devastated by fire in 1877, it was taken over as a Methodist East End Mission in 1885. Ironically this preserved it so that it remains Britain's oldest surviving music hall. Alongside a burgeoning class of purpose-built halls which increasingly rivalled the 'legitimate' theatre in their splendour, the smaller, informal pub singalong survived. In 1870 Bethnal Green had 31 public houses licensed for music and dancing.

Victoria Park was the first London park specifically established for the benefit of the working classes, envisaged by the supporters of 'rational recreation' as an alternative to dogfights and drunkenness. The venture was funded, to the tune of £72,000, by the sale to the Duke of Sutherland of a Crown lease on a property in the Mall. The design of the park was entrusted to Sir James Pennethorne (1841-71), who became chief government architect in the year of its completion, 1845. In 1847 a Chinese summerhouse (demolished in 1956) was added as a 'feature' to the boating lake. Cunningham, writing in 1849, observed that the park served "as a lung for the north-east part of London and has already added to the health of the inhabitants of Spitalfields and Bethnal Green. The leases of building-ground surrounding the Park have been delayed till the roads and walks become more perfect and the plantations in a more advanced state." As an open space of almost three hundred acres, well planted with

105. Arrival of the Prince of Wales to open the Bethnal Green Museum in 1872.

trees, the park did in due course encourage the building of up-market residential properties in the streets nearby. The planting of the park itself would be elaborated by the addition of a rose garden, an 'Old English garden', a poplar grove, carpet bedding, a picnic area and tea gardens. In 1879 it was noted that Victoria Park "differs from the West End parks in being supplied with various appliances for amusement" – a reference to the equipment of the outdoor gymnasium – but eventually there would also be tennis courts, a bowling green, cricket nets and an athletic track, separate lakes for bathing and for sailing model boats, playgrounds and a bandstand, an aviary and a deer enclosure.

Considering the importance that sport would in due course assume in male working-class culture its development in the East End was retarded by the lack of adequate facilities. A Victoria Park cricket club was formed in 1846, very soon after the park was opened and in 1860 Poplar and Blackwall Rowing Club was founded. Poplar Recreation Park was laid out in 1867.

The flight of the middle classes was accompanied by corresponding changes in the cultural landscape. The Spitalfields Mathematical Society was finally dissolved in 1845 after more than a century of existence. In 1856 the Baptist Academy abandoned Stepney Green for Regent's Park. Associational life was increasingly represented by working-men's clubs and volunteer rifle brigades. The politically conscious were attracted to Chartism and radical meetings held on Bonner's Fields. Pigeon-fancying, dog-fights and skittles probably aroused more interest with most locals. The opening of Bow and Bromley Institute in 1870 represented an effort to rejuvenate more elevated interests. In 1872 the Bethnal Green Museum was opened as a branch of the then South Kensington Museum (now the Victoria & Albert Museum). Avowedly intended for a working-class clientele, this novel attraction was housed in novel accommodation – the temporary iron buildings first erected in 1856 and affectionately known as 'the Brompton Boilers'. Contrary to pessimistic predictions, the working-classes did not reel in drunk or smash up the exhibits, but nor did they become particularly fervent patrons, either.

THE LURE OF THE RIVER

Like his creation Sam Weller, Charles Dickens (1812-70) had a knowledge of London which was both "extensive and peculiar". The first article Dickens ever had printed was *A Dinner at Poplar Walk*. Whitechapel, dismissed by Sam as "not a wery nice neighbourhood", figures as a point of arrival for the hero in *David Copperfield* and as a point of departure for Joe Willett in *Barnaby Rudge*; the area is also featured in Dickens' essay *On Duty with Inspector Field*. But it was the riverside, now bustling with commerce, now brooding with nameless evils, which fascinated the author most consistently. Ratcliff Highway is described in *Sketches by Boz* as a "reservoir of dirt, drunkenness and drabs". In *Dombey and Son* Captain Cuttle is domiciled in Brig Place, near the West India Docks. The docks figure most prominently in *The Commercial Traveller*, which includes detailed descriptions of *The Six Jolly Fellowship Porters*, a barely-disguised version of *The Grapes* in Narrow Street, and of Titbull's Alms Houses, based on the Vintner's Almshouses in Mile End Road. Much of *Our Mutual Friend* is set against the background of Limehouse. Shadwell is the probable site of the opium den in *The Mystery of Edwin Drood*, located in "a miserable court, specially miserable among many such".

It was the riverside which also provided immediate inspiration for the youthful American artist James Whistler (1834-1903) when he arrived in London from Paris in 1859 after tasting success with his first series of etchings. Wapping provided Whistler with a temporary home and the major focus for his 'London Set'. *Thames in Ice, Black Lion Wharf, Thames Warehouses* and *Thames Police* were to confirm his reputation as an artist of the highest promise. A Thames-side conversation-piece in oils, entitled *Wapping* and featuring Whistler's red-haired Irish mistress, begun in 1861 and exhibited successfully at the Royal Academy in 1864, was bought by the collector Thomas Winans and in 1866 became one of the first Whistlers to be exhibited in the USA.

A decade after Whistler's essays in depicting the many moods of the Thames at Wapping James Tissot (1836-1902), a refugee from the Franco-Prussian war (and also with a red-haired Irish mistress), found similar inspiration for *La Thamise (The Thames)* a louche depiction of an unchaperoned woman on a leisurely cruise, a picture which unsettled English critics as both accomplished and somehow not quite nice.

From these artists the painterly succession passed to William Lionel Wyllie (1851-1931). Trained at the Royal Academy schools, Wyllie began as an illustrator of maritime subjects for *The Graphic* magazine, then took up etching and made his reputation with a painting exhibited at the Royal Academy in 1883, *Toil, glitter, grime and wealth on a flowing tide,* a starkly unromantic depiction of the Thames as a working river. This was hailed by a contemporary critic: "The Thames Mr Wyllie paints is the Thames as it is... its material embodiment of British supremacy and prosperity and its testimonies to the dark romance of these coal and iron times." Wyllie was to find the gigantic Beckton Gas Works a subject of personal fascination, likening the cast-iron pillars of its coal jetty to the ruins of Karnak or Baalbec. Wyllie was elected a Royal Academician in 1907. The National Maritime Museum houses a collection of seven thousand of his drawings.

Visiting London in 1893 the exiled writer Emile Zola announced his intention – unfulfilled – of writing a novel about the metropolis and especially about its river:

> "I shall introduce the river above all, as it so deeply impressed me. The Thames from London Bridge to Greenwich I can only compare to an immense moving street of ships ... the docks are stupendous ... but what impressed me most were the splendid arrangements for unloading vessels, which came close up to the quays and disembarked their cargoes into the shops as it were. One can understand the secret of London's greatness after having seen these things."

DISASTER!

A source of inspiration to writers and artists, an object of contemplation for wondering visitors, the Thames was a sphere of recreation to many who lived along its banks. Public holidays and weekends occasioned a lively traffic for paddle-steamers packed with day-trippers. On 3 September 1878 just such an excursion

106. Identifying the dead after the Princess Alice disaster in 1878.

ended in the worst ever disaster to occur on a British waterway. The *Princess Alice*, returning from a trip to Gravesend, entered Galleons Reach to collide with the collier *Bywell Castle*, which had just been repainted at Millwall. In the absence of strict and generally understood 'rules of the road' ships using the Thames passed each other according to the varying strengths of currents and tides. When the collier's captain saw the paddler heading across his bow, he altered course to pass astern of her. This, however, confused the captain of the oncoming vessel who changed his direction to turn into the path of the collier. Although the *Bywell Castle* reversed engines when the ships were still a quarter of a mile apart, the manoeuvre was made too late and it split the steamer in two. The *Princess Alice* sank in just four minutes. Few passengers would have been killed directly by the collision but hundreds were trapped inside the vessel. Those thrown clear found themselves in waters heavily polluted by the waste-products of the many industries located along both banks of the river at

that point and by the raw sewage discharged from the northern outfall sewer at Beckton. Swimming was not a common accomplishment and women especially would have been burdened by the voluminous clothes of the period. In the absence of a passenger list the number of fatalities could not be gauged with precision. Nearly five hundred bodies were recovered in the first week after the disaster. When the two halves of the stricken ship were raised scores more were founded jammed around the exits. The total death toll seems to have been around 640. A Board of Trade Enquiry led to the introduction of new regulations in 1880 which clarified navigational protocols on the river, reduced the number of passengers ships were allowed to carry and increased the number of lifebelts they were obliged to have. It was also recommended that the river police should be equipped with steam launches to enable them to provide rescue assistance in case of future emergencies. The *Bywell Castle* disappeared in the Bay of Biscay in 1883 and is still officially listed as missing.

Years of Struggle, Years of Hope

"Two millions of people, or thereabout, live in the East End of London.... They have no institutions of their own to speak of, no public buildings of any importance, no municipality, no gentry, no carriages... they have nothing ... this immense, neglected, forgotten great city of East London ... even neglected by its own citizens, who have never yet perceived their abandoned condition."
Sir Walter Besant: *All Sorts and Conditions of Men* (1882)

UNREST THREATENS

It was in the 1880s that the term 'East End' first came into common usage, thanks to the exposure of the area's ills by novelists, pamphleteers and social investigators and to the public unease, to put it at its mildest, aroused by three new social phenomena – the advent of tens of thousands of East European refugees, perceived as alien in race, religion, language, manners and appearance; the gruesome murders attributed to Jack the Ripper, and the unprecedented labour militancy represented by strikes successfully mounted by sub-proletarian match girls, gasworkers and dockers.

Mass unrest in the West End of London in February 1886 and November 1887 brought home to the propertied classes even more forcefully the potential, or at least imagined, threat represented by the denizens of the slums which stretched away without apparent end eastwards beyond Aldgate. The huge funeral procession which accompanied the corpse of Alfred Linnell, an alleged victim of police brutality, to its last resting-place in Tower Hamlets cemetery in 1887 was said to be the largest since the turnout for the Duke of Wellington in 1852 and served as a further reminder that whole armies could be recruited from those who identified with his fate. The fact that the graveside oration was given by William Morris might have given others pause for thought. The man once famed as the author of *The Earthly Paradise* and celebrated as a designer of stained-glass and aesthetic wallpapers now proclaimed himself to be a revolutionary socialist.

Canon Samuel Barnett writing in 1896, bemoaned the continued flight of the bourgeoisie to the suburbs: "... it leaves large quarters of the town without the light which comes from knowledge and large masses of people without the friendship of those better taught than themselves." As if to endorse his observation Bancroft's School abandoned Mile End in favour of leafy Woodford Green that same year. (Canon Barnett and his wife Henrietta were themselves to later aid the diaspora of the middle class by developing Hampstead Garden Suburb.) Only one in fifty of the East End's population could be reckoned middle class by the 1890s, too few to provide personally supervised charitable efforts of the old-fashioned type. Of course there were still individual initiatives, by no means all of them futile. But would they prove sufficient to ward off revolution and sustain the social fabric? The formation of the Metropolitan Boroughs of Stepney, Bethnal Green and Poplar in 1900 would at least create the possibility of more vigorous municipal action.

PROMISED LAND?

In 1880 there were about 46,000 Jews in London, by 1900 135,000, mostly concentrated in the two square miles of the Aldgate-Spitalfields-Whitechapel area. This great increase was a direct consequence of Russian pogroms which drove industrious but impoverished Jews ever westward from their homes in the Ukraine, Poland and the Baltic seaboard. Those who

107. Emblem, designed by anti-fascist artist Arthur Szyk (1894-1951), denoting the former offices of the now defunct Jewish Daily News in Whitechapel High Street.

108. *Archway to the former Rothschild Buildings, 2004. The original sponsors were promised a 4% return on their contributions. In practice Rothschild put up most of the money himself.*

109. *Sandys Row, Spitalfields, was built as a chapel in 1766 and taken over by Dutch Jews working in the tobacco trade in 1854 and is London's oldest Ashkenazi synagogue.*

arrived in London, often penniless and invariably bewildered, speaking no English and usually dressed in the garments of the ghetto, were perceived by the capital's existing and increasingly assimilated Jewish community as a threat to their own hard-won acceptance. The editor of the *Jewish Chronicle*, Ashley Myers, crystallized the reaction of many of his co-religionists in declaring "we may not be able to make them rich but we may hope to render them English in feeling and conduct." The *de facto* leader of Anglo-Jewry Nathan Meyer, first Baron Rothschild (1840-1915) agreed, observing briskly "we have a new Poland on our hands in East London. Our first business is to humanise our Jewish immigrants and then to Anglicize them." It was essential that the newcomers should not become – or even appear to become – a burden on Gentile philanthropy. Rothschild's personal contribution was the establishment of the Four Per Cent Industrial Dwellings Company, which undertook the construction of model housing, 90% of whose

tenants would be Jewish. In 1885 an official Jews' Temporary Shelter was opened in Leman Street to provide new arrivals with food and lodging for a fortnight while more permanent accommodation and employment were arranged. In the same year the Jewish Association for the Protection of Girls and Women established a refuge in Tenter Street North in an effort to close off temptations to prostitution. Attempts were also made to stem and, indeed, even to reverse the influx of newcomers. In the quarter century after 1881 the Jewish Board of Guardians arranged for the repatriation of some 31,044 would-be Jewish settlers. Over thirty times that number would be hastened on to different destinies in New York or Cape Town or Buenos Aires.

Such efforts scarcely served to placate alarmists like the Revd C S Reaney who denounced the denizens of the emerging ghetto with a notably unChristian vehemence:

"as they come, so they remain – aliens, children of another race, amongst us, yet not of us

... the East End produces no type of man or woman so unfit, so un-English and morally and personally so alien as the pauper immigrant."

These harsh words were penned in 1893. Perhaps Reaney would have been a little reassured by a closer inspection of what was actually happening. Those charged with the task of inspection certainly were. In 1894 the official report on the Jews' Free School in Bell Lane would note approvingly that pupils entered it as "Russians or Poles and emerge from it almost indistinguishable from English children". Headed by the sternly dynamic Moses Angel (1819-98) the JFS had developed since its foundation in 1817 as a prime instrument of Anglicization, committed to safeguarding the heritage of Judaism and simultaneously exorcizing the taint of Yiddish language and culture. With almost four thousand children on its roll at the time of Angel's death, this remarkable establishment claimed, plausibly, to be the largest school in the world. Foremost among its former pupils was Israel Zangwill (1864-1931) of nearby Fashion Street, who would return as a teacher and with *The Children of the Ghetto* distil his surroundings into the pioneering Jewish genre novel. Zangwill's play about the immigrant experience, *The Melting Pot,* would add a metaphor to the English language. Other alumni would include the Spitalfields painter Mark Gertler (1891-1939) and the flamboyant diamond millionaire Barney Barnato (1852-97). Supportive institutions reinforcing the anglicization offensive were the Jewish Girls' Club, founded in 1896, and the Jewish Lads' Brigade established in 1895. Offering a sectarian version of corresponding Gentile institutions, they did so in English.

While the JFS and its allies anglicized the future, the present Judaized itself. Grodzinski's bakery was but recently established in Fieldgate Street and soon joined by Rinkoff's in O'Leary Square. Wentworth Street became lined with kosher butchers and poulterers. The dairy in Old Montague Street, kept as was common throughout the capital by a Welshman, Mr Evans, adapted its marketing to offer 'Milch Frish Fun Di Ku'. Black Lion Yard had shops selling religious tomes, Sabbath candles and bridal jewellery. Kosher regulations were effectively enforced in the area's street markets, offenders fined and defaulters ostracised. The former Huguenot, then Methodist, chapel at the junction of Fournier Street and Brick Lane

110. The Jews' Free School in Bell Lane after rebuilding in 1883. It subsequently moved to Camden Town in 1958 and to Brent in 2003.

became a synagogue in 1897. Just opposite Shewzicks' steam baths opened to cater to its congregation. In Princelet Street No. 6 (then 3) was used as a makeshift theatre where Jacob and Sarah Adler put on melodramas in Yiddish until a fire panic caused a stampede which crushed to death seventeen men, women and children. One can imagine the reproachful tut-tutting of Anglo-Jewry ...

Writing of Whitechapel in 1898 Charles Booth's investigators noted a "great improvement in this district since the incoming of the Jews", despite friction with the remaining English. The observation that "Jewish children all look particularly well fed" perhaps constituted a pointed, if indirect, swipe at the haphazard provision made by some Gentile parents. Approval was, however, by no means universal. In Bethnal Green, where Jews constituted only about 3% of a population which was otherwise overwhelmingly not only white and English but locally born, the Jews were characterised as "regular rent payers and respecters of authority ... but dirty ... and great cheats." Dutch Jews, a Spitalfields minority distinct from the Ashkenazi masses and mostly engaged in cigar-making, constituted a special case and were stigmatised as "the lowest and roughest".

It was also noticeable that, in contrast to the indigenous population, Jews confined their drinking to their clubs and avoided pubs – as they also avoided pawnbrokers – and that therefore public drunkenness was rare among them. Another profound distinction was that "women as a whole lead happier lives than Gentile women ... more respected by their husbands and more faithful."

THE LODGER

It was therefore cruelly ironic that just as Anglo-Jewry began to devote time, effort and money to the task of easing the transition out of the ghetto and into the mainstream of London life, the attention of the entire metropolis should become fixated on the epicentre of Ashkenazi cultural adjustment by an outbreak of hideous homicides. Aficionados of the genre insist on referring to the Ripper killings as 'the Whitechapel murders' but, while these overlapped in time and location, they may not have been identical. Ten East End women were murdered between April 1888 and September 1889 and another one, Frances Coles, in February 1891. Most of these killings occurred in Whitechapel but one each took place in St George-in-the-East, Aldgate, Spitalfields and Poplar. All the victims were horrendously mutilated, though not in identical ways, one being reduced to an unidentified torso. All the cases remain unsolved. Those traditionally attributed to Jack the Ripper include Mary Ann Nichols (31 August 1888, Buck's Row), Annie Chapman (8 September, 29 Hanbury Street) Lizzie Stride and Catherine Eddowes (30 September, 40 Berner Street and Mitre Square) and Mary Jane Kelly (9 November, 13 Miller's Court, 26 Dorset Street). The name 'Jack the Ripper' was signed on a letter, claiming responsibility for the murders, sent to the Central News Agency on 25 September 1888. A further postcard was sent the day after the double murder of 30 September and simultaneously chalk graffiti appeared on a wall in Goulston Street, proclaiming "The Juwes are The men that Will not be Blamed for nothing." This, and the fact that two victims were found in locations over-

whelmingly populated by Jewish residents, undoubtedly raised tensions throughout the East End. It was widely said that no Englishman could have perpetrated such vile and perverted acts. But there was no general outbreak of inter-ethnic violence.

The speed and accuracy with which many of the victims were mutilated, coupled with their distribution around a) the London Hospital and b) the capital's main area of Jewish settlement has prompted much speculation that the murderer (if there was, indeed, just the one) was either medically trained or a Jewish ritual slaughterer. Other candidates, among the more than seventy since proffered, have included members of the royal family, the Queen's physician, Sir William Gull, the writer George Gissing, the painter Walter Sickert and even Prime Minister Gladstone. The investigating officers narrowed their suspicions to four major suspects – Kosminski, a destitute Jew; Montague Druitt, a barrister who committed suicide in December 1888; Michael Ostrog, a periodically deranged Russian-born petty thief and conman; and Dr Francis Tumbelty, an American quack who jumped bail and fled Britain in November 1889 after being arrested for gross indecency.

The wider significance of the Whitechapel murders lies in the attention they drew to their physical setting and social context and the deprivation suffered by the inhabitants, a point not lost on local philanthropists eager to exploit the publicity generated by police investigations, coroner's inquests and background colour material generated by a prurient press.

Interest in the Ripper was rekindled in 1913 with the publication of Marie Bello Lowndes' sensationalist re-imagination *The Lodger,* which passed through thirty-one editions, was translated into eighteen languages and was used as the basis for five films, most notably the youthful Alfred Hitchcock's first essay in spine-chilling *The Lodger,* filmed in 1926. The story of the Ripper continues to be re-imagined as in Iain Sinclair's first novel *White Chappel, Scarlet Tracings* (1987) and Paul West's *The Women of Whitechapel* (1990), which confected the murders into a royal conspiracy implicating Gull, Sickert and the half-witted Prince Eddy. Contemporary coverage of the murders has received scholarly analysis in L Perry Curtis's *Jack the Ripper and the London Press* (2002).

111. *A typically lurid tabloid depiction of the Jack the Ripper murders. Alleged police incompetence was exploited by a new type of illustrated, sensationalist press appealing to popular anxieties.*

EAST END EXPOSED

In 1882 novelist Walter Besant published *All Sorts and Conditions of Men: An Impossible Story*. More a polemical call for social regeneration than a ripping yarn (plot was never his strong point) the central motif was supplied by a fictitious 'Palace of Delight' which would offer alternatives to the oblivion of drink and drudgery. The book sold better than any of Besant's usual historical efforts "but on other than purely literary grounds" as the *Dictionary of National Biography* tactfully puts it. Besant's vision caught the imagination of the well-intentioned and was to be realised in the form of a 'People's Palace' in the Mile End Road. Of the £75,000 needed to establish it £13,000 came from the bequest of John Barber Beaumont, the local philanthropist who had died back in 1841, the rest coming from voluntary subscriptions. The Drapers' Company chipped in a further £20,000 so that a technical institute might be tacked on to it. The Prince of Wales, going through a social concern phase with an eye to placating his irascible parent, came to lay the foundation stone in 1886 and the Queen came in person to perform the opening ceremony in the year of her Golden Jubilee. With a main concert hall capable of holding 4,000, the complex also boasted a library, gymnasium, swimming bath and winter garden, as well as numerous facilities for lectures, classes and meetings. Besant himself edited a *Palace Journal* and took part in the management of the institution but was disappointed in the realisation of his dream. House rules against betting and drinking were routinely flouted and the formal educational side of the venture quite overshadowed its social and recreational aspect after the East London Technical College was established in 1892.

Even more influential than Besant's novel, though more diffuse in its effects, was the Revd Andrew Mearns anonymous penny pamphlet *The Bitter Cry of Outcast London*, published in 1883 by the London Congregational Union. Mearns, who was based in the historic Orange Street chapel, off Leicester Square, proclaimed that "the churches are making the discovery that seething in the very centre of our great cities, concealed by the thinnest crust of civilization and decency, is a vast mass or moral corruption, of heart-breaking misery and absolute godlessness and that scarcely anything has been done to take into this awful slough the only influences that can purify or remove it." This assertion may seem to have rather ignored the heroic efforts of the Salvation Army or of slum priests in the mould of Stewart Headlam but it hit home with its intended audience. The existence of urban deprivation, depravity even, was scarcely unknown to the comfortable classes of Victorian England; what shocked readers was the claim that, despite the massive mid-century church-building boom and an apparent plethora of philanthropic initiatives, the sheer scale of the challenge had simply not been grasped: "we are simply living in a fool's paradise if we suppose that all these agencies combined are doing a thousandth part of what needs to be done."

Mearns supported this assertion, with evidence that he argued was neither misleadingly selective nor at all exaggerated – a relentlessly grim account of non-attendance at worship, vile overcrowding, homelessness, prostitution, incest, alcoholism, sweated labour, pollution, malnutrition, chronic ill health and blinding ignorance. Conceding that state intervention might well be needed to create a stable and effective framework within which philanthropy might operate Mearns argued that the matter was too urgent to allow that to be any excuse for further delay. Instead he called for mission, for charitable not sectarian objectives, with the highest immediate priority to be given to the abject poor', himself pledging the Congregationalists' own commitment to action in the three target areas of Ratcliff, Shadwell and Bermondsey. Campaigning journalist W T Stead greatly enlarged the impact of Mearns' pamphlet by reprinting extracts from it in his *Pall Mall Gazette. The Bitter Cry* was at least partly responsible for the appointment in 1885 of a Royal Commission on the Housing of the Working Classes and for the success of novels depicting crusading Christian self-sacrifice in the slums such as Mrs Humphry Ward's *Robert Elsmere* and Margaret Harkness's *Captain Lobe,* which depicts the heroism and self-sacrifice of a Salvation Army officer.

Margaret Harkness (?1861-1921), writing under the pseudonym of John Law, produced three polemical novels exposing East End life. In *Out of Work* (1888) she presented a dissentient view of the supposedly cordial relations between the monarchy and the masses, describing the day after Queen Victoria's visit to open the People's Palace. The cheering crowds,

112. *The People's Palace provided swimming baths, a winter garden, gymnasium and a library. It is now part of Queen Mary College, University of London.*

113. *Frederick Charrington's Great Assembly Room in the Mile End Road was opened in 1886. Its Assembly Hall could seat 5,000. Other facilities included a coffee palace, a book salon and rooms for the Band of Hope and YMCA.*

she alleges, consisted of carefully orchestrated and biddable groups, like the medical students at the London and the employees of the great breweries and their families. While journalists and artists concocted misleadingly positive accounts of the royal foray "no one would speak about the hisses which the denizens of the slums had mingled with faint applause ... no one would hint that the crowd ... had a sullen, ugly look which may a year or so hence prove dangerous", a rather prescient observation, as it turned out.

In 1886 the Fabian idealist Beatrice Potter (1858-1943), a cousin of Margaret Harkness, was acting manager of a bleak housing block, Katherine Buildings, in Whitechapel. Physically and socially isolated, she was constantly aware of a surrounding culture of low-level but constant demoralisation, not so much vice as "monotonous and yet excited life ... quarrels and fights; the greedy street-bargaining, and the petty theft and gambling ... as a society it is an ever-increasing and ever-decomposing mass." Even the 'model' dwellings for which she was responsible she judged a failure in which the worse elements always threatened to overwhelm the better and the "respectable tenants keep rigidly to themselves." Even the redeeming "sociability and generous sharing of small means" brought "in its train quarrels and backbiting". Drink, above all, she held responsible for a misery which passed from one generation to the next.

The monumental investigation of London poverty undertaken by Charles Booth (1840-1916) was prompted by the claim made in 1885 by H M Hyndman of the Social Democratic Federation that a quarter of the population of the capital city of the world's greatest empire was living in dire poverty. Determined to disprove what he considered to be a wild exaggeration, in 1886 Booth began to recruit a team of researchers to investigate conditions in the East End of London. His collaborators included his cousin Beatrice Potter (the future Beatrice Webb) and university-trained Clara Collet who, between them, paid detailed attention to the problems of women's labour. The reports of School Board visitors proved to be an especially valuable source of information. In a pioneering work of social cartography Booth created a poverty map colour coded to indicate the income and social class of its inhabitants, ranging from 'Black – Lowest Class. Vicious,

114. *Beatrice Webb, née Potter. Her attempts to work under cover in a sweatshop were betrayed by a posh voice and a bossy manner.*

semi-criminal', through 'Dark Blue Very poor, casual. Chronic want'; Light Blue, Purple, Pink and Red to 'Yellow. Uppermiddle and Upper Classes. Wealthy'. A first sheet, covering the East End, was published as part of *Labour and Life of the People,* Volume 1: East London in 1889. This demonstrated that the area's poverty was in fact markedly worse than Hyndman had claimed, afflicting some 35% of its inhabitants. Almost 45% of the population of Bethnal Green was living below subsistence level, although that was not the highest proportion in the metropolis, a dubious honour shared by Southwark and Bermondsey. Booth's great enterprise was subsequently expanded to take in the entire capital, the results being published in seventeen volumes over the period 1891-1903.

In 1890 William Booth published his own contribution to the poverty debate In *Darkest England and the Way Out.* His prime preoccu-

115. *The quintessential East End rag and bone man, a familiar sight until the 1950s.*

116. *Frederick Charrington (1850-1936) was born in Bow Road. He was heir to the famous brewery, but with his substantial income he instead advocated the causes of temperance, the pursuit of Christianity and with it the abolition of vice. After a grand temperance meeting in the Strand in 1873, he set about establishing a headquarters for temperance organsiations and for his evangelical missions in general. Opened in 1886, the mission complex included a GreatAssembly Hall (ill. 113) and many other facilities. Charrington often displayed aggressive behaviour in his zeal to root out local brothels or in his fight against demon drink.*

pation had always been the salvation of souls rather than the relief of poverty but throughout the crisis-ridden 1890s, while the Salvation Army spread rapidly across the nation and overseas, it had significantly failed to attract new recruits in the East End. Opportunistically, if reluctantly, Booth refocused his message to emphasise social as well as spiritual redemption. His remedial programme envisaged an unfolding process of rehabilitation involving a) 'city colonies' – urban workshops to teach work habits and basic skills; b) 'farm colonies' – ditto, plus the restoration of physical health; and c) 'overseas colonies' – to decant the UK's 'surplus population', thus prepared, into labour-hungry Canada and Australia. Booth also envisaged subsidiary measures such as refuges for single mothers and children and specialised centres to deal with the specific challenges posed by drunks, prostitutes and ex-prisoners. Booth's personal contribution to the book which appeared under his name was almost certainly less significant than the ideas put forward by socially-aware Salvationists like Frank Smith and Suzie Swift or others lifted from the Church Army, the whole being drafted into coherent prose by W T Stead. The farm and overseas colonies projects were established but fizzled out by 1906 although the urban workshop programme became a permanent feature of Salvationist strategy.

Unlike most of the writers who explored and then exposed the East End to a wider world Arthur Morrison (1863-1945) was himself an East Ender. Born in Poplar, he worked as a clerk at the People's Palace before becoming a journalist and recycling his first-hand knowledge in fictionalised form in 1894 as *Tales of Mean Streets*, a book that went through five US editions in two years, appeared in German and was to be republished five more times between 1913 and 1997. Morrison is best remembered, however, for *A Child of the Jago*, published in 1896. Within two years this book had appeared in two British editions, plus an American and a German one; ten more would appear between 1902 and 1996. Set in the criminal quarter, actually known as the Old Nichol, just north of Bethnal Green Road, it tells how Dicky Perrot's good instincts are poisoned by the vile environment of the Jago. His father is hanged for murder and Dicky himself is killed at seventeen in a street brawl, The Nichol really was appalling, with a death rate over twice as high as the London average. One single street was home to no less than sixty-four persons who had served prison sentences. Although he rejected the label of a 'realist' author Morrison scarcely bothered to disguise his locations or central character. Boundary Street became Edge Lane, Chance Street Luck Row and Mean Street Honey Lane. The saintly tough guy Father Sturt is based on Father Arthur Osborne Jay, vicar of Holy Trinity, Shoreditch, who introduced Morrison to his parish after reading *Tales of Mean Streets* and informing him that the Jago was a good deal worse than anything described therein. Jay was himself the author of *Life in Darkest London* (1891), *The Social Problem and its Solutions* (1893) and *A Story of Shoreditch* (1896) and it was mainly his campaigning that led to the clearance of the Nichol and its replacement by the London County Council's model Boundary Street estate. Morrison went on to write stories about a Sherlock Holmes-type private detective, Martin Hewitt, which found a large following among German and French readers, as well as nine other works and two one-act plays. In later life he became an expert collector of Japanese art.

THE MISSIONARY IMPULSE

Attempts to mitigate the misery of the East End clearly predated both the influx of East European Jews and the nefarious activities of the Ripper but these occurrences added a new urgency to such efforts.

Samuel Augustus Barnett (1844-1913) came to the East End in 1873 "to decrease not suffering but sin". He had asked the bishop of London to assign him to the worst parish in his diocese and was given St Jude's, Whitechapel, "inhabited mainly by a criminal population". On his very first day in post Barnett was mugged by one of his own parishioners. Within a short time he was, nevertheless, deeply involved in supplying information which led to the passage of reformist legislation of national, rather than merely local, significance, namely the Artisans' Dwelling Act of 1875 which authorised slum clearance schemes and set minimum construction standards. In 1877 Barnett set up a Children's Country Holiday Fund which would eventually evolve into the Youth Hostels' Association. Unlike the Anglo-Catholics who tried to seduce the unchurched with elaborate pomp and colourful solemnity, Barnett tried

117. *Samuel Augustus and Henrietta Barnett.*

to appeal to them with a Sunday evening 'worship hour' of music and readings. His use of pictures as teaching aids developed from 1881 onwards into an annual art exhibition which would eventually inspire the creation of the Whitechapel Art Gallery. Barnett also used his position to lever art and technical education onto the curriculum of his parish schools.

In 1884 Barnett became the first warden of Toynbee Hall, which was initially located at 28 Commercial Street. This settlement was named in honour of Arnold Toynbee (1852-83), an idealistic Oxford don who had pioneered the study of economic history in the hope of improving contemporary industrial conditions. In addition to his duties at Balliol College Toynbee had taken on extramural lecturing to working men and supported Barnett's efforts in the East End. The strain of these self-imposed burdens killed him at thirty-one.

Toynbee Hall's aim was "to educate citizens in the knowledge of one another, to provide teaching for those willing to learn and recreation to those who are weary." The teaching

118. *The courtyard of Toynbee Hall, 2004. Memorials recall the contributions made by Jane Addams, Viscount Milner, Jimmy Mallon and Clement Attlee.*

would be provided by Oxford student volunteers who would live in the settlement and staff its outreach programmes; in a sense their presence would compensate for the absence of a resident gentry class. Barnett had always emphasised that education was mutual, regretting that at Oxford "I made the mistake of using my time to grind at books, rather than to know men." Barnett pointedly renewed his links with his *alma mater* by harassing it into organising its first vacation courses for school teachers. Oxford belatedly returned the compliment, if such it was, by establishing Barnett House as a pioneering centre for the study of social problems.

Toynbee Hall's purpose-built premises were designed in a Tudor Gothic style, reminiscent of an Oxford college and thus symbolizing amidst their slum surroundings the Ruskinian values of aestheticism, social justice and learning for which a university at its best might stand. Perhaps the buildings also brought the comfort of familiarity to Oxonian residents,

beleaguered on all sides by slums. In 1887 Barnett founded the East End Dwellings Company to tackle that problem, too.

Toynbee Hall was to prove of immense influence, early attracting the involvement of Jane Addams, who took the university settlement model to North America where her Hull House in Chicago inspired six hundred similar ventures. Another early beneficiary was bookbinder J M Dent (1849-1926) whose trip to Italy with the Toynbee Travellers' Club in 1890 inspired him to publish a series of books on Medieval Towns and later to launch the Everyman Library of affordable classics, a landmark in the history of publishing. In 1902 Dent published an edition of Dante translated by a fellow alumnus of the Toynbee Italy expedition, Thomas Okey (1852-1935), a Spitalfields basketweaver who later became the first Professor of Italian at Cambridge.

Toynbee Hall's extramural teaching programme inspired the foundation of the Workers' Educational Association and its library evolved into the Whitechapel Public Library which the polymath Jacob Bronowski would hail as 'the University of the Ghetto'. In 1898 Toynbee Hall began to offer free legal advice and in 1908 raised one of Britain's first scout troops.

Barnett resigned from St Jude's in 1894 and as Warden of Toynbee Hall in 1896 but remained one of Whitechapel's Poor Law Guardians until 1904. Although he was made a Canon and then Sub-Dean of Westminster Abbey, where he has a memorial, Barnett directed that his funeral service should be conducted at St Jude's. His redoubtable wife and lifelong helpmeet, Henrietta (1851-1936) devoted her later years to the development of Hampstead Garden Suburb, founding the girls' school named after her in 1911.

In the same year as Toynbee Hall, Oxford House was established in Derbyshire Street, Bethnal Green. The moving spirits behind its foundation came from Keble College, Oxford a bastion of high-minded Anglicanism, intending that it would enable tutors, graduates and future ordinands to learn at first hand about the problems of the urban poor. The venture's early heads certainly moved on to distinguished ecclesiastical careers, Hensley Henson (1863-1947) as bishop of Durham and Arthur Winnington-Ingram (1858-1946) as bishop of London. Oxford House is now secular, with programmes focused on the arts, youth work, asylum-seekers and especially the needs of the Somali community.

In the wider provision of spiritual nourishment to the East End an increasing emphasis was placed on mission rather than formal worship. In 1884 a mission was established in Lodore Street, Poplar, which in 1893 became St Frideswide's, its unusual dedication to the patron saint of Oxford betraying its university origins. St Nicholas, Blackwall Stairs was another mission initiative but failed to achieve parochial status, despite the distinction of being the first building in Poplar to be lit by electricity. The Methodists took over Wilton's music hall in 1885 and were to retain it until 1956. In 1893 the Holy Child Settlement was founded at Tower Hill. There was, however, still some belated church-building. St Mary Matfelon at Whitechapel was rebuilt in 1882. St Peter in Garford Street, Limehouse was consecrated in 1885, St Faith, Shandy Street in 1891 and St Andrew, Bromley-by-Bow in 1901.

IT JUST WENT LIKE TINDER

Bryant & May's began manufacturing in Liverpool in 1861 but soon opened a London base in Fairfield Road, Bow, where previously crinolines and candles had been made. The workforce was overwhelmingly female, largely teenage and included many Irish from a part of Bow so rough it was known as 'the Fenian barracks'. The local police inspector described these Amazons circumspectly as "rough and ready but not bad morally. They fight with their fists to settle their differences ... and are not interfered with by the police." Disciplined by fines and blows, girls worked a minimum ten-hour day standing up and in poorly ventilated conditions. Eating at their benches, they could ingest toxins causing hair loss, yellow skin and cancerous 'phossy jaw', which rotted teeth and bones. The business, however, prospered, paying dividends of 20% or more. Supplying an article of daily necessity in an age of coal fires, gas lighting and tobacco smoking, the emerging industrial giant soon attracted the unwelcome attentions of the Chancellor of the Exchequer but managed to organise the defeat of a proposal to put a halfpenny tax on every hundred matches. To celebrate this triumph in 1872 Bryant & May's employees had their wages docked to pay for the construction of a thirty-foot high Testimonial Fountain outside Bow railway station. Ten years later they were docked again to pay for a statue of prime minister William Gladstone to mark his half century in British politics. Theodore Bryant was a fervent admirer of the 'Grand Old Man' and perhaps also wished to ward off any temptation that the latter might have to revive the notion of taxing matches. In 1885 the workers attempted resistance against proposed wage-cuts but not until 1888 did they find the missing ingredients for successful action – effective leadership and external support.

On 23 June 1888 an exposé of the 'prison-house' conditions endured by the 'white wage slaves' of Bryant & May appeared in a campaigning journal, *The Link*. The author was Annie Besant (1847-1933), estranged wife of an Anglican clergyman and sister-on-law (doubtless to his embarrassment) of Walter Besant. Her personal odyssey had already taken her via atheism, secularism and campaigning for birth control into socialism, enabling her en route to discover in herself great gifts of oratory and organisation. When the Bryant & May

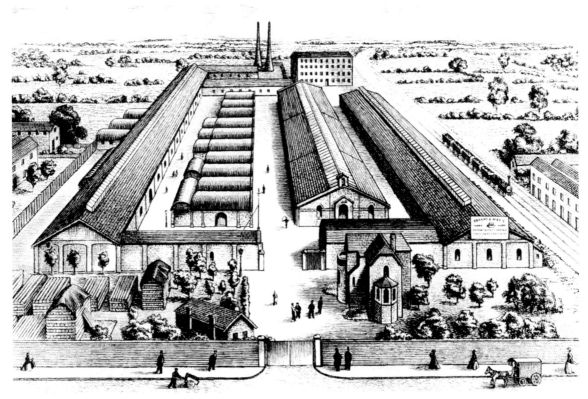

119. *The old Bryant & May factory at Fairfield in the 1860s, conveniently served by the railway. The rural aspect to the rear is unconvincing as this area had already been covered by streets.*

120. *Memorial for a memorial – this plaque on the north side of Bow Road proclaims:*
Near this spot stood the testimonial fountain erected by public subscription in 1872 to commemorate the part played by Bryant & May and their work people in securing the abandonment of the proposed match tax. Demolished in 1953.

management tried to force their employees to sign a statement of satisfaction with their working conditions, the organisers of a refusal campaign were sacked. On 5 July two hundred girls walked out in protest, to be joined by over a thousand more. Bryant & May denounced "the twaddle of Mrs Besant and other social-ists" and harrumphed about legal action against *The Link*. Mrs Besant, aided by Karl Marx's daughter, Eleanor Marx-Aveling, re-sponded by organising a strike fund and form-ing a Union of Women Matchmakers. Toynbee Hall and philanthropist Frederick Charrington both made facilities available for girls to reg-ister as members. Powerful publicity was given by Stead's *Pall Mall Gazette* and by Catherine Booth of the Salvation Army; together they called for a boycott of Bryant & May's matches. Cru-cially support came from the London Trades Council, which had traditionally safeguarded the interests of the labour aristocracy and held itself aloof from the unskilled. Meetings were held on Mile End Waste, a deputation went to

121. *The Bryant & May employees' strike committee. Herbert Burrows, reformer of factory conditions, is in the centre; to his left is Annie Besant.*

Parliament and on 16 July the Bryant & May management opened negotiations with joint representatives of the girls' strike committee and the trades council. The following day marked a famous victory – reinstatement of the victimised 'ringleaders', abolition of the hated apparatus of fines and deductions and even the provision of a breakfast room. In terms of its wider impact the significance of the strike lay in the fact of the successful formation of a union by the supposedly unskilled – and unskilled females at that. This triumph became a landmark in the history of the British labour movement, giving birth to a 'New Unionism' which would ultimately embrace millions previously excluded from the 'New Model' unions of skilled craftsmen in printing, engineering and similar elite occupations based on long apprenticeships.

The reputation of the Match Girls as irrepressible rebels was celebrated in a music hall song of 1901, *The Girls from Bryant and May*, which described them forsaking their usual Bank Holiday resort of 'appy 'ampstead' in favour of gate-crashing the Henley Regatta, a wildly improbable scenario but a neat reversal of the convention whereby toffs went 'slumming' to penetrate the mysterious world of the East End, rather than vice versa.

The Salvation Army kept up the campaign against industrial poisoning by opening its own model match factory in 1891 at Old Ford, just north of the Bryant & May complex. This used red, rather than the highly toxic yellow, phosphorous. Bryant & May's meanwhile continued to hazard the lives of their employees, half a dozen dying of what were identified by inspectors as preventable causes between 1893 and 1898. Only in 1901 was the firm's use of yellow phosphorous finally discontinued. Rebuilt in 1911, Bryant and May's match establishment was claimed at that time to be the largest single-site factory in the world. The Testimonial Fountain was demolished in 1953 to make way for road-widening. In 1966 Willy Russell and actor Bill Owen wrote a musical,

122. *Match girl strikers, 1888. An image that has acquired an iconic status, compounding pathos and defiance.*

123. Home manufacturers of matchboxes received even less money than those in the factory, but housebound housewives had little other means of earning cash.

124. Annie Besant, reformer, socialist and theosophist. Her activism induced her brother-in-law, Sir Walter Besant, to change the pronunciation of his name to rhyme with 'crescent'.

The Match Girls, to celebrate once more the memory of Annie Besant's shining hour.

For Annie Besant there would be many more shining hours. Her services to the people of the East End found a new direction in 1889 when she was elected to the local School Board and used her position to get the Board to pay its own employees union rates and to promote the provision of free school meals and medical inspections, pioneering advances which were eventually adopted as nation-wide policy by the reformist Liberal government which came to power in 1906. By then Annie Besant had taken up Theosophy, a syncretic cult formulated by the Russian mystic Helena Blavatsky. With typical commitment Besant settled in India, mastered Sanskrit, studied the Hindu scriptures with a disciplined intellectual thoroughness far exceeding that of her mentor and by 1907 was President of the Theosophical Society. A decade later her support for the cause of Indian independence led to her election as fifth President of the Indian National Congress. At her death she was cremated on the seashore of her adopted country in traditional Hindu fashion.

VICTORY AT BECKTON

Beckton gas-works, the largest in the world, opened in 1870. It was actually in today's Newham, but it employed many Tower Hamlets workers, especially those dockers who despaired of the uncertainties of employment in the docks. An attempted strike for high wages in 1872 led to the leaders' imprisonment, damping militancy for a decade. Efforts to form a union in 1884 and 1885 both failed. But the success of the match girls' action inspired a new combativeness. The demand for gas for domestic lighting and heating fluctuated with the seasons. When the usual large-scale summer lay-offs were announced in March 1889 a union was formed to resist the move under the leadership of Will Thorne (1857-1946) and Ben Tillett (1860-1943). Neither were local men. Thorne, son of an alcoholic Brummie brickmaker, had started work at six years of age and was still illiterate when he was taken on at Beckton in 1884. Taught to read by Eleanor Marx-Aveling, he became the secretary of the Canning Town branch of the Social Democratic Federation, of which they were both members. A powerfully-built man, Thorne was qualified by his physique to become an effective mob orator and was to prove a shrewd negotiator

125. *Ben Tillett in full flow at Covent Garden.*

as well. Tillett, a Bristolian, had been an acrobat, shoemaker, sailor and docker before becoming general secretary of a minor union, the Tea Operatives and General Labourers' Association. In 1888 he had attempted, unsuccessfully, to organise a strike at Tilbury Docks. Tillett shared Thorne's commitment to socialism but was a Christian rather than a Radical and also an ardent Temperance man.

Thorne, Tillett and other members of the hastily-formed strike committee formulated clear demands and a new militant posture. Aiming at an eight hour day and a six day week, they determined not to adopt the 'benefit fund' policies of traditional craft unions, which relied on relatively high subscriptions to fund payouts to members encountering unemployment, illness or injury. Funds would be devoted solely to fighting specific disputes and thus the weekly 'sub' could be set at just twopence, a fraction of the conventional rate, and

thus affordable to far more. Thorne argued that the achievement of a standard eight-hour day would oblige the company to retain men who would otherwise be thrown out of work. Victory was achieved in weeks, without even having to call the men out. Within a year the Gasworkers' Union had recruited fifty thousand members. By slashing the standard working day from twelve hours to eight it claimed to have protected five thousand jobs and thus the well-being of as many families. Thorne held the position of general secretary of the Gasworkers' Union until 1934, serving West Ham as a councillor or alderman for over half a century and sitting as MP for West Ham from 1906 and for Plaistow from 1918 until his death. He died a member of the Privy Council and CBE. Tillett, whom he had beaten in the election for general secretary, would find his glory on a different path.

126. *Will Thorne, PC CBE.*

THE DOCKER'S TANNER

The ultimate origins of the great dock strike of 1889 lay in the chronic chaos of the working conditions endured by the mass of dockside workers as 'casuals', aggravated by the advent of steam-powered shipping for the transportation of bulk cargoes. Whereas in 1871 a ship of 400 tons would be unloaded over the course of seven days, by 1889 much larger vessels of 1,500 tons would expect to be discharged in just seven hours. The result was to exaggerate daily fluctuations in the demand for labour so that one day a dock might need 3,000 men and the next as few as 200. Writing in 1886 Charles Booth, himself a shipowner with first-hand knowledge of the working of docks in both Liverpool and London, reckoned that there were some 75,000 'dock labourers', accounting for about 8% of the East End's population and ranked in his categorisation as Class C, the third lowest of eight classes.

Amongst dockside employees a new status and earnings hierarchy had emerged, based primarily on security of employment. At its apex were the literate administrative and gate-keeping staff who selected and directed the labour of the rest. Below them a pool of 'Permanents' included a minority who could read and write well enough to be entrusted with minor clerical and checking tasks. 'Irregulars' might work a day or a full week, depending on demand, a pattern of employment which meant that often substantial earnings were dissipated by a culture of celebratory drinking and compensatory debt. 'Casuals' were those employed only by the day. Booth observed damningly that "the casual by misfortune is subject to exactly the same economic and social conditions as the casual by profession. Taken on one day, he is overlooked the next. He may stave off starvation but he cannot rise to permanent employment. To have worked at the docks is sufficient to damn a man for other work."

The proximate causes of the crisis lay in the emergence of new socialist organizations, the harsh depression of 1886-87 and the inspirational example of the successes won by the match girls and the gasworkers in 1888-89. The event which actually precipitated the strike was a dispute over the division of a 'plus' (bonus) for the swift unloading of the *Lady Armstrong* on 12 August 1889. Two days later Ben Tillett led out the men of his Tea Operatives' Union in the West India Dock. Strike demands were rapidly drawn up – that men should be taken on a for a minimum of four hours at a stretch, that they should be paid sixpence an hour rather than five pence and that overtime should gain twopence extra rather than a penny. Other demands were that men should be 'called on' twice rather than four times a day, so that they wasted less time in the intervals between and that the contentious 'contract' and 'plus' payment systems, so easily abused by gangmasters, should be abolished. Within a week all the docks were paralysed. Crucial to this achievement was the widespread support received from the already unionised dockside elite of stevedores, lightermen, watermen, firemen and seamen. In Will Crooks (1852-1921) the movement found a local partisan already well known to many. Crooks had been born and would die in Poplar, showing a devotion to its people only to be rivalled by Lansbury and Attlee. Escaping childhood poverty by becoming a cooper, he

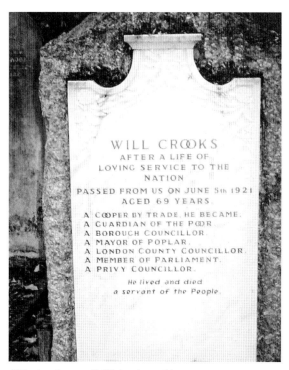

WILL CROOKS
AFTER A LIFE OF
LOVING SERVICE TO THE
NATION

PASSED FROM US ON JUNE 5th 1921
AGED 69 YEARS

A COOPER BY TRADE, HE BECAME
A GUARDIAN OF THE POOR
A BOROUGH COUNCILLOR
A MAYOR OF POPLAR
A LONDON COUNTY COUNCILLOR
A MEMBER OF PARLIAMENT
A PRIVY COUNCILLOR

*He lived and died
a servant of the People*

127. A tribute to Will Crooks on his gravestone in Tower Hamlets cemetery.

had educated himself by voracious reading and developed into a skilled speaker by haranguing open-air meetings which locals dubbed 'Crooks's College'. Crooks' radicalism had won him a reputation as an agitator, routinely rejected by employers and thus forced into casual dock work.

Outside the docks the movement enlisted the backing of the engineers' leader, John Burns, Tom Mann, a master tactician in the organisation of mass-pickets, and Will Thorne, who was the main speaker at the first mass-meeting of strikers and came with the laurels of a recent victor. Other allies from outside the ranks of organised labour also proved invaluable. H H Champion of the *Labour Elector* won the sympathy of the Liberal press. The Salvation Army distributed food tickets from its headquarters in Whitechapel Road, where Eleanor Marx-Aveling acted as supervising clerk. The Methodists used their mission at the former Wilton's music hall as a feeding-centre for strikers' families. A strike headquarters was established in the more convivial surroundings of the *Wades Arms* pub in Jeremiah Street, Poplar.

Daily processions of strikers were mobilised

to march down to the City and assemble at Tower Hill to hear morale-boosting speeches from leaders and sympathisers. Involving anything from 20,000 to 80,000 participants, these monster demonstrations kept idle men from other mischiefs, gained publicity and raised funds from sympathetic by-standers. Through strict discipline and the involvement of children, cheery bands and fancy dress costumes invoking patriotic icons such as Britannia and Neptune, the organisers underlined the non-violent, unrevolutionary character of their protest and sharply distinguished themselves from the bloody riots of recent memory in 1886-87. The parading of Friendly Society and Temperance banners conveyed a further aura of respectability. And, as H H Champion acutely noted in the aftermath, five weeks of continuously fine summer weather proved that the dockers enjoyed the favour of more than the pagan gods of legend. Unseasonal storms would have put a severe damper on boisterously good-natured demonstrations and undoubtedly have kept sympathisers indoors.

Behind the scenes blacklegs brought in to London by train were skilfully turned back at their stations of arrival by a para-military corps of 16,000 pickets, without incurring prosecutions for intimidation. By the end of August the employers' initial solidarity had begun to fragment. The dock companies, whose profits largely depended on holding down wage costs, kept to a hard line. Their customers, the ship-owners and wharfingers, whose businesses were under immediate threat because they could not shift existing cargoes, were more willing to press for compromise. But at the same time the dockers, having only philanthropy and the pawnbroker to fall back on, were in imminent danger of being starved back to work, certainly with the onset of autumn and colder weather.

At this pivotal point sympathisers in Australia – many, doubtless, recent migrants who had known London dock work at first hand or still had relatives along the riverside – despatched relief funds of £30,000. This raised the spectre of a long strike – or even a general strike. With such a prospect in view the highly respected Roman Catholic leader Cardinal Manning intervened, supported by the Lord Mayor and a reluctant Bishop of London. Their Mansion House Committee sought to effect an early end to the dispute through reconciliation. On 16 September a settlement was announced.

The 'docker's tanner' would be payable from November onwards and a minimum payment of two shillings per shift guaranteed. The 'contract' system of hiring men in gangs run by gangmasters, who had to be bribed with kick-backs or treated with drink, was abolished.

Ben Tillett went on to make his union a national organisation and to encourage unionism as a means of discouraging blackleg labour. In due course he would become a driving force behind the unionisation of transport workers and a founding member of the Independent Labour Party and of the Labour Party. Will Crooks, whose exertions in the course of the strike brought on a severe illness, recovered to graduate into Poplar politics as its representative on the newly-formed London County Council and as chairman of its Board of Poor Law Guardians. In 1901 he became London's first ever Labour Mayor and in 1903 Labour MP for Woolwich. He relied for his income on 'Will Crooks's wage fund', a pool of voluntary subscriptions from sympathisers, which never topped more than £4 a week but enabled him to remain a full-time servant of the people until the introduction of payment for MPs in 1911.

The dockers' strike inspired simultaneous outbreaks in many smaller East End industries, notably among garment workers, who needed a five week struggle to gain such minimal rights as a twelve-hour day, a lunch break and payment for working overtime. There were also walk-outs by boiler-makers and engineers at the Thames Ironworks. The dock strike also inspired James Connell to write *The Red Flag*, which became the anthem of the labour movement. The membership of unions affiliated to the Trade Union Congress doubled between 1889 and 1891 and in the latter year Pope Leo XIII himself endorsed the legitimacy of trade unions. Cut-throat competition continued, however, among the dock and shipping companies. Blackleg labour continued to be employed. The call-on was not abolished until the very eve of the docks' closure, in 1967. And the unions were to develop destructive rivalries of their own.

WORLDS OF WORK

The economy of the East End continued to diversify while the intensification of the tram system, the extension of the Underground as far as Bow Road, the perfection of the pneumatic-tyred 'safety bicycle' in the 1880s and the opening of the Blackwall tunnel in 1897 and of the Greenwich foot tunnel in 1902 combined

128. The Blackwall Tunnel, northern entrance, c.1905. The imposing gateway has gone but its counterpart at the southern end survives.

to enlarge significantly the radius within which East Enders could seek employment. In 1881 the first cargo of Australian frozen meat was successfully landed at Millwall, creating a new link in an international food chain that was becoming truly global. In 1882 the Royal National Lifeboat Institution headquarters was opened in Broomfield Street, Poplar. Forrest's shipyard continued to dominate the niche market in manufacturing lifeboats.

In 1897 Maconochie's opened their large processed food factory in West Ferry Road. Initially specialising in the manufacture of the pickles so beloved by cockneys, its name was to become synonymous with the glutinous meat-and-veg stew it created as a standard ration for the British army. Spratt's, which established the world's biggest dog biscuit factory just off the Limehouse Cut in 1899, likewise found that their basic product could be doctored for military consumption. Both firms benefited hugely from massive orders placed as a result of the outbreak of the Second Boer War in South Africa in 1899, as did local manufacturers of military tents.

Thanks largely to falling world food prices which worked their way down the social scale from the 1880s, those who had regular work could spend more and had more opportunities to spend it, whether at new theatres like the Pavilion, opened in 1892, in local landmark stores such as Gardiner's or Wickham's or at the stalls of Watney Market or in Brick Lane where the 93 authorised stalls of 1893 had become 206 by 1901.

In a world in which work both occupied most of the waking week and defined the social identity of adult males its focus often overshadowed leisure hours as well. In 1885 workers at Morton's Jam Factory on the Isle of Dogs formed themselves into a soccer team, initially called Millwall Rovers. As most of them came from a Scottish background they chose the national colours of blue and white for their team strip. The Stuart lion of Scotland may also explain the club nickname of 'The Lions'. In its early years the club occupied four different grounds on 'the island' before moving south of the river to the Den in 1910, having changed its name to Millwall Athletic and then plain Millwall. Historians have surmised that the remote location of Millwall's early grounds may have discouraged the attendance of away team supporters thus encouraging the ferociously partisan character of the Millwall crowd which has become an integral feature of the club's identity.

With the encouragement of managing director Arnold Hills employees of the Thames Ironworks and Engineering yard formed their own football team in 1895, largely funded by their employer. In 1898 Thames Ironworks FC turned professional and was elected to the Southern League. In 1900 the club disbanded, to be refounded as West Ham United. In 1904 West

129. The Strangers' Home, Limehouse, c.1905. Inmates paid to stay and kept safe from the dirt and dangers of dockside doss-houses. Visiting journalist George R Sims noted that Asian books and periodicals were available and that different castes and creeds could cook and eat separately.

Ham moved from Canning Town to the Boleyn Ground at Upton Park, which has been its home ever since. The first home game there resulted in a 3-0 win over Millwall. West Ham's industrial origins are recalled in the club motif of crossed hammers and the team's punning nickname 'The Hammers'.

ARTS AND CRAFTS CRUSADER

Work and what it might be, rather than what it had become, was to be a dominant passion in the life of Charles Robert Ashbee (1863-1942). Like his mentor, William Morris, Ashbee was a rich boy turned romantic revolutionary, his father being a City solicitor and his cultured Jewish mother the offspring of a Hamburg merchant dynasty. Trained as an architect under the ecclesiastical specialist G F Bodley, Ashbee developed an abiding interest in the complementary craftsmanship required to work wood, metal, textiles and glass. In 1886 Ashbee joined Toynbee Hall, started a reading class devoted to the works of John Ruskin and decorated the dining-room with the assistance of his students. He is also credited with inventing Toynbee Hall's 'tree of life' logo. Such experiences led Ashbee to appreciate the value of the East End as a reservoir of the skills whose survival was menaced by the increasing mechanisation of all branches of manufacture. In 1888 he recruited members of his Ruskin class as the nucleus of a Guild of Handicraft which was to be an instrument for preserving craft skills and promoting fellowship amongst their practitioners. Initially based in a Commercial Street warehouse, in 1891 the Guild moved into Essex House, opposite the present Mile End underground station. Ashbee's protégés aimed to produce furniture, jewellery and metalwork or to practise printing and bookbinding with the aim not only of creating items of which they could be justly proud but also to do so "in such a way as shall best conduce to the welfare of the workman". The Guild would function as both a craft co-operative and as a training-school for selected apprentices, thus ensuring the future existence of threatened skills. Ironically William Morris, having by the 1880s committed himself to political activism, dismissed Ashbee's venture as misguided and of marginal value. This view was at least in part contradicted by a prestigious commission from the Grand Duke of Hesse, who not only contracted for a range of furniture to be designed

130. *C R Ashbee.*

by Ashbee and his collaborator M H Baillie Scott but also set up an artisan colony on Essex House lines in Darmstadt. When Morris died in 1894 Ashbee bought his two printing presses and took on three of his workmen to produce a King Edward *Prayer Book* and an *Essex House Song Book*. The latter reflected the social life of the craftsman community, which revolved around musical evenings and, in summer, a cricket team, cycling expeditions and weekend breaks at country cottages.

In 1893 Ashbee attempted to mobilize opinion against the demolition of the 'Old Palace' at Bromley-by-Bow when the newly-established London County Council proposed to raze the site to put a new school on it. The rambling building's claim to palatial status – royal or episcopal – was dubious but it was almost four centuries old. True, it had fallen on hard times, having been sub-divided and variously used as a school, a working men's club and as commercial premises but it retained many internal features of artistic and historic value. Surely, Ashbee argued ingeniously, if it was appropriate for England's public school elite to be educated amidst buildings of antiquity, how much more was an historic environment needed by the children of the slums, who had so little awareness of their heritage. Ashbee failed to convince the demolitionists but he did manage to save a majestic room, complete with panelling, an Italian moulded plaster ceiling and a handsome fireplace surmounted by an imposing royal coat of arms. This can now be seen in the handsome British Galleries of the Victoria and Albert Museum.

Ashbee had better success in defending the Trinity Almshouses on the Mile End Road when the LCC proposed a similar act of vandalism in 1896. Ashbee's cavalier willingness to attribute their design to Sir Christopher Wren may have gone far beyond any available evidence to support such a claim but the mere invocation of such an icon proved sufficient to stay the wrecker's hand. Ashbee's subsequent monograph *The Trinity Hospital in Mile End: An Object Lesson in National History* served as a pioneering manifesto of the conservationist ideal and as the first report of the Committee for the Survey of the Memorials of Greater London, which evolved into the monumental and still ongoing *Survey of London,* whose first project was to record Bromley-by-Bow. As Ashbee had predicted, virtually all of the surviving late medieval High Street which it recorded would be totally destroyed within the following twenty years.

In 1902, when the lease on Essex House ran out, Ashbee sought a rural idyll in Chipping

131. Part of the State Room in the Old Bromley Palace, now in the Victoria & Albert Museum.

Campden, Gloucestershire, where he relocated the one hundred and fifty men, woman and children who had come to constitute the Guild. Commercial salvation, however, remained elusive and the venture was formally wound up in 1907, though several adherents remained faithful to the vision, stayed on and survived into the 1960s. Ashbee's own later career took him to Jerusalem where he played a crucial role in the conservation of the ancient city and the revival of Arab crafts.

GREEN AND PLEASANT

The Fabian Society, founded in 1884, favoured social improvement, not through violent revolution but through the 'inevitability of gradualness' and the realisation of concrete and specific objectives to ameliorate the condition of the disadvantaged. Derided from the left as 'gas and water' socialists, they would doubtless have retrospectively approved the opening in 1882 of the imposing George Green's School in East India Dock Road and in the same year of the Mothers' Lying-In Home at Glamis Road in Shadwell.

What a century later the quirky social critic Ivan Ilich would call 'tools for conviviality', such as spaces for learning and recreation, also appealed to the Fabian philosophy. These proliferated piecemeal throughout the East End, not in fulfillment of any grand strategy but as the result of individual initiatives. Repton Boys' Club, established in 1884, became famed for its juvenile boxing talent. In 1885 it was complemented by a Working Lads' Institute at 279 Whitechapel Road and in 1896 by Haileybury Boys' Club. Frederick Charrington's Great Assembly Hall *(ill. 113)* was dedicated in 1886 primarily to the promotion of temperance and in 1900 Catherine Phillimore opened her Jerusalem Coffee House in the same cause. In 1894 the Revd William Rogers established the Bishopsgate Institute just inside the City boundary and in the same year a public library was at last opened in Poplar High Street. In 1887 St Dunstan's churchyard became a public garden, to be joined by Wapping Recreation Ground in 1891, Island Gardens on the Isle of Dogs in 1895 and Bromley Recreation Ground in 1900.

Into the Abyss

Although best known as the author of adventure stories set on far frontiers, Jack London (1876-1916) had been a factory labourer, fisherman, gold prospector and journalist before turning himself into one of the world's most highly paid and famous writers – and then drinking himself to death. The transition had only just begun, with the publication of a first volume of short stories, when London assumed the guise of a stranded American sailor and took up lodgings in Flower and Dean Street in 1902. "I went down into the underworld of London with an attitude of mind which I may best liken to that of the explorer." The outcome of his investigations appeared the following year as *People of the Abyss, a* passionate diatribe against the brutal capitalism which treated the poor as so much human dross. The book's twenty-seven chapters recount the author's experiences in Poplar workhouse and Frying-Pan Alley and range over such topics as wages, drink, suicide, doss-houses and the coronation of Edward VII, an occasion of much rejoicing among the sovereign's less fortunate subjects. The appeal of the book lies in the author's eye for particularity, such as the spectacle of the exhausted homeless sleeping bolt upright in 'Itchy Park' by Christ Church, Spitalfields at three o'clock on a raw afternoon because the iron railings around it kept them out at night, While a more rigorously analytical reporter might have stressed the inexorability of the workings of the market economy London stressed the supervening role of chance – prolonged illness, accident or the death of a breadwinner – in tipping the vulnerable into the pit of poverty and condemning the blameless to inescapable lives of slum-bound misery. He also emphasised that the summer of 1902 would be considered by most East Enders as one of the 'good times'. But his depiction of their lives is almost unrelievedly negative, blind to the cheeriness of the market and music hall.

London's very male-oriented account of life in the lower depths prompted a complementary exploration by the equally self-invented Olive Christian Malvery (?1877/82-1914).

Anglo-Indian by birth, she had arrived in London as a music student and then rapidly passed through successive re-incarnations as a performer, elocution teacher, writer and photo-journalist. In 1904, capitalising on the interest aroused by Jack London's book, she set out to experience and expose the lives of 'London's poorer daughters'. The results of her odyssey, profusely illustrated with photographs of herself variously dressed in a sari, passing herself off as a flower girl, working as a barmaid, shopgirl or factory hand or disguised as a tramp, appeared in *Pearson's Magazine* as *The Heart of Things*. In contrast to the detached investigations of Charles Booth's team Malvery's picaresque adventures constituted a skilful exercise in self promotion in which her own ingenuity and daring were the key ingredients in an inverted travelogue through which a daughter of the Empire exposes the exotic ethnography of its metropolis. Malvery's London landscape, however, lacked the precision of Charles Booth and the specificity of Jack London. She made much of the Italian community while ignoring the far more numerous Jewish and Irish. Such deficiencies did not prevent her being commissioned to produce a follow-up series on *The Alien Question*, focused on the male immigrant Jew from eastern Europe, just when legislation was being placed before Parliament to impose restriction on their entry. In her reportage Malvery's stance switched from sympathy to hostility. She also descended from disguise to outright deception. Unable to enter the Russian-controlled parts of eastern Europe from which ghetto Jews were fleeing, she 'investigated' their background by photographing poverty-stricken locations in southern Italy. When her attempts to photograph applicants at the Poor Jews' Temporary Shelter resulted in threats from the crowd she resorted to a shot of Jews outside the socialist club in Princelet Street and an insinuating caption hinting at the arrival of unknown numbers of potentially criminal, exploitative and unassimilable newcomers. No matter – that same year Olive Malvery married an American diplomat in a society wedding at St Margaret's Westminster, complete with Cockney flower-girls in attendance and a 'royal' reception in Hoxton. Financially secure, she republished her London investigations in book form as *The Soul Market*, which went through four editions in less than two years, eleven in six years. Part of her royalties went to finance two shelters for homeless women. After giving birth to three children in six years Olive Malvery died from a sedative overdose in 1914.

George R Sims (1847-1922), prolific author of novels, ballads and melodrama, produced a well respected journalistic account of *How the Poor Live* (1883) but could also see the positive side of East End life. He positively revelled in the cosmopolitanism of the Mile End Road, nominating it as "the most interesting street in London ... packed with the pages of the Book of Life written in many European tongues. Here Asia jostles Europe and the dominant Oriental note carries you back to the Picture Bible of your childhood."

Stressing the prevalence of Yiddish-speaking Ashkenazim Sims was exhilarated by the bustle of the great thoroughfare "on a Saturday night when the Jewish Sabbath is over and brightly-dressed young Jewesses promenade with Oriental colours in their raiment ... You rarely see a sign of poverty or slatternliness among these young women, many of whom are only working girls."

CHANGING PLACES, CHANGING FACES

The depiction of East Enders as essentially victims of circumstance produced by both Jack London and Olive Malvery was vitiated by the fact that they were not only outsiders but writing primarily for other outsiders. Prosaic changes which might easily escape an observer in search of the exotic were in fact progressively changing life in the East End for the better, or at the least giving the lie to the notion that its inhabitants were imprisoned in a cesspit of economic and cultural stagnation.

Whitechapel Art Gallery, built between 1897 and 1899 in an Art Nouveau style to the designs of Charles Harrison Townsend, attracted over two hundred thousand visitors to its first event, an exhibition of the works of such conventional great names as Rubens, Hogarth and Constable. But the gallery soon adopted the adventurous policy for which it was rightly to become famed, organising shows devoted to the work of Scottish, Irish and Cornish artists, to Chinese, Japanese and Jewish art and to posters, photography, needlework and the art work produced by children in local schools.

132. The Whitechapel Art Gallery in 2004. It was built between 1897 and 1899 to the designs of C H Townsend.

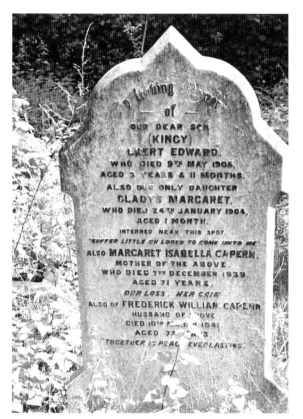

133. This tombstone in Tower Hamlets Cemetery illustrates the many premature deaths in the early years of the 20th century. One child was one month old, the other three years.

Exhibitions were also organised on locally appropriate themes such as Old London, Shipping, the Indian Empire, Engineering, Sport, House and Home and even Tuberculosis.

The passage of the 1902 Education Act led to the construction of dozens of new multistorey schools. The birth of the Workers' Educational Association at Toynbee Hall in 1903 opened up a new highway to self-improvement for adults. In 1904 the London County Council opened a new School of Engineering and Navigation at Poplar.

The revelations of poor physique and general standards of health which were thrown up by the recruitment programme for the Second Boer War led to a quest for 'national efficiency' which created a novel concern for the welfare of the rising generation, expressed in the introduction of free school meals and medical inspections as well as numerous individual ini-

tiatives, In 1907 devoted teacher Clara Grant (1867-1949) of Fern Street began her Saturday programme of distributing 'farthing bundles' of tiny treats for small children. In 1908 Margaret McMillan (1860-1931), already a pioneer of school medical inspections and nursery education, opened a children's clinic in Devons Road, Bow. In 1912 Muriel Lester (1883-1967) and her sister Doris (1886-1965) started a nursery school for working mothers at 58-60 Bruce Road.

In 1914 the Lester sisters bought a former Zion chapel at the corner of Eagling Road and Botolph Road and converted it into a mission hall, named in memory of their brother Kingsley, who had died that year. Inspired by the writings of Tolstoy, Muriel had turned her back on bourgeois comfort to "build the Kingdom of Heaven, here and now, in Bow."

The opening of the Greenwich foot tunnel in 1902 enabled residents of the Isle of Dogs to take jobs on the other side of the river at the

134. Tredegar House, the country's first institution for the preliminary training of nurses.

135. The Pavilion Theatre in Whitechapel, almost entirely given over to Yiddish productions.

Woolwich Arsenal. In the same year an extension of the District Line from Whitechapel to Bow Road station was opened. The Rotherhithe tunnel was opened to traffic in 1908. The closure of the United Horseshoe and Nail Company of Wharf Road, Cubitt Town in 1909 was a portent of the new era of motorisation.

The new Poplar Hippodrome opened its doors to customers in 1905. The Pavilion at Whitechapel became a primarily Yiddish theatre the following year. Many music halls began to show silent movies as part of their programmes. Developments at Bow included the opening of Grove Park in 1909 on the site of the former lunatic asylum, the completion of Bryant & May's fortress-like Fairfield Works adjacent in 1911 and in 1912 the opening of an imposing new police station on Bow Road and, a block to the west, of Tredegar House as the country's first institution for the preliminary training of nurses. Bethnal Green acquired a new Town Hall in 1910.

The Thames continued to dominate the economy of the eastern side of the metropolis. In 1902 a Royal Commission on the Port of London was appointed. Its recommendations led to the establishment of the Port of London Authority in 1909, a long overdue recognition of the need for some over-arching body to supersede the muddle of special boards and commissions which had proliferated over the centuries to regulate the working life of the river. Shipbuilding, however, was in its terminal stage. Although the Thames Ironworks successfully launched the Orion class 'super-dreadnought' *HMS Thunderer* in February 1911, at 22,600 tons the greatest ship ever built on the Thames, the project had bankrupted the company and the yard closed for good in 1912.

Migration out of Inner London began with the new century. Over 550,000 – 12% – left between 1901 and 1911. Some were destined for a new life in the empire. Emigration reached an all-time high in 1911-13 when some 450,000, representing 1% of the entire British population, left their native shores each year, Canada being the most favoured destination. On a less epic scale prospering artisans betook themselves to the working-class suburbs of West Ham, Forest Gate, Leyton or Walthamstow, whose tram systems still afforded access to work in the East End. Yarrow's left for the Clyde in 1907, taking three hundred Poplar men with it.

Another cause of population decline was the imposition of restrictions on immigration. The British Brothers' League, founded in 1901 by Major William Evans-Gordon, Conservative MP for Stepney, demanded an end to the uncontrolled influx of foreigners. The cause commanded support across the political spectrum with the TUC and local trades councils having passed annual resolutions to similar effect from 1892. The result of these pressures was the appointment of a Royal Commission on Alien Immigration whose recommendations were embodied in the 1905 Aliens Act. This measure was also supported by Bethnal Green's Indian-born MP Sir Mancherjee Bhownagree, a staunch defender of British imperialism. The legislation led to some four thousand would-be immigrants being turned away between 1906 and 1910. As word got round the number attempting to settle declined, reducing the annual inflow from 12,000 to 4,000.

At the same time as the number of East European immigrants was being sharply curtailed there was an increasing awareness of the existence of another, quite different, but perhaps even more 'alien', presence ensconced in the East End. Chinese settlement in Limehouse was a by-product of the expansion of Britain's commerce with the Celestial Empire stimulated by the annexation of Hong Kong in 1842 and the opening of the Suez Canal in 1869. Former sailors, settling around Pennyfields and along Limehouse Causeway, supported themselves by catering to the needs of their compatriots, mostly of employees of the Blue Funnel Line, for whom they provided accommodation, familiar food, laundry services and the distractions afforded by gambling and opium. The association between the Chinese, opium-smoking and arbitrary violence was asserted by Dickens in *The Mystery of Edwin Drood*, although he had located his setting in Shadwell – "down by the docks the shabby undertaker's shop will bury you for next to nothing, after the Malay or Chinaman has stabbed you for nothing at all".

Oscar Wilde had confirmed this literary linkage. In chapter sixteen of *The Picture of Dorian Gray* (1891), although the lurid landscape he describes is more symbolic than strictly topographic, the hero-victim being drawn inexorably into a labyrinth of sordid streets "like the black web of some sprawling spider". In 1897, however, the local police inspector for Limehouse told Charles Booth's investigator that the Chinese were essentially "tame and quiet", with "a great respect for authority," Opium smoking was, however, viewed as a problem. Even though it was almost entirely restricted to the Chinese themselves limits were imposed on its sale in 1908.

The lurid and largely undeserved reputation of the Limehouse Chinatown for vice, violence, white slavery etc., was largely the creation of Arthur Henry Ward (1886-1959) who, under the pseudonym Sax Rohmer, penned a series of lurid thrillers around the machinations of the imaginary criminal genius Dr Fu Manchu, the first of which was published in 1913. *Limehouse Nights,* published in 1916 by Thomas Burke (1888-1945) compounded the impression created by Ward, as did D W Griffith's mawkish screen melodrama of 1919 *Broken Blossoms,* although that did, at least, show the Chinese hero in a positive light as gentle and sensitive. Suffice to say that the local rector dismissed Burke's production with crisp contumely – "this may be literature but it is not Limehouse."

136. A Chinese mission house.

137. *Chinatown in 1920. Watercolour by William Monk. Note the new Chinese Nationalist flag on the right.*

138. A Chinese shop, early 20th century.

POLITICS, RED AND BLACK
From the 1880s the East End provided a bolt-hole for political refugees of all ideological complexions. Disenchanted Tsarist government official Pyotr Kropotkin (1842-1921) settled in Whitechapel in 1887 and contributed the article on Anarchism to the 1911 edition of the *Encyclopaedia Britannica*. The failed but persistent Italian insurrectionary Errico Malatesta (1853-1932) lived under police surveillance but won the admiration of Kropotkin who noted admiringly "without even so much as a room that he could call his own, he would sell sherbet in the streets of London to get his living and in the evening write brilliant articles for the Italian papers." The Scottish-born German John Henry Mackay (1864-1933) based his autobiographical novel *The Anarchists: A Picture of Civilization at the Close of the Nineteenth Century* (1891) on his first-hand contacts with Kropotkin's circle of associates in 1887-98. Published in both German and English the novel was later translated into eight other languages. Arthur Morrison's *Tales of Mean*

Streets includes an account of an anarchist band called the Red Cow Group.

Kropotkin's friend, the German Gentile Rudolf Rocker (1873-1958) came to the East End in 1895 and taught himself Yiddish. Unlike Anglo-Jewry, which insisted on Anglophone competence, the anarchists cherished Yiddish as the *mameloshn*, the mother tongue and common heritage of the working masses. Rocker became the central figure of a group of Jewish anarchists who gathered in the Sugar Loaf in Hanbury Street and at a club which met in the Alexandra Hall in Jubilee Street,. Rocker edited a Yiddish journal *Der Arbeiter Fraint (The Worker's Friend)* which continued until 1950. An intimate but unusual perspective on the Jewish anarchist coterie can be found in Fermin Rocker's 1998 memoir *The East End Years: A Stepney Childhood*.

In 1903 Lenin spoke at the Jubilee Street club in commemoration of the Paris Commune. Following the failure of the 1905 revolution in Russia he returned in 1907 to attend the Fifth Congress of the Russian Social Democratic Labour Party which assembled in the Brotherhood Church in Southgate Road, Whitechapel. Stalin and Litvinov stayed in a doss-house in Fieldgate Street. Lenin also revisited the Jubilee Street club and took the opportunity to investigate Toynbee Hall incognito to assess its counter-revolutionary potential.

THE SIDNEY STREET SIEGE
On the night of 17 December 1910 three policemen were shot dead by burglars at a jeweller's shop in Houndsditch. On 2 January 1911 police received information that the supposed perpetrators of this crime, Latvian revolutionaries known as the Gardstein Gang, were to be found at the house of a Mrs Gershon of 100 Sidney Street. Having cordoned off the area and rescued the hapless landlady, the police found themselves under fire from upstairs rooms by powerful repeating Mauser pistols. Ebullient Home Secretary Winston Churchill hastened to take personal charge of the incident and ordered in a detachment of Scots Guards marksmen from the Tower. Shooting ceased by 2.10 pm, by which time the house was engulfed in flames. Charred bodies were later identified as those of Fritz Svaas and Josef Marx. Of the third member of the gang, Peter Piatkow (*aka* Peter the Painter) there was no trace. Alexander Bloom, the enterprising proprietor of the East

139. *Scots Guards at firing positions in the Siege of Sidney Street.*

London Printing Co., not only took dramatic photographs of the Scots Guards in action and the besieged house on fire but had them printed and on sale to West End theatre queues that same evening. Police weaponry and firearms training were upgraded as a result of the inadequacies revealed by the 'Siege of Sidney Street'.

THE POLITICS OF PASSION

The initial recruiting-ground for the militant suffragette movement embodied in Emmeline Pankhurst's Women's Social and Political Union was in affluent suburbs like Kensington or the intellectual enclave of Bloomsbury. Mrs Pankhurst and her eldest daughter, Christabel, conceived themselves as generals of an army of obedient idealists, unencumbered by family ties or financial constraints, who could dedicate themselves unreservedly to the cause of winning women the vote. Sylvia Pankhurst (1882-1960) thought quite differently, believing that a movement for greater democracy must itself be democratic, reaching out to the greatest number of women and guided in its objectives by their most pressing concerns. Rejecting the

elitist strategy of the WSPU, Sylvia established her own East London Federation of Suffragettes in a former baker's shop in Bow Road. Here she enlisted the support of local women who confirmed her conviction that female enfranchisement should be part of a much broader social revolution to eliminate the poverty and squalor which stunted their lives. Sylvia was, of course, a controversial figure in her own particular way. George Bernard Shaw denounced her unfraternally as "the most ungovernable, self-interested, blindly and deadly wilful little rapscallioncondottiera that ever imposed itself on the infra-red end of the revolutionary spectrum."

Sylvia did, however, win the support of local MP George Lansbury who, in 1912, voluntarily resigned his seat to fight it again on the issue of women's suffrage. He lost, his quixotic gesture costing him more than a decade outside the Commons. Sylvia, meanwhile, endured no less than ten periods of imprisonment and hunger-strike between the summer of 1913 and 1914, yet still managed to launch her own newspaper the *Women's Dreadnought*.

The outbreak of World War One saw a widening of the rift between Sylvia and her mother

140. Sylvia Pankhurst. A trained graphic artist, she devised the distinctive Suffragette colour combination of purple, white and green.

and sister. While they turned their propaganda machine to mobilising support for the war effort Sylvia, as a pacifist, set up a toy factory in Norman Road (now Grove) to create much-needed employment for women as well as inaugurating clinics and a crèche in the Gunmakers' Arms – renamed the Mothers' Arms – at Old Ford. The boisterous children deposited there were calmed by a pioneering introduction of the learning through play programmes developed by Maria Montessori in Italy. In 1916 Sylvia renamed her organisation the Workers Socialist Federation and in 1917 renamed her paper the *Workers Dreadnought.* The outbreak of revolution in Russia won her passionate support and the WSF became, in effect, Britain's first Communist party. By the time women (over 30) were at last granted the vote in 1918 Sylvia had committed herself to the Communist cause, journeying to Moscow in 1920 to attend the Third International. Expelled from the party for refusing to hand her newspaper over to its

control, Sylvia kept it going until 1924 until she finally left the East End for the leafy charms of Woodford Green, where she lived with the anti-Fascist journalist Silvia Erasmus Corio and gave birth to a son. Her later life was to be devoted to the people of Ethiopia.

PROTEST AND PATRIOTISM

A reversal in the trend towards higher real incomes from 1906 squeezed working-class living standards and sharpened labour conflicts. In 1910 Ben Tillett succeeded in amalgamating 250,000 members into a National Transport Workers Federation and in 1911 he led a successful major dock strike on the issue of union recognition. While sensationalist 'investigators' may, as a result, have pictured the East End as a hotbed of foreign-born anarchists and traitorous native-born 'reds', the Great War would demonstrate incontrovertibly the fervent patriotism of its inhabitants. Bethnal Green alone would lose 1,122 men. Of the 685 men from the Isle of Dogs parish of St Luke's who served, 115 were killed. The recruitment drive received conspicuous support from heroes of the labour movement usually depicted as intransigent radicals. Will Thorne served as Lt. Colonel of the West Ham Volunteer Force. Ben Tillett toured three thousand miles of battle-front, successfully addressing *en masse* men who, in the words of their grateful commander, Sir John French, "would not generally attend meetings." In recognition of his efforts as a recruiter Will Crooks would be sworn of the Privy Council.

Even animals did not escape the jingoistic fervour – tram horses were requisitioned for service with the corps of transport. Volunteers drilled at Toynbee Hall; although some of the staff there opposed the war on conscientious or political grounds, thirteen past or current residents would die on active service. Toynbee Hall's secretary Clement Attlee (1893-1967), an officer in the Haileybury Boys' Club cadet force, would serve at Gallipoli and in France, be wounded twice and attain the rank of Major. Another youth worker Roland Phillips (1890-1916), the Scout Commissioner for Bethnal Green, Poplar and Stepney, volunteered for service as soon as war broke out and won the Military Cross but was killed at the Somme.

Thousands would serve in the Poplar and Stepney Rifles, which constituted the 17th battalion of the London Regiment. The existing

141. Statue of Clement Attlee. He served as Stepney's first Labour mayor and MP for Limehouse. Succeeding Lansbury as Leader of the Labour Party, he served as Prime Minister 1945-51. He died as Earl Attlee.

142. Isaac Rosenberg's plaque at Whitechapel Public Library, 'the university of the Ghetto'.

Territorial unit, established in 1909 as part of the military reform programme prompted by the inadequacies revealed by the South African war, would win its first battle honour at Loos in 1915 and nine more in subsequent Western Front engagements. A 2nd/17th battalion, raised from the volunteers of August 1914, would make its first mark at blood-soaked Vimy Ridge, then serve in Salonika and the Middle East before returning to the Western Front.

Jews, whose attachment to Britain had been sneeringly queried by the xenophobes of the British Brothers' League, proved their loyalty and paid the arbitrary price that war exacts. Robert Winthrop, born Chaim Reeven Weintrop, served with the artillery and survived being gassed and temporarily blinded to revenge himself on a sadistic sergeant-major by taking his name and making it a byword for comic absurdity as Bud Flanagan (1896-1968). Jack Cohen (1898-1979) survived shipwreck off Alexandria to return home, start up in business

by selling off surplus army rations in street-markets and build the Tesco supermarket empire. Morris Cohen (1887-1970) an alumnus of the Jews Free School and reformatory, who had picked up Chinese in Canada, supervised the Chinese labour corps in France and went on to become Sun Yat-Sen's pistol-packing bodyguard with the rank of general. Basil Henriques (1890-1961) served with distinction in the newly-formed tank corps, commanding the first tank ever to fire on an enemy; wounded on the Somme and decorated in Italy, he would return to devote his life to youth work. Artist Isaac Rosenberg (1890-1918) wrote some of the greatest poetry to emerge from the trenches before being killed in combat. Mark Gertler, a fellow student at the Slade, remained in Spitalfields to paint one of the most striking of all anti-war paintings, the unnerving *Merry-Go-Round.*

Willingness to serve at the front was matched by concern for the victims of the conflict. Belgian refugees were settled in Rothschild Buildings. The London Hospital took in some six thousand wounded and convalescent soldiers. The first batch, of one hundred, were brought from Waterloo in taxis and a fleet of vans loaned by the catering firm of J Lyons and Co. Bethnal Green Hospital became Bethnal Green Military Hospital. The London Chest Hospital specialised in treating casualties of poison gas. There were also local casualties to be treated. On 31 May 1915 there was a Zeppelin raid on the docklands. Bromley-by-Bow was bombed in

143. The Poplar Outrage memorial in Poplar Recreation Ground. The monument records the names of children who lost their lives in 1917 when the Upper North Street primary school was bombed.

1916; one bomb hit the Black Swan at the junction of Bow Road and Bromley High Street, killing four occupants. Most horrifying of all was the bombing on 13 June 1917 of Upper North Street primary school, which became known as the Poplar Outrage. The incident was part of the first German daylight raid on the capital, which was to prove twice as lethal as any other of the entire war, killing 97 persons and injuring 439 more. Flying from occupied Belgium seventeen Gotha bombers attacked East Ham, Liverpool Street Aldgate and Whitechapel before reaching Poplar where a 110-pound missile crashed through the roof of the school to explode among the five-year-olds on the ground floor, Fifteen were killed instantly; three more died of fatal injuries; twenty-seven were maimed for life.

Such atrocities intensified a hatred manifest from the outset of the war. Fierce jingoism had

its downside in repeated mob outbursts against enemy aliens. On 2 August 1914 the German supply ship *Titania*, crammed with German nationals desperate to beat the anticipated outbreak of war, pulled out of St Katherine's dock to the jeers of Wapping locals. The luckless vessel, barred by a Royal Navy blockade from a straight run home via the North Sea, fled vainly down the Channel in a futile attempt to sail right round the British Isles to safety. Boarded on 4 August, the *Titania* was taken to Falmouth where her passengers and crew were duty interned. Attacks on East End German properties, like Hagmaier's pork butchers in Poplar High Street, began even before allegations of 'Hunnish' bestialities in Belgium reached Britain. Riots reached a new peak in May 1915 with the sinking of the *Lusitania* and the first Zeppelin raid. In 1917 there were further disorders in Bethnal Green, directed at recently arrived Jews, who were not subject to conscription. Against such a background it is unsurprising that the Prince of Prussia public house in Grove Road prudently metamorphosed to become the Prince of Wales. Businesses with Russian, Polish, or other names which might be mistaken for German by the unlettered displayed prominent signs proclaiming them to be under British management.

As a major industrial area the East End made a significant contribution to the material side of the conflict. The area's myriad clothing factories made uniforms and blankets for the army and the premises of the Commercial Gas Company were converted to the manufacture of munitions. Allen and Hanbury's pharmaceutical factory at Bethnal Green was an important producer of medical supplies. A boom in ship repairing brought renewed, if temporary, prosperity to the Isle of Dogs.

While Sylvia Pankhurst was running a crèche and clinics to cushion the hardships of war for local women, Methodist minister Frederick Chudleigh (1878-1932) set up the first wartime community canteen where soup, stews and puddings were sold at twopence per portion to two thousand people a day. This initiative was soon taken up officially to be copied in other cities. At Kingsley Hall, where the Lester sisters were also declared opponents of the war, a soup kitchen was opened.

To bolster morale the Whitechapel Art Gallery put on exhibitions of war cartoons, drawings, lithographs and photographs, including not only work from allied nations, such as France, Russia, Serbia, Italy and Japan but also from neutral Spain and the Netherlands and even the German enemy. There were also themed exhibitions on Munitions of War and Allied Industries, Women's War Work and, with an optimistic view to the aftermath, on Housing and Town Planning. Walker, Harrison and Garthwaites Ltd, biscuit-makers of Ratcliff Cross, produced printed cards of VC winners as a means of combining sales promotion with patriotism.

Four local men were to be awarded the nation's highest award for valour. Sidney Frank Godley (1889-1957) was to be the first private soldier of the war to be so honoured. On 23 August 1914, during the morale-sapping retreat from Mons, Private Godley, a machine-gunner with the 4th battalion of the Royal Fusiliers, volunteered for the near-suicidal task of manning one of only two machine-guns opposing the advance of six entire German divisions. Even to get to his gun Godley had to remove the bodies of three dead comrades. For two hours he single-handedly defended a railway bridge over the Mons-Conde canal at Nimy, despite receiving a bullet wound in the head and a shrapnel wound in the back. After successfully covering the withdrawal of his comrades, Godley destroyed his gun and threw the pieces into the canal. Godley's stout resistance won the admiration even of his enemies. As a prisoner-of-war he was invited by German officers to dine with them on Christmas Day. After the war Godley became a school caretaker and, as an active worker for service charities, delighted to dress up as Bruce Bairnsfather's cartoon hero, Old Bill, having a moustache of the extravagant dimensions required for the role.

Second Lieutenant Geoffrey Woolley (1892-1969), an old boy of Parmiter's School, who had been born in Bethnal Green, was the first Territorial Army officer to receive the VC. During the night of 20-21 April 1915, twenty-two-year-old Woolley, the sole officer commanding a handful of survivors of the 9th (County of London) battalion of the London Regiment (Queen Victoria's Rifles) successfully held the vantage point known as Hill 60 against repeated German onslaughts and under con-

tinuous shellfire. Woolley was later awarded the Military Cross and the newly-created Order of the British Empire and survived the war to become a schoolmaster.

In 1915 Stepney-born Corporal Alfred George Drake (1893-1915) was serving with the 8th battalion of the Rifle Brigade at La Brique in Belgium. Reconnoitring No Man's Land on the night of 23 November as a member of a four man patrol which was hit by machine-gun fire, Drake stayed with his wounded officer when another comrade withdrew, dragging the fourth man, also wounded, to safety. Rescuers later found the officer alive and bandaged but Drake had by then been killed protecting him.

Sergeant William Francis Burman (1897-1974), another Stepney man, also serving with the Rifle Brigade, was awarded his VC for single-handedly seizing an enemy machine-gun on 20 September 1917 during the battle of Passchendaele. When the advance of Burman's company was stalled by the withering fire of a German machine-gun Burman not only killed its operator but turned the gun on the enemy to cover the advance of his comrades. Fifteen minutes later Burman led two other men in outflanking a party of Germans enfilading his battalion. Between them they killed six of the enemy and captured two officers and twenty-nine other ranks. Sergeant Burman's medals are on public display in the Imperial War Museum.

AFTERMATH

In 1919 the popular Methodist minister W H Lax, then serving a turn as mayor of Poplar decided to organise a 'peace tea' for the children of the borough and in doing so invented the street party, which became an East End institution to mark national and especially royal celebrations. Less happily the year was blighted by attacks on black seamen in Canning Town, Limehouse, Poplar and Stepney, occasioned by fears of unemployment among discharged sailors. There were also riots in Brick Lane as 135 people were evicted to make way for the building of a cinema. In 1920 the Chapel House estate was built on the Isle of Dogs as an early and, as it was to prove, isolated response to Prime Minister Lloyd George's call for 'homes for heroes'.

Making a New World?

The brief re-stocking boom which followed the end of World War I began to turn into a slump by 1921, when the national rate of unemployment passed 10%. It would not fall below that figure again until 1940. The proliferation of pawnbrokers in the East End is a clear indicator of the precariousness of many households' incomes. In 1926 Bethnal Green had twelve pawnbrokers, Stepney twenty-one and Poplar twenty-five. The very titles of items dating from the inter-war period and now deposited in the Tower Hamlets Local History Archive are indicative of a quality of life that was more often to be endured than enjoyed – pamphlets on dealing with bedbugs, a syllabus for public health education, reports of the Poplar Borough Dispensary for the Prevention of Consumption and of the Council for the Promotion of Occupational Industries among the Physically Handicapped. Reports of school medical inspections show a dramatic decline in the number of children afflicted with lice and fleas compared with the period of Booth's investigations but the infant mortality rate was still twice as high in Bethnal Green as in rural Hampshire. Overcrowding was severe. In Stepney, Poplar and Bethnal Green alike between a fifth and a quarter of the population were living at a density of more than two persons per room – i.e. above the official definition of overcrowding. In Stepney this meant some fifty thousand people, of whom almost a third were living three to a room. And rooms in the East End were invariably much smaller than in other areas where there were similar levels of overcrowding, such as in Holborn or Paddington, where the houses had at least originally been built to bourgeois standards of comfort.

Poverty was particularly severe among old age pensioners, especially those living alone; and pensioners were increasing both in absolute numbers and as a proportion of the local population because those who could and did leave the East End were predominantly from the younger age groups. Apart from the trials of daily living there were still exceptional threats to life itself. The entire metropolis suffered during the influenza pandemic of 1919 which carried off more people world-wide than the Great War had. Bethnal Green also suffered an outbreak of smallpox in 1924. Poplar was hit by typhoid in 1922 and "an outbreak of illness due to water pollution" in 1927.

POPLARISM

As one of London's poorest boroughs Poplar was hit particularly hard by rising unemployment. In August 1921, when there were 62,000 dockworkers registered as available, the highest number working on any one day was 29,000. By 1922 when fewer than one in twenty people in England and Wales was in receipt of poor relief, in Poplar the figure was one in five. Relief scales in Poplar were above those of most other Boards of Guardians and set no maximum for a family, so families with very many children could actually be better off on relief. The leading personality of Poplar's Labour council, George Lansbury (1859-1940), had refused "to tax the poor to help the poor" and from March 1921 had in effect ordered the distribution as relief the portion of local rates which should have been forwarded to the LCC and other London-wide bodies to cover the borough's assessed share of the costs of providing policing and asylums. By doing so he drew attention to the injustice of a system whereby the poorest boroughs, suffering the highest rates of unemployment, were expected to bear the greatest burden of poor relief while least able to do so. In July 1921 the government took Poplar Council before the High Court and as a result thirty Poplar councillors were imprisoned, the men in Brixton, the women in Holloway. Huge crowds turned out to cheer them on their way to their confinement. Council meetings continued to be convened, the women councillors being ferried over to Brixton by taxi. Stepney and Bethnal Green followed Poplar's lead and refused to levy rates for the outside precepting bodies. After six weeks the rate rebels were released without having 'purged their contempt'. The hasty establishment of a pooled Metropolitan Common Poor Fund conceded their principal demand that the burden of relief should be shared more fairly between richer and poorer boroughs. When the Poplar Guardians continued to pay its 29,000 recipients above the maximum set by the new Fund an official enquiry denounced its failure

144. *A slum court in Whitechapel, c.1915.*

145. *Providence Place in Stepney, c.1909. The residents have clearly made an effort to look clean and cared for. There are no barefoot children. An up-ended coster's cart is at the end.*

to force the able-bodied to work in return for relief or to discriminate between the 'deserving' and 'undeserving'. It also revealed that the Guardians' Relief Committee had in addition distributed 13,245 pairs of free boots over the course of a year, as well as unmarked second-hand clothing which "could be pawned or sold without chance of detection." Even those who had been falsely claiming relief while actually earning had not been prosecuted, merely being warned and having their relief cancelled. The 800 inmates of the Poplar Workhouse, moreover, were being treated as though the institution was more "an almshouse than a workhouse",

where butter had replaced margarine in the official dietary scales at an extra cost of £600 a year. Of Poplar's annual relief expenditure of £229,000 it was recommended that £100,000 a year should be cut. The Guardians responded with a pamphlet cheerily entitled '*Guilty and Proud of It*', stating that "the duty of the members of the Board of Guardians is to be Guardians of the POOR and not Guardians of the interests of property..."

The Ministry of Health issued an official order prohibiting excess relief expenditures above the Metropolitan Common Poor Fund scale. Poplar ignored it, spending £2,000 a week

146. *George Lansbury, editor of the Daily Herald, Leader of the Labour Party and grandfather of actress Angela Lansbury.*

over the limit. Within a year the Guardians were facing a surcharge of £110,000. No steps were, however, taken to enforce it. Lansbury's stand and policies won him enormous local popularity. In 1922 he became Mayor of Poplar and MP for Bow and Bromley. But 'Poplarism' cost him a seat in the Cabinet of Labour's first ever government in 1924.

Poplar continued self-consciously to proclaim that its Council was "in every sense a progressive one" and in 1925 issued a pamphlet celebrating its achievements over the postwar years – three hundred new homes built, library membership up by two-thirds, five *mechanical* wash-houses opened and five thousand unemployed set to work building an open-air bathing pool, asphalting five miles of roads and planting two thousand roadside trees.

THE GREAT ESCAPE

The depressed state of the local economy of the East End prompted those who could to seek a better life elsewhere. Slum clearance programmes, commercial development and the pull of semi-detached dream homes in the suburbs displaced 650,000 people from Inner London between 1921 and 1939. Stepney's population fell from 249,657 in 1921 to 225,203 in 1931. The population of Bethnal Green fell from 108,000 in 1931 to 90,130 in 1939. The romantic and the resilient were drawn by the ambiguous allure of 'chalet land' to build themselves rural retreats that looked to less sympathetic eyes like sheds or shacks on waste plots in such Essex fastnesses as Pitsea, Laindon, Canvey Island or the more fancifully named Jaywick Sands. Those who aspired to home-ownership of a more substantial nature within commuting distance of jobs repaired to Ilford, which grew by 54% in the 1920s to reach 131,040, or to Chingford, which doubled its population in both inter-war decades to reach 40,000 by 1939. Woodford, Loughton and Buckhurst Hill were other nodes of rapid growth, thanks to the extension of the Central Line and the attractions of nearby Epping Forest. Prospering Jews favoured Gants Hill or took 'the NorthWest Passage' along the Northern Line to Finchley and Edgware. Those reliant on publicly-provided housing relocated to Britain's first 'new town', the world's then largest housing estate, Becontree, which sprawled across the borders of Dagenham, Barking and Ilford. Its sturdy cottage-style homes offered occupants the often unaccustomed luxury of electricity, a bathroom and a garden but to many these comforts and an abundance of open space could not compensate for the absence of street-markets, pubs and places of entertainment. A third of Becontree's new residents either returned to the East End or moved on elsewhere within a decade.

Emigration was accompanied by the disappearance of many familiar landmarks The former mental asylum at Bethnal Green, once known as Kirby Castle, was finally demolished in 1921. The London-Blackwall railway closed in 1926. Whitechapel's ancient hay market was terminated in 1928. In 1931 fire devastated the Queen's Hall of the People's Palace. The Royal National Lifeboat Institution closed its Broomfield Street premises in 1933. From 1934 onwards Stepney began to carry through a slum clearance programme which, among other areas, demolished Pennyfields, initiating a dispersal of its Chinese community which the Blitz would shortly complete. The Pavilion theatre closed and with it ended the provision of Yiddish drama. The expansion of Spitalfields market destroyed the Dorset Street area where the Ripper's last victim had died. As if in compensation the East End began to memorialise its own past. In 1927 a bust of William Booth was erected near the site where he first began his alfresco preaching career. In 1929 a Virginia Settlers Memorial was unveiled at Shadwell.

In-migration continued. Harry Pollitt arrived from Lancashire at the end of the war and found work repairing ships at Blackwall. Within a year he had become a trade union official, the first step on a ladder of ambition which would lead him to become secretary of the newly-founded Communist Party of Great Britain. Although most incomers of the inter-war period were attracted by the prospect of jobs offered by the booming factories of west London or domestic service in the smarter middle-class suburbs, such openings were not available to Bengali lascars from the impover-ished province of Sylhet who began to settle around Spitalfields in the 1920s and Whitechapel in the 1930s.

Despite these demographic driftings "some parts of London were more London than others", as Jerry White has neatly observed. Almost 90% of Bethnal Green residents were Londoners by birth and the figure for Poplar was almost as high. One peculiarly inward-looking community was to be found around Orchard Place at Bow Creek. Dating from the 1920s, it had been stigmatised by Booth as an "Alsatia for dock thieves ... as full of gossip and scandal as a village". The inter-married Scanlans, Lammins and Jeffries who still lived there in the 1930s were, however, doomed to dispersal when the LCC cleared the area on the eve of World War Two.

For those who remained there were compensations in the form of new amenities. Half the nation's population found distraction from the depression with a weekly visit to cinemas which were now purpose-built. The Rivoli cinema in Whitechapel Road opened in 1921 on the site of the former boxing venue known as Wonderland, the Troxy in Commercial Road in 1933 and in 1937 an Odeon was built on the former

147. Carvings by Eric Gill on the rebuilt People's Palace restate its Ruskinian inspiration.

site of Essex House, opposite Mile End station. In 1922 George V opened the Edward VII Memorial Park – overlooking the river at Shadwell on the site of a fish market which had failed to rival Billingsgate. Wickham's department store was rebuilt as a (brutally flawed) neo-Classical emporium in 1927. Poplar Baths were rebuilt in 1933-34. A new hall to replace the burned out one at the People's Palace was opened by King George VI as his first public engagement. In 1937 Poplar opened a new Town Hall in an assertive Art Deco style.

ESCAPE ARTISTS

York Hall baths opened in 1929 and became renowned as a boxing venue. The sport continued to play a prominent part in local life and the success of its local heroes was a source of communal pride. Sport and show business were unaffected by depression as avenues through which the talented could transcend the ghetto. The second generation of East European Jewish immigrants appeared to have talent in abundance.

Gershon Mendeloff, son of a cabinet-maker of 56 Umberston Street, St George-in-the-East, as the 'Aldgate Sphinx' had his first fight at fourteen and as featherweight Ted 'Kid' Lewis (1894-1970) became Britain's youngest ever boxing champion. The first boxer to wear a protective gumshield, Lewis in 1915 was the first Briton to win a world title in the USA when he became world welterweight champion by defeating the ironically named Jack Britton, whom he would meet in the ring on a further nineteen occasions. Renowned for his non-stop aggression, Lewis held thirteen other titles, fought 293 bouts in six weight divisions up to light heavyweight and won 215, 71 by knockouts. A friend of Charlie Chaplin, the spendthrift and open-handed Lewis was so politically naive that he went on the payroll of Sir Oswald Mosley's New Party as physical training instructor for his bodyguard. When Mosley's anti-Semitism finally became apparent to him Lewis resigned by knocking down both Mosley and his bodyguard.

Born in a court off Cable Street, Judah Bergman began his boxing career as a teenager at Premierland in Back Church Lane, Whitechapel. As Jack 'Kid' Berg (1909-91) he won the world junior welterweight title at twenty-one and then defended the title six times

in fifteen months in the USA. In 1934 the 'Whitechapel Windmill', became British lightweight champion. Berg continued fighting until 1945, then became a film stunt man. Over the course of 192 professional fights he won 157 (57 by K.O.), lost 26 and drew 9.

Born in Brick Lane the son of a Russian kosher butcher, Benjamin Levin (1893-77) attended the Jews' Free School and began his working life as a butcher's boy before making his stage debut at the Mile End Empire. As Issy Bonn he became an iconic crooner and comedian, invoked years after his active showbiz career had ended in *Goon Show* scripts and on the cover of the Beatles *Sergeant Pepper* album. A radio broadcaster from 1935 onwards, he also starred in two films and claimed to have sung over five hundred songs and sold over a million and a half records, being best known for *When the Lights Go On Again* and *My Yiddische Momma.* His observation that "to every problem there is a solution – if there is no solution, it's not a problem but a fact of life and you have to live with it" put him in the category of a Whitechapel Wittgenstein.

Bandleader Joe (Joshua Zalig) Loss (1909-1990) had an even longer career than Issy Bonn and was honoured with the MVO and OBE. Born the son of a cabinet-maker at 16 Grey Eagle Street, Spitalfields he won a scholarship to Trinity College of Music at thirteen and found his first professional work as a cinema violinist playing to silent films. He became Britain's youngest band leader at just twenty, EMI's longest serving artist, a great favourite with the Royal Family and a tireless worker for Age Concern as well as being instrumental in launching the careers of Vera Lynn, Eamonn Andrews, Spike Milligan and Michael Bentine.

The Winogradski family, which had emigrated from the Crimea to settle in Brick Lane in 1912, was living on the Boundary estate by 1914. Parents Isaac and Golda supplemented meagre earnings with occasional performances as singers at the Pavilion theatre. Their eldest son Lovat/Louis (1906-99) mastered English in six months but was barred from a scholarship at Parmiter's School because his father had not become a British national. Nevertheless the lad had his own Aldgate-based clothing company by the time he was sixteen and leisure to indulge in the latest dance craze. In 1926 he was hailed as 'Charleston Champion of the World'. In 1930 Louis Grad, as he then was, finally stabilized his name as Lew Grade, thanks to a Parisian mis-spelling of his name. In 1934 Lew became an impresario, as did his younger brothers, Leslie and Boris, who styled himself Bernard Delfont. In the post-war period they would refashion British popular entertainment.

Further distinguished contributions would be made to post-war British culture by younger Jewish talents who grew up in the inter-war East End – dramatists Bernard Kops and Wolf Mankowitz, character actor David Kossoff, polymath scholar and TV presenter Jacob Bronowski and Louis Heren, deputy editor of *The Times.*

OUTSIDER'S EYE

George Orwell's first published work, *Down and Out in Paris and London,* was based in part on the author's experiences exploring the East End. Ex-Etonian Orwell (1903-50), dressed as a tramp, spent nights in lodging-houses in Bow and Pennyfields, as well as in Salvation Army hostels. Compared with Paris, Orwell described the East End as "much cleaner and quieter and drearier ... less drunkenness and less dirt and less quarrelling and more idling.'' This was a retrospective opinion. Orwell's East End 'fieldwork' had been conducted in the autumn of 1927, following his resignation from the Burma police. He then went to Paris for two years and only began writing *Down and Out* in 1930. More than five years in the making, it was finally published in 1933. Being almost exclusively concerned with the plight of the totally indigent, Orwell's account throws little illumination on ordinary working-class life in the East End.

In *The Face of London* topographical writer Harold Clunn set out to present "a bird's-eye view of the growth, progress and development of the world's most wonderful city" as it appeared to him in 1931. An unabashed fan of the moderniser and the motor car, Clunn's breathlessly informative tone was habitually upbeat. In Wentworth Street he was, however, temporarily disoriented by its 'alien' atmosphere: "We almost seem to have taken leave of everything English ... we might just as well be in some street in Warsaw or Cracow." But his relentless optimism was soon rekindled by the sight of "a large demolition of courts and alleys" around Petticoat Lane and he speculated – presciently if prematurely "whether in the

course of time the East End will develop into some high-class business quarter as important in a different way as even Westminster or the Strand."

Clunn's scarcely-veiled anti-Semitism surfaced again around Whitechapel: "during the last ten years the Jewish problem ... has become much less acute, since the inflow has now been stopped ..." Brick Lane, however, impressed him as "a kind of East End Bond Street ... Some of its shop-fronts and window-displays would do credit to a West End thoroughfare." Limehouse, perhaps predictably, roused reactions in Clunn similar to those provoked by Wentworth Street:

> "many of the side streets are inhabited almost entirely by Orientals and contain foreign restaurants and drinking shops hardly suitable for unaccompanied tourists ... the population consists of Chinese, Lascars, Maltese and a few Japanese ... Opium dens and fan-tan saloons still exist, despite the vigilance of the police but it is not wise for the visitor to see these establishments from the inside."

William Kent, author of a fact-packed *Ency-*

148. *George Orwell. Photo by Felix Mann, c.1949.*

clopaedia of London, published in 1937, was equally judgmental beneath a veneer of objectivity. Bethnal Green he dismissed as "grimy and dismal", relieved only by being "lively with retail trade". Kent likewise shared Clunn's acute unease at the 'alien' character of parts of the East End, explicitly contrasting Stepney with Poplar. Stepney he summarised as

> "a borough of innumerable small industries, largely carried on by Jews (their synagogues are everywhere) ... The Roman Catholics are strong in Stepney ... Limehouse Causeway is the High Street of London's Chinatown – as the names over the shops reveal."

In Poplar, by contrast, "the population, unlike that of Stepney, is predominantly British and there is none of that sordid slum feature still to be seen in Stepney ... There is general breeziness; there is an astonishing number of respectable old houses; there are not a few quiet nooks; and the public houses are small and homely."

The urbane Paul Cohen-Portheim, author *of The Spirit of London* (1935) perhaps caught the paradoxical relationship between place and people better than most British observers, judging the East End to be "one of the most mysterious places in the world but of most prosaic aspect." Lacking the "picturesque squalor" of the poorest quarters of Parts, "it looks mean and drab and this impression is chiefly due to lack of height in its buildings. Apart from the great main roads it is just a maze of alleys of low little houses of darkened brick." Redemption was to be found in the inhabitants – "It is the people who give interest to the East End streets." Unlike most parts of London, where the inhabitants "vanish into their houses", the East-Enders "promenade", as Parisians do, even if the word itself was unknown to them. Speculating that the cause might lie just as much in the "lack of comfort and charm" to be found in the home as much as in love of street life itself, Cohen-Portheim, a former Great War internee who bore no grudges, celebrated the 'alien' elements which so unsettled English writers:

> "One explanation ... is the preponderance of the foreign element, amongst which the Jews predominate, and these Eastern Jews adore the life and light, bustle and noise of their Whitechapel Road. On Saturday nights, particularly, it is thronged with people parading

up and down; there is, in fact, a Corso in progress. I know of nothing quite like it in the more purely English popular parts of London ... Certainly the Whitechapel Road, with its smart if cheaply turned-out girls and the youths with their gaudy scarves and caps, does remain in one's mind ..."

Insider perspectives on the inter-war East End are to be found, not in guidebooks but in Jewish proletarian novels and works of autobiography and reminiscence, such as Simon Blumenfeld's *Jew Boy* (1935) and Willy Goldman's *East End My Cradle* (1940) or the retrospective evocations of Bernard Kops's *The World is a Wedding* (1963), Emmanuel Litvinoff's *A Journey Through a Small Planet* (1972) and Chaim Bermant's *Point of Arrival* (1975).

CARING FOR THE COMMUNITY
Battered by economic misfortune and bled of enterprising spirits seeking salvation elsewhere, the East End continued to offer limitless scope for the exercise of compassion.

Muriel Lester of Kingsley Hall, serving on Poplar council, campaigned successfully for the provision of free milk for infants and dental care for women. In 1923 H G Wells came to open the Children's House in Bruce Road, as an adjunct of Kingsley Hall. Its foundation stones proclaimed the importance of the ideals embodied in the Lesters' holistic creed: Vision, Nature, Rhythm, Music, Beauty, Health, Education, Motherhood, Fellowship and Internationalism. During the General Strike of 1926 the Lesters opened a soup kitchen for the strikers and their families. In 1928 a new purpose-built Kingsley Hall was opened in Powis Road, Bromley-by-Bow. The well-wishers who had laid symbolic bricks are a testimony to the Lesters' talent for networking and the regard in which their work was held; they included the actress Sybil Thorndike (Drama), composer Sir Walford Davies (Music) and novelist John Galsworthy (Literature). The brick representing architecture was appropriately laid by the designer of the building, Charles Cowles Voysey. Muriel had by that date befriended Gandhi, who stayed at Kingsley Hall for three months in 1931 while attending the Round Table conference which had been convened to discuss greater internal self-government for India. In 1936 the Hall provided accommodation for the Jarrow Hunger Marchers.

Mary Hughes (1860-1941), daughter of the

author of *Tom Brown's Schooldays*, came to live in the East End in 1895 and became associated with the work of Kingsley Hall in 1915. Following no systematic programme she subsequently "went about doing good" in a totally non-judgmental way. In 1926 this "friend of all in need" opened the Dewdrop Inn in a former pub at 71 Vallance Road as centre for the homeless and hapless, living there until her death.

Toynbee Hall continued to make its own distinctive contributions under the leadership of the irrepressible Irish Mancunian Jimmy Mallon (1875-1961). In 1929 the Youth Hostels' Association was launched there. The concept of children's theatre was pioneered under its auspices. A summer seminar for American community workers became a regular feature. Mallon's contacts ranged from Lady Astor to George Bernard Shaw. A fund-raiser he put on in 1938 was able to call on the talents of Constant Lambert, Frederick Ashton and Rex Harrison.

Born in Whitechapel in 1892 Dr Emmanuel Miller pioneered the treatment of 'psychological maladjustment' among children and in 1927 founded the East London Child Guidance Clinic – Britain's first – at the Jewish Hospital on Stepney Green. In 1930 Miller published *Modern Psychotherapy* and later presented a BBC series on 'How the Mind Works in the Child'. Dr Jonathan Miller, the theatre director and broadcaster, is his son.

The role of Thomas Becket in the film version of T S Eliot's *Murder in the Cathedral* was played by an Australian Anglo-Catholic of imposing height and mien, whose performance was applauded by *Variety* as "impressive amid the welter of wordage" Being impressive amid various kinds of welter would serve as an appropriate judgment on the career of Father St John Beverley Groser (1890-1966), the archetype, if not a reincarnation, of the original 'turbulent priest'. Arriving in the East End in 1922 as curate at St Michael's, Poplar, Groser got to know local trade unionists and Communists by allowing them to meet in his rooms in Teviot Street. During the General Strike of 1926 he had his arm broken by the police as they broke up a dockers' meeting outside Poplar Town Hall. As a consequence Groser's clerical licence was temporarily revoked but in 1928 he was invited to take over run-down Christ Church, Watney Street, then under threat of demolition. His success in rebuilding its congregation won its

reprieve. Groser rapidly became one of the best known priests in the East End and by 1938 was being invited to preach in Canterbury Cathedral.

William Lax (1868-1937), minister of Poplar Methodist Church in East India Dock Road from 1902 until his death, also featured in a film. Himself convinced of the potential value of film as a medium for teaching and mission Lax ran his own shows and was featured in the first film J Arthur Rank ever made, *The Mastership of Christ,* a twenty minute documentary through which Rank, an ardent but ineffectual propagator of the gospel, celebrated the powers of a gifted one. The community saluted him in its own way. Lax's Methodist church was universally referred to as just that – Lax's.

BEATING THE BLACKSHIRTS

The first East End branches of Sir Oswald Mosley's British Union of Fascists were formed in Bow and Bethnal Green in 1934, over a year after the movement's foundation. The attraction of the East End was that, alongside self-evident concentrations of poverty, the area also had almost half Britain's Jewish population, mostly concentrated in a couple of square miles, an irresistible attraction for a movement which had by then become overtly anti-Semitic and added the cognomen National Socialist to its official name. Jews were repeatedly denounced as the prime or sole cause of many of the afflictions so evident in the East End – unemployment, sweatshop working conditions, rack-renting, overcrowding, infectious diseases, criminality etc. Protests against anti-Semitic graffiti, threatening behaviour and provocative recruiting marches were made by four local MPs but failed to elicit police action. Indeed, many believed that the police, warning off hecklers, were actually protecting the fascists.

When Mosley proclaimed that the biggest ever BUF march would be held on 4 October 1936 to mark the fourth anniversary of its foundation the mayors of Bethnal Green, Stepney, Poplar, Hackney and Shoreditch went to the Home Office to urge – in vain – that it should be banned. A mass-petition organised by the Jewish People's Council against Fascism and presented by Father Groser had no more success.

On the Sunday appointed the Blackshirts assembled in military formation in the historic shadow of the Tower of London, intending to march through and hold street meetings in Limehouse, Bow, Bethnal Green and Shoreditch. Protected by 6,000 constables representing a third of the total strength of the Metropolitan Police, as well as by its entire mounted division, the would-be marchers, despite repeated police baton charges, became stalled at Gardiner's Corner at Aldgate while further police battled vainly to force an alternative way through to Wapping via barricaded Cable Street. Defeated by a hail of bricks, stones, bottles and marbles, the police cancelled the march after a three-hour confrontation and marched the fascists westwards to ignominious dispersal along the Embankment.

Conflicting historical myth attributes the fascist defeat alternately to a well coordinated conspiracy of Communist outsiders or to the spontaneous uprising of the entire local community, united in righteous anti-racist anger. In fact the Communist party, as a party, was far less important than it later claimed to be, having been going through a phase of seeking political respectability by restraining its mem-

bers from indulging in street brawls. Individual local Communists undoubtedly did play a prominent part in the resistance, as did Labour party and trade union activists, both of whom had been advised by their respective institutions to leave matters to the police; but the most significant organisations to be involved were the Independent Labour Party, which had broken away from Labour in 1932, and the Jewish Ex-Servicemen's Association.

Nor did outside *agents provocateurs* play a sinister directive role as sections of the right-wing press alleged. The overwhelming majority of the eighty-odd persons arrested were nabbed within a mile or so of their own homes. Total communal anti-fascist solidarity is also a myth. Jews were certainly prominent among the resisters as were Irish and Somali dockers. But there was local and persisting, if limited and localised, working-class support for the BUF. A week after the confrontation of 4 October Fascists were able to get away with smashing the windows of Jewish shops along the Mile End Road and assaulting vulnerable

149. *Planned in 1979 and completed in 1993, the Cable Street mural is based on photographs of the confrontation and incorporates portraits of individuals who took part. It was defaced with paint and graffiti several times before its completion.*

Jews. MI5 reported that up to two thousand new recruits joined the BUF after 'the battle of Cable Street'. In the 1937 LCC elections the Fascists polled a fifth of the vote in three districts, coming second in Bethnal Green. The Public Order Act, hastily passed in the aftermath of Cable Street, banned the wearing of political uniforms and strengthened police powers over public demonstrations. But it failed to stop the BUF from turning out in force in Bermondsey in 1937, provoking similar resistance from another huge assemblage of locals, of whom far more were Irish than Jewish. Once again there were baton charges and barricades. Once again Mosley's intended line of march was frustrated.

Local Labour councils probably had an impact by denying Fascists access to meeting-places and banning the use of loudspeakers in public parks. But it was the war which led to the internment of Mosley and some eight hundred of his hard core followers as Hitlerian jackals rather than the super-patriots they claimed to be, that really finished off the Fascists. An autobiographical account of these troubled times can be found in *Out of the Ghetto*, a memoir by Joe Jacobs, who was expelled from Stepney's Communist party in 1938.

BEATING THE LANDLORDS

Despite the survival of some owner-occupiers, the provision of 'model' accommodation by charities and the growth of council tenancies, most East Enders rented their homes from private landlords. Rent was the first call on the weekly income and a fully paid-up rent book was a badge of honour in the battle to show that a household was 'managing'. Tenants often knew only their rent-collector, rather than their actual landlord, who might be anything from a giant property company to the proverbial widow depending on a single decaying dwelling that might be her only asset and source of income. The rent on some houses was controlled by legislation originally introduced to combat war-time inflation. In 1933 the National Government decontrolled rents on larger (class A) houses but decreed their maintenance on the rest until 1938. Most East Enders lived in the lowest (class C) type which therefore remained controlled – unless a tenancy changed hands. Many landlords rushed to exploit this condition, registering Class C properties, as having

been thus decontrolled and facing the tenant with the task and cost of disproving this. Communal rather than individual action by aggrieved tenants could self-evidently be more effective through spreading costs and sharing information. In 1937 a tenants' defence league was formed in Poplar. Within eighteen months its eight hundred members had secured £1,395 in rent reductions, £717 in repayments for overcharging and numerous long-delayed repairs. The neighbouring Stepney league claimed in half that time to have cut rent rolls by £18,400 a year and extracted nearly £14,000 in repayments. These victories, however, applied to tenants who could successfully prove controlled status. The grievances of the decontrolled began to erupt in a series of rent strikes in the summer of 1938, assisted by local Communists whose prestige had been raised by their perceived – or claimed – role in fighting local fascism.

The first major confrontation was at Quinn Square, Bethnal Green where the occupants of 346 flats shared outside taps (one between four flats) and lavatories (one between two). The attempted eviction of a woman who was eventually proved to have been long overcharged for a controlled tenancy provided the *casus belli*. Forming a tenants' association, the occupants of Quinn Square proposed new rent scales to the company owning their block. When it rejected them the tenants refused to pay any rents. The company capitulated in a fortnight.

The Quinn Square victory galvanized Stepney where a borough-wide Tenants' Defence League was led by Fr Groser, as president, and Communist Tubby Rosen, as secretary. Co-ordinated street by street rent strikes forced a succession of 'collective agreements' from landlords – until C & G Estates Ltd. refused to come to terms with the 320 tenants of Langdale and Brady Mansions. A twenty-one week rent strike ensued. Activists were served with, and ignored, notices to quit. Court orders were treated likewise. On 27 June 1939 bailiffs with police support evicted five families with their furniture. As word spread men left their work and a crowd of thousands gathered. By evening the families were reinstalled and the police station was under siege. The Bishop of Stepney's intervention then allowed the company to negotiate its way out of the impasse by agreeing to cut decontrolled rents and pledging an immediate £2,500 on repairs. Stepney celebrated for a week.

THE PEOPLE'S WAR

In 1938 an eyewitness watching the filling of sandbags at Bethnal Green noted "such an air of gaiety and so many sightseers that the atmosphere was ... more akin to children playing ... than to the potential horrors of total war." Bethnal Green was to suffer over a thousand casualties. The mayor of Stepney later confessed that "ARP had been looked upon as a joke." Stepney would lose 747 civilian dead. Fortunately the LCC organised a small-scale practice evacuation of school-children in 1938, from 'which many valuable lessons were learned so that at least chaos was minimised when mass-evacuation was required in the autumn of 1939. The Jews' Free School in Bell Lane departed and never returned to the East End, being refounded in Camden Town over a decade later.

In fact bombs did not begin to fall on the East End until 24 August 1940. The Blitz proper began on 'Black Saturday', 7 September when Beckton gasworks became London's first civilian target and the docks at Limehouse were hit. A quirk of geography, of which the East Ender might be largely unaware at street-level, made the area peculiarly vulnerable. While a major provincial city like Sheffield could erect a dummy town on neighbouring hills to deceive Luftwaffe pilots the sheer size of London made it almost impossible to miss or mistake the massive and distinctive U-shaped bend of the River Thames round the Isle of Dogs which provided a recognition and aiming point right at the heart of the docklands and constituted the enemy's prime strategic target. That so many transport facilities, factories and homes were clustered around the docklands as their prime *raison d'être* was an added bonus.

The Metropolitan Commissioner of Police recorded encouragingly on 12 September that "... there is no sign of panic in the East End ... the inhabitants are shaken by lack of sleep but no sign of panic and no rush to evacuate. No defeatist talk." Mass-Observation reporters, by contrast, concluded that

> "The whole story of the last weekend has been one of unplanned hysteria ... the press versions of life going on normally in the East End on Monday are grotesque. There was no bread, no electricity, no milk, no gas, no telephones ... The press version of people's smiling jollity and fun are gross exaggeration. On no previous investigation has so little humour, laughter or whistling been recorded."

On 15 September Communist activist Phil Piratin led a hundred East Enders to the Savoy hotel and successfully demanded admission to its shelter – though the cessation of enemy action after a quarter of an hour was followed by their rather anti-climactic departure. Tory backbencher and man of letters Harold Nicolson noted in his diary on 17 September "Everyone is worried about the feeling in the East End ... There is much bitterness. It is said that even the King and Queen were booed the other day when they visited the destroyed areas." If they were, it didn't deter them from coming back repeatedly. Writing in 1969 historian Angus Calder would observe that "had the East End lost all heart, the chain reaction might have crippled London's morale. This nearly happened, but not quite, and after a few days the attack shifted noticeably westward."

Further major assaults concentrating on the East End were mounted on 15/16 October and 15/16 November 1940 and 19/20 March, 19/20 April, 10/11 May and 27/28 July 1941. The March raid – 'the Wednesday' involved an aerial armada of five hundred bombers which started almost two thousand fires, killed 750 people and seriously injured 1,200 more. During the April attack a direct hit on Old Palace School at Bromley-by-Bow killed thirty-four firemen using it as a. temporary headquarters, the worst single fatal incident involving firefighters of the entire war. The May onslaught set over two thousand fires blazing. These raids severely damaged or destroyed seventeen churches in Poplar and Stepney alone. Burdett Road station was blitzed out of existence.

The attentions of the Luftwaffe were largely diverted to the Russian front from 1941 but many East Enders continued to occupy shelters or the tube by night, for reasons elaborated by an investigator employed by Mass Observation:

> "people don't go to the tubes merely for extra safety ... some who went for shelter ... found ... not only shelter but a whole new life in a new society ... where they could start from scratch and for the first time in their lives make a name for themselves and shine in their social group. Others came from solitary bedsitting rooms with a gas ring and found they could spend

150. *Normality in the Blitz – a family sits down to a
meal with a backdrop of bomb damage.*

evenings in light and gaiety ... Harassed housewives found that they could halve their house-
work if the family spent the main part of its
leisure time - i.e. the time when it makes the
most mess and wants the most food - some-
where other than in the home. The trouble of
preparing sandwiches ... was ... small compared with the work they would otherwise have
to do ... Some found themselves possessed of
unsuspected talents for organising ... which for
the first time found scope and appreciation."

But it was a panic-stricken flight for sheer
physical safety that caused the worst single
British civilian disaster of the entire war, taking
the lives of 27 men, 84 women and 62 children,
who were crushed or suffocated on the steps of
Bethnal Green Underground station as they
rushed for shelter on Wednesday, 3 March 1943.
The panic was caused not by enemy action, but
by the sudden and unannounced test firing of
a battery of sixty anti-aircraft rockets secretly
assembled in nearby Victoria Park and tragi-
cally mistaken for hostile fire.

The first V-bomb to fall on London exploded
at Grove Road, Mile End on 13 June 1944. On
27 March 1945 the last V-2 to hit the capital

demolished Hughes Mansions in Vallance
Road, killing 134 residents, almost all of them
Jewish. Poplar, East India Dock Road, reput-
edly achieved the unenviable distinction of
being Britain's most bombed passenger station.
Damaged beyond repair by a V-bomb in 1944,
it was demolished in 1947; the site is now
occupied by All Saints DLR station. Bow station was also destroyed irreparably in 1944.

Despite the Blitz the East End contributed
significantly to the sinews of war. The
Chisenhale Works at Old Ford made cockpit
interiors for Spitfires and Hurricanes. The
historic Whitechapel Bell Foundry switched
from bells to castings. Components of the D-
day Mulberry harbours were assembled in the
East India Dock and at London Yard in Cubitt
Town, where motor torpedo boats were also
repaired. In December 1941 Bethnal Green
challenged Bermondsey to a waste-paper col-
lecting competition.

In this, 'the People's War', civilian morale
and involvement were recognised as crucial to
victory. The Whitechapel Art Gallery organised a reassuring 'Might of Britain' exhibition
of photographs in the spring of 1940 but of-

151. Sixty years on – local schoolchildren investigate the War Memorial in Tower Hamlets cemetery.

fered nothing comparable again until the tide of conflict began to turn in 1943 when it put on 'Wings of Victory', 'Artists Aid Jewry' and 'Stepney Reconstruction Plans'; in 1944 came 'Salute the Soldier' and a photographic tribute to three Russian cities. The Bethnal Green Museum was converted into a public restaurant serving a thousand shilling meals a day, as well as preparing food for schools. Less happily the Heavy Rescue Service took over Davenant Foundation School and inflicted irreparable damage, vandalising honours boards to cover broken shop windows and destroying much of the school's archive.

Individuals as much as institutions 'did their bit'. Sculptor Henry Moore immortalised the exhausted denizens of shelterers in East End Underground stations in a series of pencil drawings which have since attained iconic status – to the extent that it is easily forgotten that most civilians preferred to take their chances in their own homes.

Comediennes Elsie (1894-1990) and Doris Waters (1904-78), both born in Bromley-by-Bow, toured for ENSA in their stage incarnations as 'Gert and Daisy' and did invaluable propaganda work on the radio for the Ministry of Food. The ubiquitous Father Groser won the admiration of government ministers for organ-

ising relief for bombed-out families. Kingsley Martin, editor of the left-wing *New Statesman,* hailed Groser as "the happiest example of a priestly saint". Maverick Tory MP Robert Boothby, then Under-Secretary to the Ministry of Food, recalled Groser in his memoirs as a "dominant figure ... He never failed. He seemed to be everywhere all the time." Dr Hannah Billig MBE (1901-87) – 'the Angel of Cable Street' – was awarded the George Medal for her untiring efforts in tending victims of bombing. Sergeant Maurice Rogers (1919-44) was awarded a posthumous VC for taking out two enemy machine-gun posts at Anzio single-handed in June 1944.

By 1945 just under 20% of the East End had been laid waste, compared with 5% 'up West'. Of Stepney's 34,000 homes over 32,000 were more or less seriously damaged. Of Poplar's 25,000 dwellings just one escaped unscathed. The Port of London was Britain's most consistently bombed civilian target but its docks were never closed down. The displacement of much of the population through evacuation and enemy action, however, accelerated a demographic decline already in progress, while the destruction of workplaces in particular hastened the contraction of the area's manufacturing base.

No New Jerusalem

The comprehensive destruction wrought upon the East End by the king's enemies at least opened the theoretical possibility of reconstruction and renewal on an equally far-reaching scale. In 1946 the LCC did indeed accept the designation of a Stepney-Poplar Comprehensive Development Area which envisaged a thirty-year timetable for the demolition and replacement of some 1,300 acres of buildings, housing 75,000 people. In the same year the extension of the Central Line from Liverpool Street to Stratford opened up a major new transport axis. In 1951 the Lansbury estate in Poplar was built as the 'living architecture' showpiece of the Festival of Britain but proved too far from the event's South Bank site to attract the hoped-for hordes of admiring visitors. The reality of East End life proved to be less resurgence than continued depopulation. The foundation of the East London History Society in 1952 in retrospect seems strangely prescient in the light of the rapid disappearance of much of the life its members would set themselves to chronicle or recapture. Raymond Mortimer's 1950 revision of Paul Cohen-Portheim's *The Spirit of London* noted the virtual extinction of the Limehouse Chinatown:

> "it was always insignificant and now there is not much of it left; Limehouse Causeway has been largely bomb-obliterated; there and in Pennyfields there are some nondescript Oriental shops and mean restaurants, but the Chinese population wear European dress and it is hard to believe that opium smoking or anything sinister is going on behind those small tight-closed doors. There are expanses of rubble-strewn waste from which rise large blocks of brand-new workmen's dwellings. As an area Chinatown is more than ever a failure and a disappointment even if a visit to it may still be included in sightseeing motorcoach itineraries."

By contrast the emphasis in *Family and Kinship in East London* was on the continuing prevalence, significance and durability of family relationships among the white working-class community of Bethnal Green. Published in 1957, the book was based on 933 interviews conducted by Peter Willmott and Michael Young.

Young (1915-2002), founder of the Institute of Community Studies, which had its headquarters in Victoria Square in Bethnal Green, had been responsible for drafting the 1945 Labour manifesto and would go on to found the Consumers' Association and the Open University. The study would become a sociological classic and prescribed reading on university campuses for over a quarter of a century. The authors emphasised the central importance of the bond between mothers and their married daughters both to the emotional solidarity and the practical welfare of the extended family. They also demonstrated that the prevalent housing and planning policies of the decade, physically epitomised by the high-rise housing block, were antithetical to the needs and wishes of the people they were supposed to benefit. The mother-daughter bond was likewise undermined by the process of relocation by which many former East End residents, especially young marrieds, were resettled in post-war New Towns such as Harlow or Basildon or to the LCC estates at Debden (Loughton), Harold Hill (Romford) or Oxhey (Watford}.

This outward movement from the East End reflected a general trend common to the entire capital. Inner London's 1951 population was still 15% down on its 1939 level. By 1971 it had dropped by a further 17%, and by 1981 it was down to 2,350,000 – half what it had been in 1901. Bethnal Green's population, which stood at 60,500 in 1948, had already dropped to 58,000 in 1951 and 53,960 by 1955. By 1981 it was a mere 30,000. Although this was in fact part of a much broader shake-up affecting the structure of government across the entire metropolis the creation of the London Borough of Tower Hamlets by the amalgamation of the previously separate boroughs of Stepney, Bethnal Green and Poplar in 1965 could also be seen as a necessary act of rationalisation in the face of communal erosion.

At the same time as the population of the East End was contracting it was also becoming even more multi-ethnic. The exodus of many Jews doubtless contributed to the closure of *Die Zeit* in 1950 and of the Pavilion Theatre in 1962. The reclusive cabalistic scholar David Rodinsky who suddenly and inexplicably disappeared from his upstairs room at 19 Princelet Street in the 1960s seems strangely symbolic of this process of ethnic self-erasure. West Indian settlement around Cable Street was estimated at around 450 in 1951 and was blamed for making the area notorious for prostitution and drug-dealing. Race relations were further aggravated by competition for housing in the decade after the war when accommodation was at a premium.

Former Bengali seamen had been living in the Brick Lane area since the 1920s. In 1956 a Dhaka travel agent opened for business in Sandys Row off Petticoat Lane. In 1961 the (then) Pakistani population of Stepney amounted to only 800. An anti-Asian riot took place in Brick Lane in 1970. By 1991 Spitalfields and its environs would be home to some 38,000 Bangladeshis, as they had been redesignated by the break-up of Pakistan in 1971.

Demographic decline was matched by instances of cultural contraction. The Poplar Hippodrome was demolished in 1950. In 1958 Christ Church, Spitalfields had to be closed as unsafe – it would remain semi-derelict for two decades until the Spitalfields renaissance kick-started its reclamation. Lacking a willing purchaser in either the Antipodes or British Columbia, Captain Cook's house in the Whitechapel Road was knocked down in 1959. The demolition of Poplar workhouse in Stoneyard Lane the following year marked the closure of another historical chapter, doubtless with little regret. In 1963 the Troxy cinema became the London Opera Centre, a reincarnation which saved it from demolition until it achieved Grade II listing in 1991 and restoration as a bingo hall. The less architecturally distinguished Odeon, Mile End closed in 1976 and was demolished to make way for a post-modern office building. In the same year the historic church of St Matthias, Poplar closed and in the following year St Bartholomew the Less, Bethnal Green was converted into flats.

If literally dozens of places of worship were amalgamated or demolished altogether there were at least a few distinguished replacements. In 1954 St Mary and St Joseph's RC church was rebuilt to the designs of the architect Adrian Gilbert Scott. St Paul's, Burdett Road, consecrated in 1960 and designed by Robert Maguire, would be hailed by critic Ian Nairn as "the one worthwhile new church in a city-region of ten millions". Structured around a top-lit central altar, the building was entered through an almost detached porch proclaiming "This is the Gate of Heaven." St Paul's would be des-

152. *The Foundation of St Katherine, Butcher's Row – the memorial plaque honours Father Groser.*

ignated a Grade II* building in 1988. Maguire, whose first building this had been, became head of Oxford's School of Architecture.

There were also some positive counter-currents in the spiritual life of the locality. In 1948 the Royal Foundation of St Katherine moved to Butcher Row, Stepney. In 1958 Bromley-by-Bow church and community centre in Bruce Road reopened although it was only decades later, under the dynamic leadership of the Revd Andrew Mawson, that it would spawn a vigorous programme of activities, a state-of-the-art health centre and the Pie-in-the-Sky café while attracting the active interest and support of Diana, Princess of Wales and Cherie Booth, wife of Prime Minister Tony Blair. In 1965 R D Laing established the Philadelphia Association as a 'therapeutic community' at Kingsley Hall. Loosely described by the media as a controversial American psychiatrist, Laing was in fact an anti-psychiatrist who denied the reality of mental illness and not only tolerated but encouraged what many local residents considered bizarre and even offensive behaviour in his charges. When Laing moved on after five years he left Kingsley Hall more or less comprehensively trashed. Its reinstatement would wait upon its use as an historically authentic set in the making of Richard

Attenborough's bio-pic of the life of Gandhi.

The East End also showed that it could still attract a 'turbulent priest' when in 1968 the uncompromising anti-apartheid campaigner Trevor Huddlestone became suffragan Bishop of Stepney. His successor a decade later, 'Big Jim' Thompson, would also become nationally known through his commonsensical contributions to Radio Four's *Thought for the Day* slot and locally known for his efforts to promote inter-faith dialogue and to combat racism.

GAIN AND LOSS

Much rehousing was achieved. By 1972 54% of the dwellings in Tower Hamlets had been built since 1945. But it was not only squalor that disappeared with the slums that the new high-rises replaced. In the 1960s the topographical artist Geoffrey Fletcher set out with his sketch-book "to record some carefully chosen portions of the East End before they are wiped out." The result was *Pearly Kingdom* (1965), whose arch title belied its anger. In a passionate Introduction to his impressionistic illustrations Fletcher denounced the relentless 'redevelopment' creating "happy homes for healthy State controlled people, who, no doubt, would prefer to be left alone." The outcome was the dissolution of "the old closely knit life of the East End", which Fletcher blamed on "an army of welfare workers ... social observers, planners and all the sickening busybodies who flourish under the dreary conditions of post-war England." The physical expression of their endeavours could be seen in "blocks of flats, utterly at variance with the old East End, lawns that are piebald before the turves have knitted together, abstract sculpture, play areas, useless mural decorations, community centres, centres for the aged, centres for discussions ... The old familiar monotony of seemingly endless streets, all apparently identical, is being replaced by a new monotony of giant blocks of a barrenness considerably more chilling than the old humble streets, mean as they undoubtedly were". On the other hand Fletcher could not but note the impact of a prosperity undreamed of in the 1930s – the disappearance of scarecrow children and secondhand clothes dealers, of soleless shoes and bread and dripping, of sodden drunkenness and wife-beating, of costermongers and gin-palaces, free dispensaries and oyster stalls. Pawnbrokers had given way to betting-shops, donkey-carts to cars and

motor scooters. Nevertheless, inspired by the 1960s craze for 'package tours' abroad, Fletcher still thought enough of the past survived for him to indulge a whimsical flight of fancy regarding the possibilities of basing one in an East End doss house, with

"tours of Peabody flats ... meals ... taken at a selection of Yiddish restaurants, cheap caffs, coffee stalls and the like. Docks, warehouses and former music halls would add to the delights ... One of the highlights would be a visit to the Abbey Mills Pumping Station ... Optional extras ... would include mildewy church halls, the Jack the Ripper area, a day in Cable Street and a leisurely inspection of the remaining Victorian lavatories...".

Idiosyncratic architectural critic Ian Nairn, writing in 1966, came to much the same conclusion:

"Of all the things done to London this century, the soft spoken, this-is-good-for-you castration of the East End is the saddest. All the raucous, homely places go and are replaced by well-designed estates which would fit a New Town but are hopelessly out of place here. This is a

153. Featured as a case-study in the Life of Grime TV series this tower block on the Crossways estate was proposed in 2004 for a fast-track, hi-tech makeover.

154. The closing of London Docks, Wapping, May 9, 1969. Oil by Charles Hardaker,1969.

hive of individualists and the last place to be subjected to this kind of large-scale planning. Fragments survive and the East Enders are irrepressible – and no doubt satisfied by the undoubted increase in material amenities; but they could have had so much more, so easily."

In his 1979 study of *The Streets of East London* Bill Fishman likewise denounced the extent to which reconstruction had led to deconstruction:

> "a crime has been committed against the past
> ... the little streets and their ancient communities have fallen before the demolishers – a development now recognised, too late, as an error... Dirt piles high in the crumbling streets. Why clean up when the bulldozer is on the march? And the waste-land continues to extend itself as the rubble heaps replace the cosy ... brick structures, which once nurtured the same families for generations."

DEMISE OF THE DOCKS

On the eve of World War Two London was still the greatest port in the world with docks generating employment for 100,000 people, over 30,000 of whom were actually employed by the Port of London Authority itself. Following the repair of war damage a major strike in 1949 showed that the dockers had lost none of their traditional militancy. London's docks reached their peak of activity, in terms of volume of goods handled, in the early 1960s, when sixty million tons passed through them each year. The Borough of Stepney's official Guide still proudly boasted that it was "probably the world's most highly developed trading centre." At that time and into the following decade it was generally assumed that the docks would continue to expand in capacity and, implicitly, in extent. Major infra-structural improvements appeared to confirm this assumption. In 1958 a new power station opened on the site of the former Brunswick Hotel. 1967 witnessed the opening of a second Blackwall tunnel and the

were costly wharfside warehouses as goods inside containers required neither further protection nor security. At the same time specialised vessels were built for transporting containers and built to such a scale that they became far too large to penetrate right upstream to the heart of the city. Specialised facilities for handling containers and bulk products like cement were developed downstream at Tilbury and along the east coast at Felixstowe and Lowestoft, sites where there was room for expansion and the possibility of recruiting non-union labour unattached to traditional practices. Unsurprisingly the strongly unionised dockers proved themselves to be a bastion of unyielding conservatism in the face of these changes. Resistance to rationalisation even extended to the maintenance of the traditional twice-daily 'call-on' for work right up until 1967, just a year before dock closures began. A major strike against containerisation in 1972 proved as futile as it was damaging. Dock closures were inevitable as even the dockers' best known spokesman, the Communist Jack Dash, admitted privately, even while his famed combination of rogueish rhetoric and intransigence continued to make the headlines.

The contraction of cargo-handling was accompanied by a broader trend of deindustrialisation, although this, too, was certainly not anticipated in the locality. In 1958 a list of Stepney industries included marine- and auto-engineering, sailmaking, the manufacture of machine tools, surgical instruments, bottles, paints, plastics, paperboard, veneers, chemicals, sugar, beer and asbestos, as well as the typical smaller-scale East End trades of clothing, printing and cabinet-making. Local specialisms included the manufacture of industrial sewing-machines, factory stools and tropical helmets. The borough boasted of being home to Britain's largest firm of salmon smokers and of producing the new bells for Liverpool's new cathedral. But over succeeding decades many industrial facilities would relocate beyond the capital. Others would simply go out of business. Wall Paper Manufacturers Ltd of Wick Lane closed down in 1966 as did Bryant & May's Fairfield Works in 1980. Brewing, one of most large-scale and capital-intensive of East End industries was particularly hard hit. The Barley Mow brewery in Church Road, Limehouse ceased brewing in 1960, the Anchor brewery in 1975 and the Albion Brew-

Bow flyover, complemented in 1969 by the Bow underpass and in 1973 by the rebuilding of Bow Bridge. In 1969 also the Blue Bridge was opened on the Isle of Dogs.

The rapidity of the docks' decline can be seen therefore to have been generally unanticipated. It arose in part from changing patterns of international trade consequent upon Britain's loss of empire, which gave former colonies the option of seeking new markets for their exports and new sources of supply for their imported manufactures. Important aspects of this realignment included the remarkable recovery of the economies of defeated Germany and Japan and the emergence of Rotterdam as a formidable rival for the entrepot trade of northern Europe. The most fundamental factor underlying the demise of London's docks, however, was the advent of containerisation in cargo handling. The traditional skills of the stevedore who was capable of handling a wide range of cargoes in barrels, bundles or boxes were suddenly rendered redundant – and so

ery at Whitechapel in 1979. In 1976 the Black Eagle brewery was redeveloped by one of post-war Britain's most distinguished architectural practices, Arup Associates, an early but as yet isolated indicator of future trends.

VILLAINS

The Shoreditch-born Kray twins, Ronnie (1933-95) and Reggie (1933-2000), and elder brother Charlie (1927-2000) were the offspring of an Irish/Jewish/Austrian/Gypsy secondhand clothes dealer of whom they saw little. The dominant influence in their childhood was their mother ('our Queen') who presided over the family home at 179 Vallance Road, to which they had moved in 1939. 'Fortress Vallance' would later serve as a depository for the arsenal of firearms and edged weapons that they would later accumulate. As teenagers both Kray twins were keen amateur boxers, appearing in bouts at the Albert Hall in 1951. As adults they would patronise boys' boxing clubs with random generosity to burnish their Robin Hood image. The twins signalled their entry into National Service by decking an NCO on day one. Most of the rest of their terms of service was spent either in military prisons (including the Tower) or on the run, until both were dishonourably discharged.

The Krays' first criminal headquarters was the run-down Regal snooker club in Bethnal Green, from which they built up a network of protection rackets. In 1956 Ronnie was sentenced to three years for GBH. While his brother was serving time Reggie opened the Double R Club on Bow Road. In 1960 it was Reggie's turn for a spell inside. Ronnie meanwhile took control of a Knightsbridge casino by putting the squeeze on the notorious Notting Hill slum landlord Peter Rachman who had unwisely tried to stiff the Krays.

By the early sixties the Krays had achieved celebrity status, rubbing shoulders with minor showbiz stars and some of the sleazier denizens of the Tory party. Such contacts might have offered avenues for turning respectable but instead they chose to provoke their own nemesis, though it took time to unfold. In 1966 Ronnie shot dead George Cornell, a decrepit surviving member of the former rival South London Richardson gang, who was imprudent enough to be drinking in the Blind Beggar pub at Bethnal Green. Apart from sullying the Krays' manor by his presence Cornell had sealed his

155. *Rebuilt in 1894, the Blind Beggar dates back to at least Pepys's time, its name recalling a local legend of true love rewarded.*

fate by calling Ronnie a 'fat poof'. Despite the presence of dozens of eyewitnesses to the point-blank shooting no one saw anything. In 1968 Reggie, blind drunk, stabbed Jack 'The Hat' McVitie through the eye in a house at Stoke Newington. The body was never found. Neither murder had any rational motive in terms of criminal advantage but appear to have been acts of psychopathic bravado. In 1969, thanks to information divulged by their former accountant, both Kray twins were at last found guilty of murder and sentenced to thirty years. Ronnie passed most of his sentence in Broadmoor, a prison hospital for the criminally insane. In 1982 they were allowed out, under close guard, to attend their mother's funeral. In 1990 their life story was filmed as *The Krays*, starring brothers Gary and Martin Kemp, former members of Spandau Ballet. In 1995 Ronnie's elaborately Victorian funeral cortège attracted huge crowds to line the streets of the East End. In 1997 Charlie – 'the quiet one' – who did not share his brothers' penchant for gratuitous violence, was found guilty of masterminding a £39,000,000 cocaine deal and sentenced to twelve years. Reggie married Roberta Jones in Maidstone prison in 1997 and was released on compassionate grounds when suffering terminal cancer. He was buried beside his twin in Chingford cemetery.

"EVENING ALL"

In an ironic case of art resolutely refusing to imitate life, just as the Krays were building their empire of intimidation, the nation's rapidly-expanding television audience became loyal fans of the avuncular copper personified by actor Jack Warner (1895-1981) as *Dixon of Dock Green.* Born in Bromley-by-Bow and educated at the Coopers' Company School in Mile End, Warner's real name was Horace John Waters but he changed it while building his acting career in a scrupulous effort to avoid trading on the established fame of his sisters, Ethel and Doris, who had become a national institution as the Cockney comediennes 'Gert and Daisy'. Warner's initial career as a mechanic took him to Paris, the centre of European car production before World War One and, perhaps unusually for a working-class English lad, he became a fluent French-speaker. His show business apprenticeship proved to be a long haul through wartime concert-parties to amateur dramatics, cabaret and finally the West End stage, radio and film. The major breakthrough in Warner's career, however, came with a role in Basil Dearden's 1949 film *The Blue Lamp,* whose wider significance is emphasised in Leslie Halliwell's definitive Film Guide:

> "A young man (Jimmy Hanley) joins London's police force. The elderly copper who trains him is killed (by teenage tearaway Dirk Bogarde) but the killer is apprehended. Seminal British police film which spawned not only a long line of semi-documentary initiations but also the twenty-year TV series *Dixon of Dock Green* for which the shot PC was happily revived. As an entertainment, pacy but dated; more important, it burnished the image of the British copper for a generation or more."

While *The Blue Lamp* was set against the background of a visibly impoverished post-war Paddington, the *Dock Green* TV series (1955-76) was relocated to an organic East End riverside community in which Warner as PC George Dixon could personify kindliness, courage and common sense in equal mixture and keep crime under control with a lifted eyebrow, a cautionary word or a clip round the ear. Warner complemented the success of his televi-

156. *Jack Warner als PC George Dixon als Pa Huggett.*

sion persona with a long-running radio role as fictional paterfamilias of the Lord-luvva-duck but lovable Huggett family. The *Dictionary of National Biography's* judgment on Warner's career was acute as well as complimentary: "the character that he developed, growing from cockney irreverence to maturity will be interesting for social historians as a picture of the working-class hero of the first half of the twentieth century, romanticized but not unreal."

East End show business talent of a later generation which also found fame in the post-war decades was to include singers Alma Cogan and Georgia Brown, comic actors Alfie Bass and Bernard Bresslaw, entertainer Des O'Connor, rock star David Bowie, actor Terence Stamp and actress Barbara Windsor. Her first starring role was in a self-consciously Cockney comedy *Sparrows Can't Sing* (1963), for which the versatile but self-destructively drunken journalist Daniel Farson (1927-97) had recruited extras from the docks. Farson had himself the previous year used his inheritance to buy the tenancy of the Waterman's Arms in Cubitt Town with a view to using it as a venue for traditional music hall. It lasted a year and cost him perhaps £34,000 – enough to have bought a whole terrace of houses at the time.

Phoenix in the East

"Looks Like Venice, Works Like New York"
LODC slogan

St Katherine's Dock, sold by the Port of London Authority to the Greater London Council in 1969, was redeveloped by Taylor Woodrow as a marina, complemented by upmarket housing, touristically-oriented shops and the unlovely 800-room Tower Hotel. Certain historic features were preserved, notably the Ivory House, a pioneering example of the early use of iron as a structural material, and sections of the original curtain wall. An eighteenth-century wooden warehouse, obscured by later brick accretions, was discovered in the course of reconstruction and disassembled for relocation and reincarnation as the *Dickens Inn.* Immediately adjacent to the Tower and Tower Bridge, the new development could reasonably anticipate to benefit from an almost inevitable spillover effect in terms of visitor interest. What could replace declining docks less fortunately placed down river was more problematic.

157. Sailing ships at St Katherine's. Instead of handling wealth, the dock came to handle the wealthy.

Studies commissioned by the government and GLC led to the formation in 1974 of a Docklands Joint Committee consisting of representatives of the GLC itself and from five affected riverside boroughs – Tower Hamlets and Newham on the north side of the Thames and Southwark, Lewisham and Greenwich on the south. In 1976 this body published a Strategic Plan which envisaged regeneration through new (mainly council-owned) housing and the provision of new manufacturing jobs for their putative occupants. In retrospect this vision looks like a mere restatement of post-war pipedreams thirty years on but, given that so many voters in Labour-dominated riverside boroughs were unionised workers in industry or occupations dependent upon it, the plan's dogged determination to reshape the past rather than contemplate a radically different future is entirely understandable. One far-sighted proposal – to extend the Jubilee line eastwards to attract private investment – was quashed by the Treasury.

Given that the riverside boroughs seemed incapable of envisioning a practicable path to their own salvation the incoming Thatcher government revived the post-war corporatist device used to develop the New Towns but inverted it to put businessmen rather than bureaucrats at the helm. Planning powers for the eight-and-a-half square miles deemed to constitute the Docklands area were simply taken away from the boroughs and in 1991 conferred on a London Docklands Development Corporation which was to continue in existence until 1999. Although the target area for redevelopment stretched as far east as the site of the

158. The Dickens Inn at St Katherine's. From tonnage to tourists.

159. A model for the new Docklands.

former Beckton and sprawled along both banks of the river, the epicentre of activity was the Isle of Dogs, which was designated as an Enterprise Zone in 1982.

Apart from the sheer push to try something new to break the Docklands deadlock, accompanied by the opportunistic thrust of the 'greed is good' philosophy of the decade, there was also a plausible rationale for radical redevelopment, not, of course, because it would benefit the existing local population but because it would benefit London as a bastion of contemporary capitalism. As computerisation transformed the day to day operations of the financial markets and associated information-based industries, from insurance to journalism and the legal profession, many institutions based in the City or West End feared that their existing premises, constructed for the dignified conduct of business at a more leisured pace, could not be adapted to keep up with the seemingly exponential pace of technological change.

Moving out *en masse* to state-of-the-art buildings designed for the 'Information age' seemed to offer a way of reassuring New York and Tokyo that London was still up with the race and keeping Frankfurt, Paris etc. firmly in their properly subordinate place. The more imaginative business gurus provided a further rationalisation in the vague mirage of powerful 'synergies' which would spontaneously emerge as the capital's by definition most energetic enterprises found themselves among new bedfellows. As if to symbolise the willingness of even the most tradition-bound of trades to break away and make the leap in 1982, Billingsgate fish market abandoned a site it had occupied for a couple of decades short of a millennium to relocate to Poplar.

Beguiled by generous tax concessions and investment incentives an avalanche of cash poured in, over two-thirds of it from overseas, from boardrooms where perhaps the name of Millwall suggested its origins as a defensive

160. Canary Wharf station – the name became synonymous with Canada Tower which overlooked it.

wall punctuated by picturesque mills rather than a football team famed for the ferocity of its fans and Poplar likewise conjured a vision of feathery sylvan luxuriance.

The lead project co-ordinated by the Canadian Reichmann brothers' Olympia & York consortium, was the development from 1985 onwards of Canary Wharf, which took its name from the place where bananas from the Canary Islands had once been landed. The centrepiece was to become Britain's tallest building, the 824 foot, fifty-storey Canada Tower, over twice the height of St Paul's, designed by an American-based architect of Argentine birth and Italian descent, Cesar Pelli. The tower and surrounding complementary scheme dramatically enhanced both the pace and the scale of the transformation of the Isle of Dogs. Whereas previous projects had been typically of no more than 100,000 square feet, henceforth the noughts ran to six figures – despite the fact that Olympia & York went into bankruptcy in 1992.

Marketing magicians meanwhile conjured up notions of a lifestyle to match the dizzy heights arising all around – an end to tiresome commuting, a brisk bout of windsurfing at the end of an invigorating and well-rewarded day and then home in minutes to admire the vista from an ultra-stylish hi-tech apartment. It was known that maverick politician David Owen had acquired a new neighbour in Narrow Street, Limehouse when film director David Lean undertook the conversion of redundant warehouses into a spectacularly spacious residence complete with its own private cinema. Alas, early residents of 'the Island' were to find the bars and bistros that seemed the natural setting for the charismatic and the creative were still miles – or a decade – away.

The first section of the Docklands Light Railway was opened by the Queen in 1987 but initially it did not run at weekends or in the evenings. This meant that when the London Arena opened in 1989 it was possible to get to an evening event on the DLR – but not to go home from it in the same way. Canada Tower itself was completed in 1991. And in 1993 the Limehouse Link, in terms of cost per mile one of the most expensive road-building projects ever undertaken, was opened.

161. *Canada Tower.*

According to the 1995 *Rough Guide to London,* Docklands was still "a fascinating open-air design museum, not a place one would choose to live or work – most people stationed here see it as a bleak business-orientated outpost – but a spectacular sight nevertheless." 'Stationed' is revealing as a choice of verb, suggestive of an involuntary isolation in obedience to corporate imperatives rather than a freely-chosen option eagerly embraced for its promise of a vibrant new lifestyle. The Isle of Dogs in the mid-1990s was characterised by the *Rough Guide* as "surreally lifeless, an uneasy mix of drab high-rises, clapped-out housing, warehouses converted into expensive apartments and a lot of new architecture – some of it startling, some of it crass, much of it empty." Stephanie Williams, author of the *Phaidon Architecture Guide,* declared witheringly that the Docklands "contains one of the worst collections of late twentieth-century architecture to be seen anywhere in the world. It is a marvel, if it were not so embarrassing, that so many very bad buildings from the same period can be found in such a comparatively small area." Honourable ex-

ceptions were held to include the quirky, quasi-maritime Cascades apartment block on Westferry Road, John Outram's post-modern Storm Water Pumping Station in Stewart Street, Richard Rogers' Reuter's headquarters in Blackwall Yard, the hi-tech Telehouse in Leamouth Road and Nicholas Grimshaw's *Financial Times* Printing Works in East India Dock Road – the latter deserted within a decade. The London Arena would also be condemned to oblivion and redevelopment. Seemingly almost as an afterthought an impressive Museum of Docklands was finally opened at West India Quay in 2003.

Elsewhere de-industrialisation continued. 1997 witnessed the closure of Limehouse Paperboard Mill and Blackwall Engineering, formerly known as Siley, Weir & Co. Brewing ceased at the Black Eagle brewery in 1988. In 1989 Brunswick power station was demolished. The disappearance of characteristic local institutions was even more relentless. In 1982 eighteen East End synagogues were amalgamated under the aegis of the survivor at Nelson Street. The East London Synagogue closed in 1987 although, after some years of dereliction, it was to be rescued and reopened as a block of residential apartments a decade later. Poplar Baths also closed in 1987, though the baths in East India Dock Road clung on until 1998. The Railway Tavern, Limehouse, far better known as 'Charlie Brown's' and long renowned for its bizarre collection of exotic curios, was finally demolished in 1999 to make way for the construction of the Limehouse link. In 1991 Spitalfields market relocated to Leyton. Bloom's kosher restaurant at Aldgate closed in 1996, just short of its half-century on that site, although most of those who knew would probably have sworn that it had been there far longer.

THE REAL EAST ENDERS?
Between 1971 and 1981 Tower Hamlets lost a further one seventh of a population that was already in decline, falling from 164,349 to 139,996. Much of this contraction reflected the continuing out-migration to 'Cockney Essex' which had been in train at varying rates throughout the century as the white working-class and their offspring were finally able to take advantage of rising incomes and widening educational opportunities to join the ranks

162. *A DLR train on original London-Blackwall arches.*

of owner-occupiers and City commuters. This was also true of the other five east London boroughs – Hackney, Waltham Forest, Newham, Redbridge and Barking and Dagenham – all of which lost population over the course of the same decade, though to very different extents, ranging from under 6% in affluent Redbridge to almost 18% in Hackney. But whereas Hackney would lose a further 10% in the 1980s, and the other four boroughs would also continue to experience a demographic haemorrhage, in Tower Hamlets the population loss was to be uniquely reversed into a gain of 7.5%, representing just over ten thousand additional residents. One major cause of this reversal was the in-migration of young urban professionals taking advantage of new occupational and residential opportunities in the renascent Docklands. But this was overshadowed demographically by the impact of the fertility of the borough's expending ethnic minorities. During the 1980s the immigrant population of Tower Hamlets increased by some 14,000 so that by 1991, 27% of the borough's residents had been born outside the United Kingdom. In

that year Tower Hamlets had the highest proportion of children aged fifteen and under in all London, representing over a quarter of the borough's population, with the figure for the under-fives standing at double the national average. In 1991 nearly half of all births were to women from the New Commonwealth, a figure twice as high as that of London as a whole. Offsetting the expansion of the juvenile population was a decline in the proportion of pensioners locally resident, many older inhabitants joining the eastward exodus on retirement or loss of employment or, in the case of the more fortunate, taking advantage of the Thatcher government's 'Right to Buy' legislation to purchase and then swiftly to re-sell their council accommodation to finance their own resettlement in the suburbs, in the country or at the coast.

Changes in age-structure were paralleled by changes in family structure – or perhaps loss of structure. Whereas in 1974 some 15% of Tower Hamlets' births were outside marriage by 1991 the proportion had almost doubled to 29%. Uniquely, again, among the East London

163. The Albion brewery site was redeveloped as a Sainsbury's with the administration block retained as apartments and a health centre.

boroughs Tower Hamlets also witnessed a rise in the number of families with three or more children under five. But this trend was also matched by a rise in single person households to account for a third of the total, comprising a category grossly disparate in age, lifestyle and income as it consisted primarily of students, partnerless pensioners and high-earning yuppies.

Even within the conventional nuclear family household lifestyles had changed markedly since the 1950s when Willmott and Young had conducted their classic study of working-class life in Bethnal Green, contrasting the street oriented lives of the East Enders with the home-centred suburbanites of leafy Woodford barely five miles away. A follow-up study, conducted in 1985, observed

"how home-centred most Bethnal Green families had now become ... it was noticeable how many husbands ... were almost as much around, when they could be, as Woodford husbands. DIY, even in rented property, and television – not to mention the baby – were clearly strong

competitors of the pub and the football ground ... the corollary was the emptiness of the streets and corridors and staircases of the housing estates. Markets still flourished. Children sometimes played outside. Small groups of adults occasionally congregated. But no longer could it be said that people in Bethnal Green were vigorously at home in the streets."

The influx of well-paid service sector workers was reflected in a dramatic shift in the profile of housing tenures. In 1981 Tower Hamlets still had the largest proportion of council housing in the entire United Kingdom, with only 2,440 of its households in owner-occupation. The combined impact of the 'Right to Buy' initiative and the development of new residential enclaves in the Docklands was to raise the proportion of owner-occupied households from a mere 4.6% to 23.3% in a single decade – though this was still far below an Inner London average of 38.6% and a national average of 66%. Over the same period the proportion of households in council accommodation dropped from 82% to 58% and the number of new local authority dwellings built fell from 442 in 1981-85 to just 90 in 1986-91 as planning priority was given over to provision by housing associations, which doubled to represent almost 10% of all local households by 1991. Meanwhile Tower Hamlets house prices rose rapidly to an average of £88,000, compared with £72,000 for East London as a whole.

As if spurred on by the locality's architecturally embodied embourgoisement the proportion of Tower Hamlets teenagers committed to education beyond the statutory minimum leaving age rose rapidly. Whereas in 1981 only a quarter of seventeen year olds were still attending school or college, by 1991 almost half were doing so, an increase matched by improved examination performance at GCSE level. Less happily there was also a marked increase in the proportion of 'economically inactive' adult males who, by 1991, represented nearly one fifth of the 16-64 cohort, an increase of over 50% on 1981. This reflected the loss of jobs consequent upon the final round of dock closures, the continuing decline of local manufacturing and the mismatch between the skills of the displaced and the opportunities emerging in the financial and service sectors which demanded high levels of formal qualifications or computer literacy. Female participation in the labour force also fell. By 1991 Tower Hamlets had the lowest proportion of economically active women of any London borough – 57%. Those who were in work, however, both male and female, were earning more on average than in any of the other East London boroughs and more than the average in Greater London as a whole. Over half were in service sector employment, many in senior positions. Between 1981 and 1991 the proportion of professional and managerial workers in Tower Hamlets doubled from 8.5% to 17%.

CREATIVE QUARTER

The changing nature of the community was reflected in the advent of new structures and services. The domed East London Mosque, funded by the government of Saudi Arabia and capable of accommodating two thousand worshippers, opened in Whitechapel Road in 1984. The *East London Advertiser* hailed its blend of Islamic motifs and polychrome brickwork as "a touch of the Taj Mahals". In 1986 Onyx House, designed by architect Piers Gough, opened opposite Mile End station on the site once

164. *The permanence of a local Muslim population was emphasised by the opening of a major purpose-built mosque in 1984.*

occupied by C R Ashbee's Essex House. In the same year the London Independent Hospital opened in Beaumont Square. 1990 saw the inauguration of the Royal London air ambulance helicopter service and of the Ragged School Museum in Copperfield Road.

Ethnic diversification continued in the 1990s, impelled as much by political as economic imperatives, with influxes of refugees and aylum-seekers from the Horn of Africa, the Kurdish homelands and the Balkans. Among 'the ethnics', as some local residents derisively designated the newcomers, it was the South Asian and especially Bangladeshi presence which most detectibly provoked a nativist reaction in surviving white working-class redoubts such as the Isle of Dogs, leading to a renewal of local British National Party activism and the election in 1993 of a BNP councillor. The major alleged grievance was unfair-

165. Limehouse Basin – where workers once unloaded the world's wealth: the wealthy now contemplate the water.

ness in housing allocation – reflecting in part the spiralling cost of dwellings and the contraction in their public provision. In the light of this it was perhaps doubly ironic that the soap opera *East Enders* in the same decade achieved a distinctly higher proportion of loyal viewers among older Bangladeshis than it did among the corresponding age-cohort of whites whose lives it was supposed to mirror.

Nativist hostility was also directed at the LDDC, 'developers' in general and unspecified 'planners' – all of whom were perceived as outsiders whose interventions were to be interpreted as disruptive of a coherent social and moral order rather than regenerative of the energies and aspirations of a community in decay and despair. The 'media' were similarly reviled for concocting unrealistic representations of the East End, whether in the form of alarmist profiles of resurgent racism, patronising conjurations of fading Cockneydom or gushing PR affirmations of profit-driven 'urban renewal'.

Although its occupants might have justifiably been preoccupied with the tide of local changes engulfing them Tower Hamlets enjoyed no special exemption from the social conflicts of the eighties and nineties. The apparently motiveless murder of garment-worker Altab Ali in 1976 galvanised the previously passive Bangladeshi community into a march on Downing Street and proved a catalyst for its political mobilisation, leading over subsequent decades to the election of Muslim councillors and eventually Tower Hamlets' first Muslim mayor. The demise of traditional 'hot metal' technology in the newspaper industry precipitated a general exodus from Fleet Street and gave employers the opportunity to challenge the restrictive practices which had long been upheld by the entrenched power of the printers' and journalists' unions. In 1986-7 Rupert Murdoch's News International moved into what become known as 'Fortress Wapping' and began a long, bitter and violent industrial dispute which embraced employees of *The*

166. *Asian stall-holders supply vegetables unfamiliar to the older inhabitants of Bromley-by-Bow.*

167. *Share past? Local schoolchildren investigate historic almshouses in Puma Court, Spitalfields.*

168. *The former Frying Pan pub in Brick Lane, now a Balti house.*

Studio opened at Canary Wharf as early as 1983. A decade later Rachel Whiteread's cast of a house immediately prior to its demolition – engagingly entitled *House* – concentrated attention for its few months of existence on Mile End Park. In Spitalfields long-term residents Gilbert and George were joined by Britain's highest-paid female artist Tracey Emin, while Californian eccentric Dennis Severs realised his personal fantasy of life in the eighteenth century by turning his home at 18 Folgate Street into a multi-storey stage-set for the imaginative re-incarnation of the imaginary Jervis family of Huguenot silk-merchants. Social historian Raphael Samuel, a local resident reasserted the significance of understanding 'history from below', while architectural historian Dan Cruickshank helped to mobilize the Save Spitalfields campaign which successfully resisted the radical redevelopment (i.e. projected annihilation) of the locality envisioned by would-be developers of commercial Behemoths. Extensive excavations of the crypt of Christ Church recovered, identified and analysed the bodies of almost a thousand past inhabitants of Spitalfields interred there between the 1720s and the 1850s. This was followed by extensive

169. *The former Lord Napier, now a halal grocer.*

Times, Sunday Times, Sun and *News of the World* and ended, perhaps predictably, in victory for the employers. In 1996 an IRA bomb at South Quay, considerately detonated on a Friday evening when the area was supposedly deserted, still managed to kill two innocent shopkeepers working 'all hours', as well as shattering windows for miles around. In 1999 a lone bomber, who subsequently proved to be both racist and homophobic, left a nail-bomb in Hanbury Street on a Saturday morning; this was moved by a well-intentioned by-stander to Brick Lane where it exploded, injuring six people.

More positively the expansion of Britain's creative industries brought new types of service worker to the East End in the form of high-profile artists, makers of television programmes, advertisements and videos, website designers, 'fashionistas' and gallery-owners. From 1995 the area was supposedly portrayed on the screen as the setting for *East Enders*. In reality it was to be the birthplace of cult programmes such as *Big Brother*. Limehouse Productions

170. South Quay – London marathon competitors pass buildings shattered by an IRA bomb.

171. Dennis Severs' house, 18 Folgate Street, home to the Jervis family.

refurbishment of the fabric of the building and the successful establishment of an annual Spitalfields Music Festival. Aspects of this localised renaissance were reflected in the il-luminating pages of wannabe priest William Taylor's autobiographical odyssey *This Bright Field*. Monica Ali's account of marital tensions among the Bangladeshi community, *Brick Lane,* gained critical acclaim but was less than warmly received by older members of the com-munity itself. Brick Lane itself increasingly became a vibrant creative corridor, dominated by food and fashion – just the sort of culture-and-consumption arena which the early Docklands had so conspicuously lacked.

OLYMPIC BID

Britain's decision in 2003 to bid for the Olym-pics of 2012 depended to no little extent on the availability of some 1,500 acres of semi-derelict land immediately to the east of Tower Hamlets along the line of the Lower Lea Valley, running

from Hackney Marshes down to the river at Blackwall. This locality was already envisaged as part of a larger project to regenerate a 'Thames Gateway' region of urban decay stretching far downriver along both banks of the Thames, which would over the course of two decades acquire 200,000 new homes and 30,000 new jobs, in effect adding a new city the size of Leeds to the capital's eastern extremities. Pre-viously labelled the Thames Corridor (what the shift of metaphor to 'Gateway' betokened re-mained obscure) this massive area had been belatedly recognised as the neglected obverse of the Heathrow-M4 nexus which had bestowed such affluence on the western approaches to the capital in the post-war period.

If the entire Docklands adventure and the abortive Millennium Dome fiasco are seen as successive attempts to kick-start an eastern renaissance by means of a French-style *grand projet*, the Olympic bid therefore represented a third bite at this seemingly indigestible urban

172. *The Ragged School Museum runs Victorian schooldays for local children and has a popular teashop for canal-side walkers.*

173. *The former George Green's School overshadowed by a post-war tower block.*

174. *Bryant & May's factory in Fairfield Road, Bow, has now been converted into a gated community called Bow Quarter. The polychromatic Gothic building dates from 1874, the tower from 1911.*

175. *Kingsley Hall (see p. 125) has lost its specifically religious orientation to become a general community facility.*

176. St Paul's, Bow Common, built 1958-60, hailed by architecture critic Ian Nairn as 'the one worthwhile new church in a city region of ten millions.' Designed by Robert Maguire.

177. Going out in style: a traditional East End funeral with horse-drawn hearse is about to take place.

178. *Before the railways the Thames sailing-barge was the major means of bringing bulk goods like grain, fodder or lumber into Loondon. Its small crew made it much more economical than road carriage.*

179. *A narrow boat parts the summer algae on Bow Backs, 2004.*

180. Ideal for power lunches – a generator hall becomes the smart café.

181. The Georgian headquarters of the Society for the Protection of Ancient Buildings in Spitalfields.

cherry. The decision to open a Eurostar terminal at Stratford, the historic repair and maintenance base of the old London and North Eastern Railway, in 2007 made the area between it and the wealth of the City particularly attractive as a potential site for an Olympic village of four thousand housing units, plus a state-of-the-art stadium, velodrome, swimming-pool and media centre. It was not, however, entirely a blank canvas, including as it did some 5.5 kilometres of waterways along the Bow Back Rivers and an assemblage of Grade I industrial archaeology around the Three Mills conservation area. It was hoped that, should the bid for the Games prove successful, in the short run it would create a

thousand new businesses and five times that number of permanent new jobs. In the longer term the hope was for 30,000 new homes and 40,000 new jobs. All local residents could *count on* was that their council tax would include an extra impost of £20 to fund the bid ...

In the same year that London decided that it wanted to host the Olympics 60% of the working population of Tower Hamlets were in jobs paying less than £10,000 per year. Six out of every ten children were receiving free school meals. Child poverty was the worst in Britain. This book was written in Bromley-by-Bow, in the second poorest ward in the entire United Kingdom. From most parts of it you can see Canada Tower quite clearly.

Reading and Reference

Robert Barltrop and Jim Wolveridge: *The Muvver Tongue* (Journeyman Press, 1980)

Chaim Bermant: *Point of Arrival, A Study of London's East End* (Eyre Methuen, 1975)

Walter Besant: *All Sorts and Conditions of Men* (Oxford University Press, 1997)

G Black: *JFS: The history of the Jews' Free School, London, since 1732* (Tymsder Publishing, 1997)

Noreen Branson: *Poplarism 1919-25: George Lansbury and the Councillors' Revolt* (Lawrence and Wishart, 1979)

Asa Briggs and Anne Macartney: *Toynbee Hall* (Routledge and Kegan Paul, 1984)

Jane Cox: *London's East End* (Weidenfeld and Nicolson, 2000)

Margaret Cox: *Life and Death in Spitalfields 1700 to 1850* (Council for British Archaeology, 1996)

Andrew Davies: *The East End Nobody Knows: A History, A Guide, an Exploration* (Macmillan, 1990)

John Eade: *Placing London: From Imperial City to Global City* (Berghahn Books, 2000)

Harold Finch: *The Tower Hamlets Connection: A Biographical Guide* (Tower Hamlets Library Services and Stepney Books, 1996)

William J Fishman: *East End Jewish Radicals 1875-1914* (Duckworth, 1975); *The Streets of East London* (Duckworth, 1979) *East End 1888* (Duckworth, 1988)

Geoffrey Fletcher: *Pearly Kingdom* (Hutchinson, 1965)

Brian Girling: *East Enders' Postcards* (Tempus, 2002)

Robin D Gwynn: *Huguenot Heritage* (Sussex Academic Press, 1985, 2001)

Louis Heren: *Growing Up Poor in London* (Hamish Hamilton, 1973, Phoenix 1996)

Dick Hobbs: *Doing the Business: Entrepreneurship, The Working Class and Detectives in the East End of London* (Oxford University Press, 1988)

Joe Jacobs: *Out of the Ghetto – My Youth in the East End, Communism and Fascism 1913-1939* (2nd. ed. Phoenix Press, 1991).

Colm Kerrigan: *A History of Tower Hamlets* (London Borough of Tower Hamlets Community Services, 1982)

Tony Kushner and Nadia Valman: *Remembering Cable Street: Fascism and Anti-Fascism in British Society* (Frank Cass, 2000)

Vera Leff and G Blunden: *The Story of Tower Hamlets* (Research Writers, 1967)

Peter Linebaugh: *The London Hanged: Crime and Civil Society in the Eighteenth Century* (Verso Books 2nd ed. 2003)

Jack London: *The People of the Abyss* (Pluto Press, 2001)

Peter Marcan: *An East End Directory* (Peter Marcan Publications, 1979)

Kevin McDonnell: *Medieval London Suburbs* (Phillimore, 1978)

Philip Merrick: *A Pictorial History of Victoria Park* (East London History Society, 1996)

Derek Morris: *Mile End Old Town 1740-1780: a Social History of an Early Modern London Suburb* (The East London History Society, 2002)

Arthur Morrison: *Tales of Mean Streets* (Academy Chicago Publications, 1997); *A Child of the Jago* (J M Dent, 1996)

Venetia Murray: *Echoes of the East End* (Viking, 1989)

Gilda O'Neill: *My East End: Memories of life in Cockney London* (Penguin 2000); *Our Street: East End Life in the Second World War* (Viking 2003)

Alan Palmer: *The East End: Four Centuries of London Life* (Revised ed. John Murray, 2000)

John Pearson: *The Profession of Violence: The Rise and Fall of the Kray Twins* (4th ed HarperCollins, 1995)

Phil Piratin: *Our Flag Stays Red* (Lawrence and Wishart, 1978)

Charles Poulsen: *Victoria Park: A Study in the History of East London* (Stepney Books & Journeyman Press, 1976); *Scenes from a Stepney Youth* (THAP, 1988)

John Pudney: *London's Docks* (Thames and Hudson, 1975)

Winston G Ramsey: *The East End: Then and Now* (After the Battle, 1997)

Fermin Rocker: *The East End Years: A Stepney Childhood* (Freedom Press, 1998)

Millicent Rose: *The East End of London* (Cresset Press 1951, Cedric Chivers, 1973)

Raphael Samuel: *East End Underworld: chapters in the life of Arthur Harding* (Routledge and Kegan Paul, 1981)

Survey of London Volume I Bromley-by-Bow (1900); Volume XXVII Christ Church and All Saints (Spitalfields and Mile End New Town) (1957); Volumes XLIII, XLIV Poplar, Blackwall and the Isle of Dogs: The Parish of All Saints (1994)

Survey of London Monograph Series
1. Trinity Hospital, Mile End
2. St Mary Stratford Bow
3. The Old Palace, Bromley-by-Bow
6 The Church of St Dunstan, Stepney
Rosemary Taylor: *Walks Through History: Exploring the East End* (Breedon Books, 2001)
Rosemary Taylor and Christopher Lloyd: *Stepney, Bethnal Green and Poplar in Old Photographs* (Sutton, 1995); *The changing East End: Stepney, Bethnal Green and Poplar 1860-1960* (Sutton, 1997); *The East End at work* (Sutton, 1999); *A century of the East End* (W H Smith/ Sutton, 1999); *The East End at War* (Sutton, 2000)
Victoria County History of Middlesex (ed. T F T Baker): Volume XI Stepney – Bethnal Green (Institute of Historical Research/Oxford University Press, 1998)
Gillian Wagner: *Barnardo* (Weidenfeld & Nicolson, 1979)
Michael Young and Peter Willmott: *Family and Kinship in East London* (Routledge and Kegan Paul, 1957, Penguin 1990)
Jerry White: *Rothschild Buildings: Life in an East End tenement block 1887-1920* (Routledge and Kegan Paul, 1990, Pimlico 2003)
Jim Wolveridge: *Ain't it Grand (or This was Stepney)* (Journeyman, 1981)

WEBSITES

East End Life www.eastendlife.com
East London History Society www.eastlondonhistory.org.uk
East London Family History Society www.eolfhs.org.uk
Island History Trust www.islandhistory.org.uk
Jack the Ripper www.casebook.org
Jewish History www.olamgadol.pwp.blueyonder.co.uk
London and Middlesex Archaeological Society www.middlesexpast.net
London Borough of Tower Hamlets www.towerhamlets.gov.uk
London Docklands Development Corporation www.lddc-history.org.uk
Museum in Docklands www.museumindocklands.org.uk
Museum of London www.museum-london.org.uk
Port Cities www.portcities.org.uk
Ragged School Museum www.raggedschoolmuseum.org.uk
Tower Hamlets History On Line www.thhol.org.uk
Whitechapel Mission www.whitechapel.org.uk

Chronology

3rd Century AD: Roman settlement at Old Ford.

959 St Dunstan appointed Bishop of London.

1086 Domesday Book lists eleven Tower hamlets in Stepney.

1101 (ca.) Bow Bridge built; Priory of St Leonard, Bow founded.

1108 Priory of the Holy Trinity, Aldgate founded.

1148 St Katherine's Hospital founded by the Tower (refounded 1273).

1158 River Thames runs dry.

1197 St Mary's Spital founded by Walter Brune.

1228 Canons of St Paul's granted an estate in Shadwell.

1230 Earliest known record of Old Ford.

1235 Priory of St Mary Spital founded.

1270, 1317, 1391 Famine.

1280 First mention of St Mary Matfelon, Whitechapel – rebuilt 1362.

1288 First documentary record of Mile End.

1293 Convent of the Sisters of St Clare (Minoresses) founded.

1299 Parliament held in Stepney Green home of Lord Mayor Henry le Waleis.

1302 Whitechapel parish established.

1309 Stepney tournament celebrated the coronation of Edward II.

1311 Chapel of St Mary, Bow consecrated.

1348-9 Black Death.

1350 Abbey of St Mary Graces founded.

1361, 1369, 1407, 1499, 1562, 1581, 1603, 1625, 1665 Plague

1362 Earliest recorded reference to lime-burning at Limehouse.

1380 Chapel known to be established on Stepney Marsh (Isle of Dogs).

1381 Peasants' Revolt – men of Essex meet Richard II at Mile End Waste.

1410 and 1434 River Thames frozen.

1419 First record of brewing in Stepney.

1448/9 Stepney Marsh (Isle of Dogs) inundated after breach of embankment.

1450 Jack Cade's Kentish rebels rendezvous with Essex men at Mile End.

1471 Falconberg's 47-ship fleet lands at Blackwall in a failed attempt to release Henry VI from the Tower of London.

1485, 1518 and 1551 Sweating sickness.

1515-16 *Mary Rose* fitted out at Blackwall.

1518 Mercers' Company acquires ninety acres of farmland in Stepney.

1532 Dissolution of Holy Trinity Priory.

1535-6 Draining of Wapping marsh authorised by Act of Parliament.

1542 Road paved from Aldgate to Bow.

1544 Wapping embanked – breached 1565 and 1571.

1551 Manor of Stepney granted to Thomas, Lord Wentworth.

1553 Sir Hugh Willoughby sets out from Ratcliff.

1570 Kirby Castle built at Bethnal Green.

1580 Bow Bridge damaged "by reason of great inundations".

1583 Bell Foundry moves to Whitechapel.

1593 Irish Immigrants known to be settled in Wapping.

1598 John Stow *Survey of London.*

1600 Foundation of the East India Company.

1605 Tower Hamlets designated as a military district.

1606 Settlers of Jamestown, Virginia set sail from Blackwall.

1612 First East India Company ships built at Blackwall.

1629 Charles I kills a stag at Wapping after chasing it from Wanstead.

1633 Particular Baptist congregation established in Old Gravel Lane, Wapping.

1635 Surviving remains of St Leonard's Priory, Bow demolished.

1643 Defensive fort and mound raised at Whitechapel.

1644 Stepney Meeting House of Independents inaugurated.

1647 Civil war fortifications slighted.

1648 Royalist insurgents seize Bow Bridge.

1650 (ca.) Netteswell House, Bethnal Green built.

1654 East India Company chapel at Poplar (St Matthias) consecrated.

1656 Readmission of Sephardi Jews from the Netherlands.

1657 Jewish cemetery at Mile End (now 243 Mile End Road).

1660 Kirby Castle bought by Sir William Rider, hemp merchant. Major breach in Isle of Dogs flood defences.

1661 Stepney Watch House built.

1664 Stepney Michaelmas Fair originated at Mile End Green. First record of Quakers in

Stepney.

1665 Great Plague – over 6,500 victims buried in St Dunstan's churchyard.

1666 Great Fire of London.

1669 Piped water supply established in Shadwell.

1670 St Paul, Shadwell parish established.

1673 Wren makes a survey of Mile End. St Mary Matfelon rebuilt.

1674 Stepney Meeting House built by Pastor Matthew Mead.

1676 Vintners' Almshouses established.

1680 Davenant's School established in Whitechapel.

1682 Spitalfields Market chartered.

1685 Revocation of the Edict of Nantes provokes Huguenot immigration.

1686 Bow Lane almshouses erected.

1691 Dame Jane Mico founds Mercers' Almshouses, Stepney.

1694 Wapping parish established.

1695 Trinity Almshouses built.

1696 Danish church built in Wellclose Square.

1697 Ashkenazi cemetery established.

1698 Skinners' Almshouses built.

1701 Pirate William Kidd hanged at Execution Dock. Coborn school founded.

1702 First record of Spring Gardens.

1703 Map of Stepney and Bethnal Green by Joel Gascoyne. Hurricane drives ships from London Bridge to Limehouse.

1706 Drapers' almshouses erected at Bow.

1708 Ratcliff hay market relocated to Whitechapel.

1711 Fifty New Churches Act.

1714 Mile End Old Town charity school established. Major cattle plague.

1715 Limehouse parish established.

1716 Collapse of St Leonard's, Shoreditch.

1717 Spitalfields Mathematical Society founded. Ireland Row, Mile End Road built.

1719 Riots in Spitalfields against imported calicoes. Bow parish established. Wapping brewer Henry Raine endows a charity school in Farthing Fields, Charles Street, St George's-in-the-East.

1721 Calico Act passed.

1722 Ashkenazim establish synagogue at Duke's Place. Whitechapel-Shenfield turnpike established. Parmiter's School established in Bethnal Green.

1724 St Anne's Limehouse completed. Jack Sheppard hanged.

1725 Wapping blockmaker Daniel Day founds Fairlop Fair.

1726 St George's in the East completed. Swedish church built in Princes Square, Wapping.

1729 Christ Church Spitalfields consecrated. Goodman's Fields Theatre opened.

1730 Barley Mow brewery opened at Stepney. St Mary, Bow established as a parish. St Anne's, Limehouse established as a parish.

1735 Bancroft's Almshouses erected.

1736 Spitalfields riots against Irish labour.

1738 Bancroft's School opened. Fitzhugh House built. Whitechapel bell foundry moves to its present site.

1741 Spitalfields Madrigal Society founded. Malplaquet House, Mile End Road built. London Hospital moves to Prescot Street. Ratcliff workhouse built. David Garrick's first London appearance at Goodman's Fields theatre.

1743 Fournier Street chapel opened. St Matthew, Bethnal Green parish established. Jack Broughton of Wapping draws up rules for prize-fighting.

1744 Edward Heylyn and Thomas Frye establish a porcelain factory at Bow.

1746 John Rocque maps of London. St Matthew's, Bethnal Green (architect, Dance the Elder) completed.

1748 West Ham Water Company reservoir established near Bancroft Hospital.

1757 Anchor brewery established in Mile End Road.

1758 Magdalen Hospital to reform prostitutes founded in Prescot Street.

1759 London Hospital completed in Whitechapel.

1760 Coalheavers riot at Shadwell.

1761 Jewish cemetery opened in Brady Street, Whitechapel.

1763 Silkweavers riot in Spitalfields. St George's Lutheran church, Alie Street.

1764 New rectory built for St Dunstan's.

1764-8 Assembly Row, Mile End Road built.

1765 Spitalfields weavers march against imports.

1766 Ban on the importation of foreign silks.

1768 Riots in support of John Wilkes. Irish riots in Spitalfields against low pay. Limehouse sawyers burn down Dingley's sawmill.

1769 Spitalfields weavers riot against imported technology; two are hanged at Bethnal Green.

1770 Limehouse Cut opened.

1772 Mystic Immanuel Swedenborg buried at Swedish church, Wapping.

1773 Spitalfields Act establishes tariff protection against foreign competition

1775 Closure of New Canton porcelain factory.

1776 St Matthias, Poplar rebuilt.

1780 Gordon riots against Catholics

1783 Merchant Seamen's Orphanage Asylum established in Merchant Street, Bow. Evangelical Academy established in Mile End Old Town.

1785 London Hospital medical school opened.

1787 Royalty Theatre opened off Wellclose Square.

1790-1 Perry's wet-dock dug at Poplar. Daniel Mendoza becomes champion of England.

1791 Thames floods Wapping.

1794 Fire devastates Ratcliff.

1795 Patrick Colquhoun founds soup kitchen in Spitalfields.

1797 Patrick Colquhoun *Treatise on the Police of the Metropolis*. Spitalfields Soup Society founded.

1798 Establishment of the River Police.

1800 Huddart's Patent Cable Manufactory established in Limehouse. Patrick Colquhoun *The Commerce and Police of the River Thames*.

1802 West India Docks opened.

1803 Commercial Road developed.

1806 East India Docks opened.

1807 Whitechapel Mount demolished.

1808 Albion Brewery, Whitechapel Road built.

1809 Wesleyans purchase former Huguenot chapel in Brick Lane.

1810 Poplar manor house demolished. East India Dock Road and West India Dock Road opened.

1811 Ratcliff Highway murders.

1812 West Ferry Road built. Baptist Academy established in Worcester House. Brown Lenox, manufacturers of anchor cables, relocate from Ratcliff to Millwall.

1813 Tobacco Dock completed.

1814 Infirmary for Asthma, Consumption and other Diseases of the Lungs established in Brushfield Street, Spitalfields.

1816 Father Barber founds Wade Street (later Holy Family) RC School.

1817 All Saints', Poplar established as a parish. Poplar workhouse opened. Jews' Free School opens in Bell Street, Spitalfields. Independent chapel opened in West Ferry Road.

Mercers' Company develops side streets along Commercial Road. Ratcliff Gas Light and Coke Works established.

1820 Regent's Canal opened. All Saints, East India Dock Road completed (architect C Hollis).

1821 First steamship, *City of Edinburgh*, built at Blackwall. Poplar parish established. Rebuilt St Paul's, Shadwell consecrated.

1823 Bow fair suppressed.

1824 Spitalfields Act repealed.

1826 Ban on the importation of foreign silks ended.

1828 St Katherine's Dock opened. St John's, Bethnal Green dedicated (architect Sir John Soane). George Green's school built in Poplar. Tredegar Square built.

1829 Poplar Dock completed (engineer Sir John Rennie).

1830 Baptist College, Stepney Green (architect Savage) opened. Last pirates hanged at Execution Dock.

1832 First outbreak of cholera. Brunswick Wharf built for paddle steamers. Brunswick Methodist chapel built in Three Colt Street, Limehouse. Parliamentary Borough of Tower Hamlets established.

1833 George Green builds Preston Road School.

1834 Merger of West and East India Docks.

1835 William Fairbairn's shipyard opened at Millwall.

1836 Congregational chapel, Harley Street (now Grove) opened.

1838-9 Stepney Gas Works built.

1839 Holy Trinity, Tredegar Square (architect Austin). Bow Bridge rebuilt. David Napier establishes a shipyard at Millwall.

1840 Railway reaches Blackwall. Barber Beaumont established the Beaumont Philosophical Institute.

1841 Tower Hamlets cemetery opened. George Green builds Trinity chapel and school, East India Dock Road.

1843 Wapping-Rotherhithe tunnel opened. Building of Cubitt Town begins. Samuda shipyard opens in Millwall.

1845 Victoria Park opened. Dissolution of the Spitalfields Mathematical Society. Bishop of London's manor house demolished.

1847 First full-time, purpose-built school opened on the Isle of Dogs. Blackwall Iron Works, Yabsley Street opened.

1848 Hector Gavin *Sanitary Ramblings: Being Sketches and Illustrations of Bethnal Green*. Commercial Street laid out. Poplar Methodist church built in East India Dock Road.

1849 St Clement's Hospital built as City of London Union Workhouse. Cholera.

1851 Prince Albert lays the foundation stone of the London Chest Hospital. Canterbury Association establishes a settlement in New Zealand for emigrants from the East End.

1852 Christ Church, Cubitt Town (architect William Cubitt). Municipal Baths and Wash House opened in East India Dock Road.

1853 Napier's Millwall shipyard destroyed by fire. Benjamin H Cowper *A Descriptive, Historical and Statistical Account of Millwall, Commonly called the Isle of Dogs.*

1854 Soup kitchen for Poor Jews established in Leman Street.

1855 Albion brewery rebuilt. Poplar hospital opened. Limehouse District Board of Works established.

1856 Strangers' Home for Asiatics opened in West India Dock Road. Spitalfields Market sold to Robert Horner. Cholera outbreak. Limehouse Ragged School opened by Barnett Tabrum in Three Colt Street. Poplar Baths opened. Baptist Academy moves to Regent's Park.

1858 *Great Eastern* launched at Millwall.

1859 Wilton's music hall opened.

1860 J R Green becomes a curate in Stepney. *HMS Warrior* launched at Blackwall. Poplar and Blackwall Rowing Club established.

1861 Bryant & May's match factory opened at Bow.

1862 Mast House at Blackwall demolished. Columbia Square Buildings opened. Burdett Road opened.

1864 Peabody Buildings opened in Commercial Street.

1865 William Booth begins preaching. Bow Road Methodist Mission built. Yarrow's shipyard established at Folly Wall, Isle of Dogs.

1866 Last cholera outbreak – three-quarters of London fatalities occur in St George-in-the-East. Old Ford lock opened. Overend, Gurney financial crash severely damages Thameside ship-building. St Peter's, Wapping Lane founded by Father Lowder. Mile End turnpike trust loses the right to collect tolls.

1866-7 Severe winter damages riverside trades.

1867 Peabody estate completed in Shadwell. Poplar Recreation Park laid out. Dr Barnado establishes the East End Juvenile Mission. People's Market, Whitechapel established.

1868 Millwall Docks opened. Abbey Mills pumping station completed. Charles Booth begins preaching on Mile End Waste. Mrs Wigram founds the East London Nursing Society.

1869 Columbia Market opened.

1870 First Barnardo home opened on Stepney Causeway. Poplar Town Hall built. Bow and Bromley Institute established. Frederick Charrington established the Tower Hamlets' Mission.

1871 Poplar and Stepney Sick Asylum for the Poor (St Andrew's Hospital) opened. Marie Hilton opens first crèche in Stepney Causeway. Old Castle Street School, London's first Board School, opened.

1872 Poplar-Bloomsbury horse-tram service inaugurated. Dock strike led by Labour Protection League wins 25% pay rise. Bryant & May Match Tax Testimonial Fountain. Jewish Working Men's Club founded. Publication of Edward Denison's Letters.

1873 Canon Barnett becomes vicar of St Jude's, Whitechapel.

1876 East London Synagogue opened.

1877 Wapping flooded. Danish Lutheran church built in King (now Ming) Street. Copperfield Road Ragged School opened. Revd Stewart Headlam established the Guild of St Matthew.

1878 Beckton Gas Works comes on stream.

1879 Bethnal Green Road improved. Wapping High Street widened by the Metropolitan Board of Works.

1880 Grodzinski's bakery established in Fieldgate Street.

1881 Assassination of Tsar Alexander II leads to pogroms impelling mass migration of Ashkenazi Jews from Russian territories. First cargo of Australian frozen meat successfully landed at Millwall.

1882 RNLI headquarters opened in Broomfield Street, Poplar. Statue of Gladstone (by Albert Bruce-Joy) erected in Bow churchyard. St Mary Matfelon rebuilt. Walter Besant *All Sorts and Conditions of Men: An Impossible Story.*

1883 Revd Andrew Mearns *The Bitter Cry of Outcast London.*

1884 Oxford House opened. Toynbee Hall opened. The Mothers' Lying-In Home opened in Glamis Road, Shadwell.

1885 Poor Jews' Temporary Shelter opened in Whitechapel. Working Lads' Institute opened at 279 Whitechapel Road. Millwall football club founded.

1886 Jewish Girls' Club established. Bancroft's School moves to Woodford Green. Frederick Charrington's Great Assembly Hall opened.

1887 Funeral of Alfred Linnell at Tower Hamlets cemetery. East End Dwellings Company founded. Queen Victoria opens the People's Palace and lays the foundation stone for the East London Technical College.

1888 'Jack the Ripper' murders. First Salvation Army hostel opened in Limehouse. Match girls strike. Four Per Cent Industrial Dwellings Company founded. C R Ashbee establishes Guild and School of Handicraft in Toynbee Hall. Scandinavian Sailors' Home opened.

1889 Gas workers strike. Dock Strike. Jewish tailors' strike. Charles Booth *East London.*

1890 William Booth *In Darkest England and the Way Out.*

1891 Central Foundation Schools established. Guild and School of Handicraft moves to Essex House, Mile End. Wapping Recreation Ground opened.

1892 Israel Zangwill, *Children of the Ghetto.* East London Technical College opened. Pavilion Theatre opened

1893 Demolition of 'Old Palace', Bromley-by-Bow.

1894 Major drought disrupts domestic water supplies. Revd William Rogers establishes the Bishopsgate Institute. Public library opened in Poplar High Street.

1895 Arthur Morrison *A Child of the Jago.* Island Gardens, Isle of Dogs opened. Jewish Temporary Shelter established at 84 Leman Street.

1896 Haileybury Boys' Club opened. C R Ashbee, *The Trinity Hospital in Mile End: An Object Lesson in National History.*

1897 Blackwall tunnel opened. Former Huguenot chapel in Brick Lane becomes a synagogue. Maconochie's pickle factory opened in West Ferry Road.

1899 Whitechapel Art Gallery opened (architect C H Townsend).

1900 Formation of the Metropolitan Boroughs of Stepney, Bethnal Green and Poplar. British Brothers League founded. Boundary Street estate completed. St Nicholas, Blackwall opened, the first building in Poplar to be lit by electricity. Bromley Recreation Ground laid out.

1901 Passmore Edwards Sailors' Palace opened.

1902 Jewish soup kitchen opened in Brune Street. Greenwich foot tunnel opened. District Line from Whitechapel to Bow Road station opened. Royal Commission on the Port of London appointed.

1903 Workers' Educational Association launched at Toynbee Hall. Guild of Handicraft leaves Essex House for Chipping Campden. Jack London, *The People of the Abyss.* Report of the Royal Commission on Alien Immigration.

1905 Aliens Act passed to limit foreign immigration. Prince's Theatre (Poplar Hippodrome) built. Fashion Street, Spitalfields arcade opened.

1906 School of Marine Engineeering opened. Transfer of Yarrow shipyard to Scotland.

1907 Clara Grant founds Fern Street Settlement. 5th Congress of the Russian Social Democratic Party held in Fulbourne Street.

1908 Rotherhithe tunnel opened.

1909 Port of London Authority established. Grove Park, Bow opened.

1910 Millwall Football Club moves to New Cross. Bethnal Green town hall completed.

1911 Siege of Sidney Street. Bryant & May Fairfield Works rebuilt. Dreadnought *HMS Thunderer* built at Thames Iron Works. Ben Tillett leads major dock strike. Jews' memorial to Edward VII erected (designer W S Frith). Bow and Bromley Institute closed down.

1912 George Lansbury loses by-election on the issue of women's suffrage. Ben Tillett leads second major dock strike. Strikes by seamen, railwaymen and Jewish tailors. Sylvia Pankhurst founds East London Federation of Suffragettes. Bow Road police station opened. Queen Alexandra opens Tredegar House, Bow Road.

1913 Sax Rohmer (Arthur Henry Ward) *The Mystery of Dr Fu Manchu.*

1914 Sylvia Pankhurst launches the *Women's Dreadnought.* Belgian refugees settled in Rothschild Buildings. (Sir) Basil Henriques founds the Oxford and St George's Jewish settlement.

1915 Ted 'Kid' Lewis becomes world welterweight champion. Zeppelin raid on docklands, 31 May. Alien-owned businesses attacked by mobs. East London Federation of Suffragettes established the Mothers' Arms creche in Old Ford Road. Thomas Burke, *Limehouse Nights.*

1917 Gotha bombers kill 18 children at Upper North Street School, Poplar.

1918 Parliamentary borough of Tower Hamlets abolished.

1919 Methodist minister W H Lax pioneers the street party. Attacks on black seamen in Canning Town, Limehouse, Poplar and Stepney. Tubby Isaacs' seafood stall opens for business at Aldgate. London Jewish Hospital opened.

1920 Chapel House estate built on the Isle of Dogs.

1921 Poplar councillors' rate revolt. Kirby Castle demolished. Rivoli cinema built in Whitechapel Road.

1922 George V opens Edward VII Memorial Park.

1923 Children's House, Bruce Road opened by H G Wells. Nelson Street synagogue built.

1924 Empire Memorial Sailors' Hostel, Salmon Lane opened.

1926 London-Blackwall railway closed. Mary Hughes establishes the Dewdrop Inn, Vallance Road.

1927 Bust of William Booth (by G E Wade) erected. Thames floods. Wickham's department store built.

1928 Whitechapel hay market closes. Spitalfields market modernised. Virginia Settlers Memorial unveiled. Kingsley Hall built (architect C Cowles-Voysey).

1929 Youth Hostels' Association launched at Toynbee Hall. York Hall opened.

1931 Gandhi stays at Kingsley Hall. Fire devastates the Queen's Hall of the People's Palace.

1933 RNLI Broomfield Street premises closed. Fire at Poplar Rum Quay, Poplar Baths rebuilt. Troy cinema opens in the Commercial Road.

1934 Poplar Baths reopened. Pavilion theatre closed. Former East London Technical College recognised as part of the University of London as Queen Mary College. First East End branches of the British Union of Fascists formed in Bow and Bethnal Green. Stepney slum clearance programme demolishes Pennyfields.

1936 Battle of Cable Street, 4 October. New People's Palace opened. Jarrow Crusade marchers lodge at Kingsley Hall.

1937 Poplar Town Hall opened (architect E Culpin). Essex House replaced by an Odeon cinema. King George VI opens the rebuilt People's Palace.

1939 Mass evacuation of schoolchildren.

1940 First bombs fall on the East End, 24 August. The Blitz begins on 'Black Saturday', 7 September. Major raids concentrating on the East End 15/16 October, 15/16 November.

1941 Major raids concentrating on the East End 19/20 March, 19/20 April, 10/11 May, 27/28 July. 36 firemen killed at Old Palace School 19 April. East London Mosque opened in Commercial Road.

1943 Bethnal Green Tube disaster kills 173.

1944 First V-bomb falls on London at Grove Road, Mile End 13 June.

1945 Last V-2 falls on London at Hughes Mansions, Vallance Road, killing 134.

1946 Central Line extended from Liverpool Street to Stratford.

1948 Royal Foundation of St Katherine moves to Butcher Row, Stepney Dockers strike.

1950 Poplar Hippodrome demolished. Closure of *Die Zeit*.

1951 Lansbury Estate, Poplar opened.

1952 East London History Society founded. George V Mile End playing field opened.

1958 Brunswick power station built. Bromley-by-Bow church and community centre reopened.

1959 Captain Cook's house demolished.

1960 St Paul's, Burdett Road consecrated (architect Robert Maguire). Demolition of Poplar workhouse, Stoneyard Lane. Barley Mow brewery, Church Road, Limehouse ceases brewing.

1962 Pavilion theatre demolished.

1963 Troxy cinema becomes the London Opera Centre.

1965 Creation of London Borough of Tower Hamlets by amalgamation of Stepney, Bethnal Green and Poplar. R D Laing establishes the Philadelphia Association as a 'therapeutic community' at Kingsley Hall.

1966 Closure of Wall Paper Manufacturers Ltd of Wick Lane. Mile End stadium opened. George Cornell shot in the Blind Beggar by Ronald Kray.

1967 Second Blackwall tunnel opened. Dockworkers' 'call-on' abolished. Bow flyover built.

1968 Trevor Huddlestone becomes suffragan Bishop of Stepney. London Docks closed.

1969 Port of London Authority sells St Katherine's Dock to the GLC for redevelopment. Kray brothers sentenced to life imprisonment. Bow underpass built. Blue Bridge opened on the Isle of Dogs.

1970 Anti-Asian riot in Brick Lane.

1972 London dockers strike against containerisation.

1973 Tower Thistle hotel opens. Bow Bridge rebuilt.

1974 Docklands Joint Committee established.

1975 Nelson Street synagogue reconsecrated as East London Central. Anchor Brewery ceases production.

1976 London Docklands Strategic Plan published. Black Eagle brewery rebuilt by Arup Associates. St Matthias, Poplar closed. Odeon, Mile End closed.

1977 St Bartholomew the Less, Bethnal Green closed for conversion to flats.

1978 Murder of Altab Ali in Whitechapel.

1979 Statue of William Booth erected. Stepping Stones urban farm opened. Closure of Albion Brewery.

1980 Closure of Bryant & May Fairfield Works.

1981 London Docklands Development Corporation assumes planning powers.

1982 Isle of Dogs designated as an Enterprise Zone. Billingsgate market relocates to Docklands. Amalgamation of 18 East End synagogues under Nelson Street.

1983 Limehouse Productions Studio opens at Canary Wharf.

1984 East London Mosque opens in Whitechapel Road.

1985 First episode of *East Enders* broadcast.

1986 Onyx House, Mile End built (architect Piers Gough). London Independent Hospital opened in Beaumont Square.

1986-7 Wapping printing dispute.

1987 Closure of Limehouse Paperboard Mills. Closure of Blackwall Enginering (formerly Siley, Weir & Co.). First section of Docklands Light Railway opened. East London Synagogue closed. Poplar Baths closed.

1988 Brewing ceased at the Black Eagle brewery.

1989 London Arena opened. Brunswick power station demolished. Demolition of the Railway Tavern, Limehouse (Charlie Brown's).

1990 Royal London air ambulance helicopter service inaugurated. Ragged School Museum, Copperfield Road opened.

1991 Canada Tower completed. Spitalfields market relocates to Leyton.

1993 Limehouse Link opened.

1996 IRA bomb at South Quay kills two. Bloom's restaurant at Aldgate closed.

1997 East London synagogue converted to residential use. Brick Lane designated as Banglatown.

1998 LDDC dissolved. Closure of East India Dock Road baths.

1999 Brick Lane bomb injures six.

2001 William Taylor *This Bright Field: A Travel Book in One Place*

2003 Monica Ali, *Brick Lane*. London bids for the 2012 Olympics. Museum of Docklands opens.

Index

An asterisk denotes an
illustration or caption.

AARONS, Barney 62
Abbey Mills *80, 151
Ackroyd, Peter 8
Adams, William 10, 34
Addams, Jane 110
Ainsworth, Robert 48
Albion Brewery 66
Aldgate 6, 11, 17, 18, 22, 24, 38, 50,
  62, 74, *91, 100
Alexander, Daniel 64
Alexandra Hall 129
Ali, Monica 166
All Sorts and Conditions of Men 100,
  105
All Saints, Poplar 68
Allen, William 70
Almshouses 53-4, *54, *55, *56, 70,
  98, 122, *164
Altab Ali 163
America, Americans 9, 31, 34, 35,
  50, 51, 62, 80, 84-5, *86, 98, 101,
  103, 108, 110, 123, 127, 140,
  156, 165, *166
Anarchists 129-30
Anchor brewery *49
Anchor & Hope *30
Angel, Moses 102
Anglicanism 43, 45, 68, 92-3, 111
Anglo-Catholics 03, 109, 143
Anglo-Saxons 11-13
Anti-Semitism 18, 101-2, 132, 140,
  141, 143-5
Armada 32, 34, 35
Artists 59, 98, 161, 165
Ashbee, C R 121-22, *121
Asylums 20, *28, 54, 83, 126, 138
Attlee, C R 131, *132
Augustinians 17, 20
Australia 60, 67, 79, 86, 90, 108,
  118, 120, 143, 150

BAKERIES 14, 102
Bancroft's almshouses 54, *56
Bancroft's School 48, 100
Bangladeshis *40, 139, 150, 162-3,
  *164, *165, 166
Baptists *7, 43, 70, 97
Barking Abbey 16
Barnardo, Dr John 10, 86-7, *88, 90
Barnato, Barney 9, 102
Barnett, Henrietta 100, *109, 111
Barnett, Canon Samuel 100, 109-
  11, *109
Baths *91, 92, 140, 159
Bazalgette, Sir Joseph *80
Beaumont, J T Barber 70, 105
Beckton gasworks 80, 98, 115-116,
  146, 157
Becontree estate 138
Bedford, Peter 70
Bell foundry, *26, 27, 50, 147

Bentham, Jeremy 9, 51
Berg, Jack 'Kid' 140-1
Bermondsey *24, 105, 147
Besant, Annie *7, 111-13, *113, 115,
  *115
Besant, Sir Walter 100, 105, 111
Bethnal Green *5, 9, 11, 28-9, *28,
  37, 38, 39, 43, *44, 48, 50, 58,
  *60, 61, 67-8, *68, 69, 72, 74, 77-
  8, *78, *82, 83, 100, 102, 107, 131,
  135, 142, 145, 149, 154, 161
Bethnal Green disaster 147
Bethnal Green Museum 97-8, *97,
  148
Bethnal House *5
Bhownagree, Sir Mancherjee 127
Billig, Dr Hannah 148
Billingsgate 157
Bishops of London 11, 12, 13, 14,
  17, 18-19, 27, 76, 109, 111, 118
Bishopsgate Institute 122
Bishops Hall Farm *68, 72
Bitter Cry of Outcast London, The 105
Bittoon, Isaac 62
Black Death 14, 20
Blackshirts 144-5, *144
Blackwall 15, 22, 26, 30, 35, 50, 66,
  *74, *75, 78, 90, 166
Blackwall Tunnel 119, *119
Bligh, Captain William 9
Blind Beggar 154, *154
Blitz 9, 146-8
Blizard, Sir William 70
Bloom's 159
Boer War 120, 125, 132
Bonn, Issy 140
Booth, Charles 8, 102, 107, 117,
  123, 127, 139
Booth, William 88, 90, *90, 107-8,
  139
Boundary Street estate 109, 140
Bow 7, 8, *9, 15, 38, 39, 43, 46, 49,
  50-1, 70, *71, 80, 83, 94, 97, 111,
  125-6
Bow Bells public house *6, *7
Bow Bridge 16-17, *16, *17, 26, 36,
  50, 66, 153
Bow Fair 72
Bow Road *21, *38, 130, 133, 154
Boxing 9, 52-3, 60-2, 122, 139, 140-
  1, 154
Breweries, brewing 15, 29, *49, 50,
  *55, 66, 70, 80, 107, 153-4, *161
Brick Lane 15, *40, 50, 69-70, 120,
  140, 142, 150, 165, *165, 166
Brickmaking 15
British Brothers' League 127, 132
British Museum 11, 31
Bromley-by-Bow *6, *7, 9, 17-18,
  *19, 48, 71, 76, *95, 96, 121-22,
  *122, 133, 143, 147, 148, 150,
  155, *164, 171
Bromley St Leonard 17-18, *19, 53,
  *69, 72
Bronowski, Jacob 111, 141
Broughton, Jack 52-3
Brune, Walter de 19
Brunel I K 9, 74, *75, 76, 79
Brunswick Dock 67
Brunswick Wharf 66

Bryant & May 80, 82, 111-15, *112,
  *113, *114, *115, 126, 153
Burdett Road 84, 147
Burdett-Coutts, Angela 83-4, *83,
  *84, *85, 90
Burials 11, 18, 36, *44, 74, *77, 83,
  *125, 165
Burman VC, Sgt William 134
Burrough, Sir William 31-2, *31
Bus services 74
Butcher Row 15, 150, *150
Buxton, Sir Thomas Fowell 70

CABLE STREET *72, 80-1, 150, 151
Cable Street, Battle of 144-145
Cade, Jack 22
Canada 32, 90, 108, 127, 132, 158
Canada Tower *157, 158, *159, 165
Cattle trade 14, 16, 48, 138
Cemeteries *5, 38, 42, 74, 76, *76,
  *77, 83, 88, *125
Charles I 37
Charlie Brown's 159
Charrington, Frederick 93, *106, *108,
  112, 122
Chaucer, Geoffrey 10, 18
Chevalier, Albert 8
Child of the Jago, A 108-9
China, Chinese 11, 33, 127, *128,
  132, 142, 147
Chinatown 7, *8, 127, *127, *128,
  129, *129, 139, 142, 149
Cholera 59, 73, 80, 86, 91, *91, 92, 93
Christ Church, Cubitt Town 77
Christ Church Hall *7
Christ Church Spitalfields *44, 45-6,
  123, 150, 165-66
Chudleigh, Revd Frederick 133
Cibber, Gaius 43
Cinemas 126, 134, 139-40, 141, 150
Civil Wars 36-7, 43, 71
Classicianus 11
Clothing industry 119, 133, 141
Clunn, Harold P 141
Coborn, Prisca 46
Cockneys 6, 9, 120, 123, 148, 155,
  159, 162-3
Cohen, Jack 132
Cohen, Morris 132
Cohen-Portheim, Paul 142, 149
Colet, Sir Henry 22-3
Colet, John 22-3
Colquhoun, Patrick 62, *62, 69
Columbia Market *5, 84, *84
Columbia Square 85, *85
Commercial Road 65, 71, 82
Commercial Street 74, *86, 121
Compleat Angler, The 38
Communists 131, 139, 143, 144, 146,
  147, 153
Congreve, Col. *9, 10
Conservation 76, 121-2
Cook, Captain James 9, 49, 54, *56,
  150
Coopers' Company School 28
Crab, Roger 37
Crime 9, 43, 48, 51-2, 54, 57, 58, *58,
  60, 62, 64, 65, 69-70, 82, 87, 88,
  103, *104, 108-9, 127, 129-30,
  139-40, 154-55, 165

Cromwell, Oliver 37, 38
Cromwell, Thomas 23
Crooks, Will 117-19, *118, 131
Cubitt, Thomas 65
Cubitt, William 76
Cubitt Town 76-7, 79, 126, 147
Culpeper, Nicholas 36-7, *36

DANES 31, 43, *45
Davenant Foundation School 148
Davison, William 35
Defoe, Daniel 36
Dekker, Thomas 35
Delfont, Bernard 141
Denison, Edward 85-6
Dent, J M 110
Dethick family 28
Dickens, Charles *7, 84, 92, 98, 119
Dictionaries 48
Dissolution of the monasteries 18, 24, 26
Dixon of Dock Green 8, 155
Dock strikes 117-19, 131, 152-3
Docklands 146, 156-9, *157, *158, *159, 160, *160, 161, *166
Docklands Light Railway 158, *158, *159, *160
Docks 9, 62-7, 80, 98, 117-19, 152-3
Dollond, John 40-1
Domesday Book 12-13, 15
Drake VC, Cpl Alfred 134
Drake, Sir Francis 29, 32
Drapers' Company 53, 105
Dreadnoughts 9, 126
Druce, Joseph 59, 60
Duckett, Sir George 65-6
Dutch 25, 26, 28, 33, 34, 37, 38, 39, 50, 71, *101, 102-3
Dyeing 15, 50

EAST END 6-10, 23, 24, 51, 52, 58-9, 68, 71-2, 74, 81-4, 100-3, 107, 109-11, 121-2, 124-5, 138, 141-2, 146-8, 149-52, 155, 162-3
East Enders 155, 163, 165
East India Company 35, 41, 48, 50, 54, *56, 65, 66, 67
East India Docks 7, 64-5, 67, 147
East India Dock Road 65, 67, *93, 147
Eastern Counties Railway 77
Edward I 21, 37
Edward II 20, 21
Edward III 20
Edward VI 25, 27
Edward VII 123
Eglantyne, Madame 10, 18-19, *18, 26
Elias, 'Dutch Sam' 62
Elizabeth I 27, 31, 33, 35
Emigration 86, 90, 101, 108, 118, 126, 135, 138, 149
Entick, Revd John 48
Erasmus, Desiderius 6, 23
Essex House 121-2, 140, 162
Etgoos, Richard 16, 26
Etonians 33, 85, 93, 141
Execution Dock 32, *82, 72

FABIAN Society 107, 122
Fairbairn's 66, 78-9

Family and Kinship in East London 149, 161
Famine 13-15, 42
Farson, Daniel 155
Fascists 143-5, *144, 162
Fashion Street 102
Fauconberg, Thomas 22
Ferries 15
Films 103, 143-4, 154, 155, 158
Fires 21, 58, 147
Fishing 14, 15
Fishman, Bill 152
Flanagan, Bud 9, 132
Flemish 15, 21, 25
Fletcher, Geoffrey 151
Flooding 15, 36, 58
Folgate Street *40, 165, *166
Fournier Street *40, *54
Foxe, Richard 22
France, French 27, 32, 39, 40, 68-9, 82, 166
Frobisher, Sir Martin *31, 32, *33
Frye, Thomas 50-1

GANDHI M K 10, 142, 151
Gardening 29, 38
Gardiner's 120
Garnett, Alf 8
Garnett, Henry 35
Garrick, David 57, 59
Gascoyne, Joel 38-9, 48
Gasworkers' strike 115-16, *116, *117
Gasworks *5, 66, 80, 115-16, 133, 146
Gavin, Hector 77
General Strike 142
George III 42, 61
George V 140
George VI 140
Gerbier, Sir Balthazar 37
Germans, Germany 25, 43, 80, 129, 133, 134, 153
'Gert and Daisy' 148, 155
Gertler, Mark 102, 132
Gibson, Nicholas 28
Giffard, Henry 57
Gilbert, Sir Humphrey 32-4
Gladstone, W E 103, 111
Godley VC, Sidney Frank 134
Goodman's Fields and Theatre 46, 54, 57, *57
Gordon, James 48-9
Grade, Lew 140-1
Grant, Clara 125
Great Eastern 9, 79
Great Fire 39
Great Plague 22-3, *23, 30
Green, George 67, 70, 83, 112
Green J R 93
Green, Richard 67, 83, 90, *93
Groser, Father St John 143, 145, 146, 148, *150
Grove Hall asylum 83
Guild of Handicraft 121

HACKNEY 6, 11, 27
Hanbury Street *7, 103, 129, 165
Handel G W F 46
Harkness, Margaret 105, 107
Hawksmoor, Nicholas 8, *44, 45-6, *45
Headlam, Stewart 93-4, 105

Heckford, Dr Nathaniel 92
Henriques, Sir Basil 132
Henry I 16, 18
Henry VI 22
Henry VII 15, 22
Henry VIII 232, 23, 27, 28, 30
Holy Trinity, Aldgate 17, 19, 21, 24
Hospitals 14, 19-20, 54, *55, 70, 73, 86, 91-2, 103, 107, *125, 132-3
Housing 71-2, 76, 78, 84-5, *86, 94, 101, *101, 105, 107, 109, 110, 134, 135, *136, *137, 138, 145-6, 148, 149, 150, 151, 156, 150, 161-2, *161, 163, 166, *166
Hoxton 6, 93, 123
Huddart, Joseph 66
Huddlestone, Trevor 151
Hughes, Mary 142-3
Huguenots *7, *8, 25, 38-42, *40, *41, 45, 46, *47, 69-70, 165

IMMIGRATION, immigrants 7, *8, 15, 21, 25, 28, 42-3, 52, 81-2, 100-3, 127, 132, 139, 160, 162-3
India, Indians 10, 35, 79, *91, 115, 123-4, 150, 151, 162
India Pale Ale (IPA) 9, 50
Industry 9, 15, 16, 25, 26-7, *26, 39-42, 50-1, 57, 66, 78, 80, *81, 91, 133, 147, 148, 153-4, 156, 162
Ireland, Irish 7, 25, 33, 34, 42, 43, 52, 66, 73, 81-2, 83, 86-7, 98, 111, 123, 144
Ireland Terrace 54
Island Gardens 15, 122
Isle of Dogs 14, 15, 20, 48, 64, *64, 66, 76-7, 80, *92, 120, 122, 125, 131, 133, 134, 146, 153, 157-9, 162, *166
Italians, Italy 32, 50, 110, 122, 123, 129, 131, 132, 134, 148

JACK THE RIPPER, 8, 9, 100, 103, *104, 139, 151
James I 29
James, John 46
Jamrach, Charles 80
Japan 10, 34, 79, 153
Jay, Father Arthur Osborne 109
Jessop, William 64
Jews 7, 8-9, 18, 37-8, 42, 60-2, *68, 71, 87, 100-3, 123, 124, 129-39, 132, 133, 138, 140-5, 147, 148, 149, 158, 159
Jews' Free School 9, 70, 102, 132, 141, 146
Jolles, Sir John 46

KENT, William 141-2
Kenton, Benjamin 50
Kingsley Hall 125, 133-4, 142, 143, 150-1
Kirby Castle 28-9, *28, 38, 54, 138
Knockfergus 7, 81
Kray Brothers 9, 154-5
Kropotkin, Prince Pyotr 129

LABOUR PARTY 135, *138, 145, 149, 156
Laing, R D 10, 150

Lansbury, George 8, 130, 135, 137-8, *138
Lansbury estate 149
Lascars 88
Lax, Revd W H 134, 143
Lea, river 6, 11, 14, 15, 16-17, 18, 20, 38, 50, 65, 166
Leman Street *81, 87
Lenin 129
Lester, Muriel and Doris 125, 133-4, 142
Lewis, Ted 'Kid' 140
Limeburning 15
Limehouse *9, 15, 16, 26, 32, 33, 34, 35, *39, 42, 43, *44, 50, 52, 66, *66, *67, 82, 98, 127, *127, *128, *129, 141, 149
Limehouse Cut 58, 66, 120
Limehouse Link 158, 159
Linebaugh, Professor Peter 51
Linnell, Alfred 100
Little Warsaw 7, 142
Lodger, The 103
London, Jack 9, 123
London Arena 158, 159
London-Blackwall Railway 66, 74, *74, *75, 138, *160
London Chest Hospital 14, 91, 133
London County Council 121-22, 135, 146, 149
London Docklands Development Corporation 156-8, *157
London Docks *5, 64, *94, *152
London Hospital 54, *55, 70, 73, 86, 91, 92, *94, 103, 107, 132
Loss, Joe 140
Lowder, Father Charles 93
Lowndes, Marie Bello 103
Lusby's 96

MACKAY, John Henry 129
McMillan, Margaret 125
Maconochie's 120
Malatesta, Errico 129
Mallon, Jimmy 143
Malplaquet House 54
Malvery, Olive Christian 123-4
Mann, Tom 118
Manors, medieval 12-15
Maps 31, 38, *47, 48, 107
Market Gardening 38, 48-9, 72-3, 78
Markets 84, *84, 120, 139, 140, 157, 159, 161, *164
Mary Rose 30
Marx-Aveling, Eleanor *7, 112, 115, 118
Match Girls Strike 111-15, *112, *113, *114, *115
Matilda, Queen 16-17
Mansion House 70, 118
Mass-Observation 146-7
Mawson, Revd Andrew 150
Mayhew, Henry 78, 82
Mayors (and Lord Mayors) of London 15, 20, 21, 22, 29, 54, 76, 90, 118
Mearns, Revd Andrew 105
Mendoza, Daniel 9, 60-2
Merceron, Joseph 69-70
Mercers' Company 23, 36, 71

Methodists *7, 40, *40, 68, 88, 96, 111, 118, 133, 134, 144
Mile End 20, 22, 25-6, 29, 43, 46, 48-9, 54, *55, 57, 70, *95, 112, 121
Militia 27, 29-30
Miller, Dr Emmanuel 143
Milligan, Robert 64
Millwall 66, 76, 78-9, 99, 157
Millwall Docks 80, 120
Millwall FC 120, 121
Model dwellings 84-6, *85, *86, 101, *101, 107, 109
Moore, Henry 148
Morris, Derek 54
Morris, William 100, 121
Morrison, Arthur 6, 8, 108-9, 129
Mosley, Sir Oswald 140, 143-5
Mosques *40, 162, *162
Mulberry Place 7
Murder 58, *58, 103, *103, 154, *154
Muscovy Company 31
Museum of Docklands 159
Museum of London 11
Music 41, 46, 82, 113, 166
Music Halls 96, 113, 123, 126, 141, 150, 155

NAIRN, Ian 150, 151-2
New Canton works 50-1
New Zealand 60, 67, 90, 150
Normans 12-12
Novels 98, 102, 103, 105, 107, 108-9, 129, 142, 166

ODELL, Thomas 57
Okey, Thomas 110
Old Ford 11, 16, 71, 113
Old Nichol, the 108-9
'Old Palace', Bromley-by-Bow 121-2
Olympic Games 166, 171
O'Neill, Gilda 8
Orchard Place 79, 139
Orwell, George 141, *141
Overcrowding 25, 38, 74, 77, 78, 135
Oxford House 111
Oxford University 22-3, 27, 33, 36, 85, 93, 109-11, 150

PACE, Richard 27-8
Palestine Place *68
Pankhurst, Sylvia 130-31, 133
Parks 96-7, 122, *133, 145
Parmiter's School 48, 134, 141
Pavilion theatre 120, 126, *126, 139, 140, 149
Peabody, George 84-5, *85, *86, 151
Peasants' Revolt 10, 21-22
People of the Abyss 9, 123
People's Palace *5, 105, *106, 108, *138, *139, 140
Pepys, Samuel 38-9
Perkin, Sir William 80-1, *80
Perry, John 67
Pett family 30
Petticoat Lane 24, 27, 62, 141
Piratin, Phil 146
Plague 14, 24-5, 27, 35-6
Platt, Sir Hugh 29, 38
Police 54, 62, *63, 73, 93, 98, 99, 103,

*104, 111, 126, 129, 130, *130, 135, 142, 144-5, *144, 146, 155, *155
Pollitt, Harry 139
Pollution 6, 15, 24, 99, 135
Pomfret manor 13, 15
Poplar 15, 20, 26, 28, *34, 35, *35, 68, 70, 72, 73, 74, 76, 97, 100, 119, 127, 134, 135, 137-8, 142, 146, 149, 158
Poplar and Stepney Rifles 132
Poplar Outrage 133, *133
Poplarism 135, 137-8
Population 9, 14-15, 20, 24-5, 43, 48, 52, 54, 58, 74, 76, 77, 78, 138, 139, 149, 159-60
Porcelain 50-1
Port of London Authority 125, 152, 156
Potter, Beatrice 107, *107
Poverty 7, 52, 52, 68-9, 77, 81-90, 100-3, 107-8, 123, 135, 141-2, 171
Prelleur, Peter 46
Princelet Street *8, 102, 123, 149
Princess Alice disaster 98-9, *99
Printing *88, 121, 163, 165
Prospect of Whitby *25, 26
Prostitution 52, 82, 101, 105, 108, 150
Public Houses *7, 16, *25, *30, *39, 49, 61, 78, 90, 94, *94, *95, *96, 103, 131, 133, 138, 142, 154, *154, 155, *156, 159, 161, *165

QUAKERS 43, 45 70, 88
Queen Mary College 49, *139

RACISM 18, 21, 60, 101-2, 132, 133, 134, 140, 142, 144-5, *144, 150, 151, 162-3, 165
Rag Fair 52
Ragged schools 84, 87, 90, 162
Raine's Foundation 48
Railways 58, 66, 73, 74, *74, *75, 77, 119, 158, *158, 171
Raleigh, Sir Walter 30
Ratcliff 11, 15, 26, 28, 30, *31, 32, 35, 43, *47, 48, 58, *58, 66, 80, *89, 93, 9i, 105
Ratcliff murders 58, *58
Regent's Canal 65-6
Rennie, John 64
Rent strikes 145-6
Repton Boys' Club 122
Reynolds, George 77
Ricardo, David 9, 71
Richard II 10, 21-2
Richard III 22
Riots 21, 42, 52, 73, 100, 133, 134, 144-5, *144, 150
Road improvements 11, 16, 26, 48, 49, 74, 138, 142, 158
Rocker, Rudolph 129
Rocque, John *47, 48
Rodinsky, David 8, 149
Rogers VC, Sgt Maurice 148
Roman Catholics 42, 52, 70, 93, 118, 119, 142
Romans 11
Rope-making 50, 51-2, 66, 78
Rosenberg, Isaac 132, *132
Rothschild, Nathan Meyer, Baron 101
Rothschild Buildings 101, *101, 132

Royal Mint *5, 20, 66
Royal Navy 24, 30, 73, 79-80, 133
Royalty theatre 58-9, *59
Runaways 42-3
Ruskin, John 110, 121
Russell, John Scott 79
Russia, Russians 31, 32, 73, 79, 100, 102, 125, 129, 134, 147, 148

SAILORS' homes 70, 83
St Anne, Limehouse 43, *44, 45
St Clare, Abbey of 19
St Clement's Hospital 67, 83
St Dunstan, Stepney *5, 12, *12, 17, 22, 27, 30, 34, 35, 37, 48, 122
St George-in-the-East 43, 45, *45, 46, 48, 72, 91, 92-3
St George Lutheran church 43
St John-at-Wapping *43
St Jude, Whitechapel 109, 111
St Katherine, Foundation of 15, 19, 150, *150
St Katherine's Dock *5, 65, *66, 133, 156, *156
St Leonard, Bromley 17-19, 26, *69, 76
St Mary, Bow 6, 20, *21
St Mary Graces 20
St Mary-le-Bow 6
St Mary Matfelon 20, *20,111
St Mary Spital 19-20
St Matthew, Bethnal Green 93
St Matthias, Poplar *34, *35, 150
St Michael, Shoreditch 93
St Paul, Burdett Road 150
St Paul, Shadwell 68
St Paul's cathedral 11, 13, 22-3, 28
St Paul's school 22, 23
St Peter, London Docks 93
St Philip, Stepney 93
Salvation Army 9, 88, 90, *90, 105, 108, 112, 113, 118, 141
Samuda brothers 79
Samuel, Raphael 165
Sandys Row synagogue *101
Schools 28, 33, 46, 48, 70, 76, *78, 125, 143, 146, 162
Scots 62, 64, 83, 90, 120, 129, *130
Seven Years War 42
Shadwell 11, 14, *31, 42, 60, 82, 85, *86, 92, 98, 105
Sheppard, Jack 51, *51
Shipbuilding 7, 9, 15, 35, 66-7, 78-80, 120, 126, 133, 139, 147
Shoreditch 66, 11, 39, 109
Sidney Street, Siege of 129-30, *130
Silk industry 25, 39, 40-2, *41, 52, 68-9, *81, *82
Sims, George R *120, 124
Sinclair, Iain 8
Slave Trade 42-3, 54, 70
Slum clearance 109, 1138-9
Smithfield 22
Solander, Daniel 49
Somalis 111, 144
Somes, Joseph 67
Soup Kitchens 40, *62, 69, 70, 84, 87, *89, 133-4, 142
South Africa 120
Spert, Sir Thomas 30
Spitalfields *7, *8, 9, 11, 20, 25, 29,

*31, *32, *33, 35, 36-7, *36, 39-42, *31, 43, 45-6, 51, 52-3, 69, 70, *81, *89, 102, 132, 139, 150, *164, 165, *166, *171
Spitalfields Act 42, 69
Sport 38, 52, *53, 60-62, *60, *61, 97, 120, 121, 125, 166, *166, 171
Spring Gardens 57
Spratt's 120
Stead, W T 105, 108, 112
Stepney *5, 6, 11-15, *12, 20, 21, 22-3, 27, 35-6, 42, 48, 50, 58, *72, 85, 86, *87, *88, 100, 134, *137, 142, 146
Stepney Green 42, 52, 54, *56, 59, 70, 143
Stepping Stones farm 22
Stothard, Thomas 59
Stow, John 20, 24, 25-6, 30
Strangers' Home for Asiatics 87, *120
Stratford 6, 14, 20, 22, 50, 171
Street Names 71-2, 84
Strikes 52, 100, 111-15, 131, 152-3, 163, 165
Stucley, Thomas 31
Suffragettes 130-1
Sugar trade 43, *81
Survey of London 122
Sweating sickness 14, 24, 70
Sweden, Swedish 43, *46, 49
Swedenborg, Emanuel 43, *46
Synagogues *8, 38, *101, 159

TAILORING 119
Taine, Hippolyte 82
Tales of Mean Streets 108-9, 129
Taylor, William 166
Telford, Thomas 65
Tesco 132
Television 8, 9, 141, 155, 163, 165
Thames Ironworks 79, 119, 120-21, 126
Thames Tunnel 74, *75, 76
Theatres 57, *57, 58-9, *59, 102, 120, 126, *126, 139
Thorne, Will 115-16, *117, 118, 131
Thunderer, HMS 126
Tillett, Ben 115-16, *116, 117-19, 131
Tissot J-J 98
Tower of London *5, 8, 11, 17, 21-2, *24, 27, 29, 32, 35, 42, 65, 66, 92, 94, 129, 145, 154, 156
Toynbee, Arnold 109
Toynbee Hall 109-11, *110, 112, 112, 121, 125, 129, 131, 143
Trade Unions *7, 9, 42, 81, 94, 111-19, 131, 139, 143, 145, 152-3, 156
Trams 74, 127, 131
Tredegar House *125, 126
Tredegar Square 72
Trinity almshouses 49, 53, *54, 122
Trinity House 30, 34, 53, 64, 66
Tunnels 74, *75, 76, *119, 125, 126, 152
Turpin, Dick 51

UNDERGROUND 119, 126, 138, 147, 148, 149, 156
Unemployment 68-9, 116, 117, 135, 138, 162

VALLANCE ROAD 88, 143, 147,

154
Vanderdelft, Cornelius 26
Vassall, John 34-5
Victoria, Queen 91-2, 105
Victoria & Albert Museum 97-8, *97, 122
Victoria Cross 134, 148
Victoria Park *5, 11, 65, 76, 84, *85, 96-7, 147
Victualling trade 15, 26, 30, 35, 50, 78
Vikngs 11-12, 17

WALTON, Izaak 38
Wapping 8, 9, 11, 15, 25, *25, 26, 30, *32, 38, 43, 45, 48, 52, 62, *63, 64, 92, 98, *152, 163
Ward, Arthur Henry 127
Warner, Jack 8, 155, *155
Waters, Elsie and Doris 148, 155
Warrior, HMS 79, *85
Watermills 10, *10, 13, 14, 15, 17
Water supply 50, 71, 77
Webbe, Edward 31
Wellclose Square 43, *45, 48, 52
Wells, H G 80, 142
Wentworth family 27, 30, 32
Wesley, John *7, 49
Westminster Abbey 8, 27, 53, 59, *85, 111
West Ham United FC 120-21
West India Dock Road 65, 87
West India Docks 64, *64, *74, 98, 117
Whistler, J A M 98
Whitebait suppers 90
Whitechapel 9, 15, *20, 26, *26, 35, 36, 38, 46, 48-9, 51, 54, 90, *95, 98, 103, *104, 107, 109-11, *136, 138, 143, *162, *165
Whitechapel Art Gallery 109, 124-5, *124, 134, 147-8
Whitechapel Bell Foundry *26, 50
Whitechapel Mount 71
Whitechapel murders 103, *104
Whitechapel Public Library 111
Wickham's 120, 140
Wigram, Sir Robert 66-7
Wilde, Oscar 127
William the Conqueror 12, 17
Willoughby, Sir Hugh 30-1, *31
Wilton's music hall 96, 111, 118
Windsor, Barbara 155
Winogradski brothers 140
Woolley VC, Lt Geoffrey 134
Workers' Educational Association 110, 125
Workhouses *5, *71, 72, 83, 123, 137, 150
World War I 131-4, *133, 142, 145
World War II 7, 9, 146-8, *147
Wren, Sir Christopher 45, 122
Wyllie, W L 98

YARROW'S 80, 127
Yiddish 41, 102, *126, 129, 139
Young, Michael 149
Youth Hostels Association 143

ZANGWILLl, Israel 102
Zola, Emile 98